D1625328

OUTSIDER
BASEBALL

THE WEIRD WORLD OF HARDBALL ON THE FRINGE, 1876–1950

Written and Illustrated by

◆ Scott Simkus ◆

CHICAGO
REVIEW
PRESS

Published by Chicago Review Press, Incorporated
814 North Franklin Street
Chicago, Illinois 60610

ISBN 978-1-61374-816-9

Library of Congress Cataloging-in-Publication Data
Simkus, Scott.
 Outsider baseball : the weird world of hardball on the fringe, 1876-1950 / Scott
Simkus.
    pages cm.
 Summary: "With new research and revelations that will surprise even the most
ardent baseball history buffs, this engaging account tells the story of the mostly
forgotten world of the mercenaries, scalawags, and outcasts who made up the
independent professional ball clubs. Combining meticulous research with modern
analytics, the book provides a deeper understanding of how vast and eclectic the
world of professional baseball was during the first half of the 20th century. It illu-
minates an alternate baseball universe where Babe Ruth, Rube Waddell, and John
McGraw crossed bats with the Cuban Stars, Tokyo Giants, Brooklyn Bushwicks,
dozens of famous Negro league teams, and novelty acts such as the House of David
and Bloomer Girls. Written in a gritty prose style, this entertaining book shares
the stories of these unsung players and uses a critical lens to separate fact from
fiction"— Provided by publisher.
 Includes bibliographical references and index.
 ISBN 978-1-61374-816-9 (hardback)
 1. Baseball—United States—History—20th century. I. Title.

GV863.A1S6337 2014
796.357—dc23
                    2013035612

Interior design: Jon Hahn
Cover design: Andrew Brozyna

Printed in the United States of America
5 4 3 2 1

CONTENTS

For one thing, it is absolutely amazing how many minor league organizations in that era (1900–1920) didn't know a baseball player from an opera singer. One minor league team released Walter Johnson. One minor league operation had Ty Cobb under contract for a month, and cut him. The New York Giants had Tris Speaker in spring training, and cut him. The Cleveland Indians had an option on Pete Alexander; Alexander had a huge year in the minors, and the Indians didn't pick up the option. These people didn't have a clue what they were doing— and because they didn't, many of the best players in baseball played out their careers in the minors, while players had substantial major league careers just basically because they were in the right place at the right time.

—BILL JAMES
billjamesonline.com
April 2012

*This book is dedicated to my parents, Bob and Barb Simkus,
who filled our home with books, newspapers, and magazines
and introduced me to baseball.*

INTRODUCTION

◆

BROTHERHOOD OF THE TRAVELING BASEBALL PANTS

Hi, my name is Scott Simkus, and I was the worst door-to-door copier salesman in the history of the industry.

After months of getting dressed down by sadistic small-business owners, chased out of warehouses by pit bulls, and chewed up, spit out, and shit on, I'd finally given up. Instead of canvassing a sales territory (or looking for a new job), I'd go to the library and spend hours squinting at microfilm, reading about old-time baseball stuff. Baseball, and baseball history in particular, was my comfort food. My drug.

I'd walk into a building with three little mysteries I hoped to untangle and walk out with ten new ones. It was both frustrating and fascinating. Two steps forward, five steps back, and a two-by-four of new information cracking me in the forehead, jolting my understanding of a game I thought I knew.

I stumbled across a lot of weird stuff: semipro teams from New York City that drew more paid customers than the Brooklyn Dodgers; Japanese teams barnstorming across America in the 1930s; Cuban clubs who regularly defeated major league outfits; white teams sponsored by religious cults and women playing in games with legends such as Jimmie Foxx and Babe Ruth.

I'd eventually find a new job, but the spelunking and hardball time travel never ceased. Two huge file cabinets were filled with material. A computer baseball simulation company called Strat-O-Matic used some of this information to create their historic Negro league set in 2009. My name popped up in *Sports Illustrated* because of my work on that project. I was on TV and NPR. There was a story about my stuff in the *New York Times*. It was Warholian: a baseball nerd's fifteen minutes of fame. I was working as a dispatcher at a limousine company at this point, but the research never stopped.

I stumbled across a number of baseball mysteries while working for Strat-O-Matic, looking for other things. I'd been charged with two major responsibilities: finding box scores from the defunct Negro leagues, and collecting evidence that could help the company determine how talented the Negro leagues were, relative to the white major leagues. The latter was, in their estimation, the most critical requirement for producing something worth bringing to market. It's what would separate a true simulation from something produced for the Xbox 360, the Wii, or a smartphone app.

With the digitization of newspapers, the first part—collecting box scores—has become relatively easy over the last few years. But the second part, what we'll call "league quality," is a can of spring-loaded worms. A number of garden-variety baseball litmus tests can be used to compare one league to another, but they all have their limitations. For instance, you could look at the performance of players who transferred from one league to another. Did their batting averages and power figures improve or get worse after making the switch? If their performance gets worse, it usually (but not always) means the competition is stiffer. Such analysis is not definitive, and there are some adjustments that need to be considered, but it certainly beats random speculation or gut feelings.

Preferably, one can look at head-to-head records in games pitting teams from opposing leagues against one another, such as the World Series, All-Star contests, and interleague games, to determine who was better. As an example, from 1950 to 1982, the National League (NL) won 30 of 35 All-Star games versus the American League (AL) and garnered 17 of 33 World Series titles. Overall, the National League was considered stronger during this period, owing partly to a more aggressive recruitment of star-quality African American ballplayers after integration. The proof is in the tapioca. And if there hadn't been such a cluster of talent on the legendary New York Yankees clubs of the 1950s, the narrow World Series advantage enjoyed by the NL likely would have been greater.

But then there were things I saw, as I scoured the papers, that didn't make a lot of baseball sense: Babe Ruth's Yankees losing to semiprofessional teams. Class D minor league clubs defeating Satchel Paige's great Pittsburgh Crawfords squad; a team sponsored by a religious cult topping the Philadelphia Athletics; women pitching in major league spring training camps; Japanese squads playing tough with Pacific Coast League clubs in the 1930s; men dressed as clowns (as in white face paint and big red noses) playing one hundred and fifty-game schedules and defeating most of their opposition across the country.

This was the stuff I gravitated toward when the research drifted off course. The dusty box scores, game stories, and grainy photos were a treasure trove, revealing a shadow world of professional baseball that hadn't been seen in a long, long time.

◆ ◆ ◆

Let's fast-forward to what we all assume about baseball today. There can be little doubt that nearly all the best baseball players in the world currently perform in the major leagues. Nearly all the best baseball talent in the Western Hemisphere, and a good deal of the best talent in Asia, gets funneled, pretty efficiently, into the majors. Even Cuba, one of the few major talent reservoirs that doesn't feed directly into Major League Baseball (MLB), contributes many of its best players as defectors. And Japanese professional baseball, the world's other major league, has agreements in place with organized baseball that facilitate the transfer of much of its top talent to North America.

But turn the clock back, and we'll find this has not always been the case. Before 1950, enough major league talent may have resided on teams and in leagues outside MLB that it distorts our understanding of baseball history. We're not talking about Japan and Cuba this time (though they do come into it); we're referring to non–major league teams and leagues with top-notch talent in the United States. This talent came from three sources.

The Negro Leagues

Baseball history is divided in half, pivoting on 1947, the year Jackie Robinson broke the color line for the Brooklyn Dodgers. Before Jackie, an unwritten gentlemen's agreement dating back to the 1880s had kept black players (or any players who were perceived as not white) out of the big leagues. In response, African American players formed their own teams and leagues, built their own parks, and ran an entire parallel baseball world. That the Negro leagues produced baseball of the highest quality is not seriously disputed by anyone—a fact recognized by the Hall of Fame, for instance, which since 1971 has inducted some twenty-nine members solely for their playing careers in the Negro leagues. Almost everyone believes Satchel Paige belongs firmly in the discussion of the greatest pitchers of all time and that Josh Gibson is right up there with Ruth, Wagner, Mays, Williams, and Cobb as one of the greatest players the game has ever seen.

The Minor Leagues

The minor leagues did not start off as farm teams developing talent for the majors. They began as exactly the same sort of enterprise as the major leagues—associations of ballclubs trying to draw paying fans by competing for championships, just in smaller towns (most of the time, anyway). Only gradually, over the first half of the twentieth century, did the majors extend their dominion over all of organized baseball, buying up clubs to form farm systems. For much of this time, a large number of leagues and teams resisted, keeping their best players for as long as possible. A slugger named Buzz Arlett might have been among the top home-run hitters anywhere in the 1920s—yet he spent the bulk of his career not in the majors but with teams in the Pacific Coast and International leagues.

Independent Pro and Semipro Baseball

In the early twentieth century organized baseball didn't include all the high-quality hardball talent in the United States. The national appetite for the game far outstripped the ability of both the majors and minors to satisfy it. Plenty of independent teams existed, many of them semipro, along with a few genuine, full-time professional clubs, playing in small towns and cities alike, in outlaw and industrial leagues. Were any truly great players hidden inside the semipro bushes? Maybe, maybe not, but teams like the Brooklyn Bushwicks, Chicago's Logan Squares, the Killers of Philadelphia, and the Treat 'Em Roughs of New York City unquestionably featured major league–quality players. We know this because they hired *actual major leaguers*, often in the primes of their careers. Up through the 1910s and 1920s, stars like Nixey Callahan of the White Sox or Mike Donlin and Jeff Tesreau of the New York Giants thought nothing of walking out on their contracts and spending several years playing for these independent teams, sometimes for less pay (and sometimes for *more* pay) but always for more freedom.

◆ ◆ ◆

Today there is thankfully no need for the Negro leagues. Most minor leagues are symbiotic partners of the majors, and independent, semiprofessional baseball is almost nonexistent. But before the 1950s independent leagues were, to varying degrees, important competitors of the majors. What kind of talent have we missed by not having access to these forgotten players' scores and stats? How many of these men could have played big-league ball, and how would they have fared? Were there more Satchel Paiges out there? What and who has yet to be discovered?

That's what this book is about.

Using new sources and old, I've put together a vast (and always growing) database of games spanning eight decades. The evidence I've collected falls roughly into five categories:

1. Negro league statistics, from the vast amount of material I've collected as part of my research on the Negro league card set for the Strat-O-Matic computer game. I've compiled some of the most comprehensive and detailed stats ever put together, including vital and eye-opening data on platoon differentials, ballpark effects, and fielding.

2. Common opponents, through statistics for major league exhibition games against Negro league, Latin American, minor league, and semipro teams, as well as Negro league exhibition games against many of these same opponents. A *lot* of baseball happened outside league structures before 1950, so I have a large amount of data over many years to work with.

3. The records of individual players who moved between two leagues; by comparing their performances, we can collect evidence about the relative quality of the leagues. This is most useful for minor leaguers, obviously, but also for the first generation of black ballplayers in the majors, whose careers give us important information about the quality of play in the Negro leagues. Players also moved between the major leagues and semipro teams, and a few Latin ballplayers before Jackie Robinson moved between the Negro leagues and the majors.

4. Statistics for third-party leagues, especially Latin American leagues (Cuba, Mexico, Dominican Republic, Puerto Rico) and California winter leagues where Negro leaguers, major leaguers, and minor leaguers all featured in varying proportions. In these settings we actually find white and black players competing directly against each other for championships, in nonexhibition settings, during the era of Jim Crow baseball in the United States.

5. Findings from something called the STARS system. An entire chapter is devoted to explaining this metric, which helps untangle how baseball talent was distributed during the first

half of the twentieth century. It's particularly helpful for quantifying the ability of nonleague teams (the barnstorming independent semipro outfits that fanned out across the country every summer), where individual statistics are difficult to come by.

This is the world I call outsider baseball. Before 1950, many of the greatest players in baseball were making money performing on this periphery, outside the confines of the major leagues. In *Outsider Baseball*, a bottom-up account of our national pastime's evolution, I show just how extraordinary these forgotten players were.

The chapters traverse a seventy-five-year span, surveying this lost America. At the heart of *Outsider Baseball* are little mysteries and large questions. I'll spend a good deal of time using empirical evidence to debunk some of baseball's most persistent myths.

But please don't tell my boss; I'm supposed to be at the office right now.

◆ 1 ◆

THE CEDAR RAPIDS BASEBALL BUNKER

Fᴵᴠᴇ ᴏꜰ ᴜs ʜᴜɴᴋᴇʀᴇᴅ ɪɴsɪᴅᴇ ᴛʜᴇ ᴍᴜsᴛʏ ᴄᴇʟʟᴀʀ of a creaky frame house in downtown Cedar Rapids. Four white guys and an elderly black man were sitting around a wobbly card table in the middle of the space. On the limestone walls, hung haphazardly, were framed black-and-white snapshots of forgotten ballplayers throwing, running, and swinging at pitches in ballparks that no longer existed. Yellowed newspaper clippings, framed as well, bore witness to triumphs and defeats of bygone days, before the passage of time wreaked its unforgiving havoc. Family photos—personal stuff—were mixed in with all the baseball artifacts, evidence of a full, active life.

And eventually, my bladder couldn't take it anymore. We had been there a couple hours, and I was going to burst.

Our hosts had been nothing if not congenial, loading us up with bottled water, soda pop, and good cheer. I needed to piss like a racehorse. In the corner of the cellar was a little bathroom, not quite large enough for a human being, really, but it would suffice. With the door wide open (it couldn't be shut completely) I took care of my business, eavesdropping as the conversation continued. Earlier in the morning, the five of us were complete strangers, but now we were the best of buddies. Swapping stories about Tiger Woods's sexual conquests, peeing in front of one another, talking baseball. There wasn't anything off-limits here in the baseball bunker.

Everybody got up, moving around the tight quarters, stretching their legs. Everybody except the black gentleman, who remained at the table, holding court, spinning yarns. After years of playing baseball and football, his legs bugged the hell out of him, and he preferred to sit. A photographer from a local paper was there, trying to find some decent lighting, plus a reporter who'd flown in from Los Angeles, the black man's business agent, and me.

The home owner's name was Arthur David Pennington, and he was eighty-six years old at the time. He'd been nicknamed "Superman" when just a boy, back in Arkansas, and the moniker stuck with him throughout his life. His mother had tagged him with the label after she'd happened upon the teenage Arthur lifting some car tires without any assistance. He'd grow to be 5'11", 185 pounds, wiry and strong with huge, powerful hands. After becoming a professional baseball player, he'd muscle up on a fastball, lining a shot into Comiskey Park's upper deck. On the wall in the basement was a photograph commemorating the blow. It had a little arrow marking the spot where the ball landed.

We had all convened at Superman's house on a cold December morning as part of a press junket, promoting the Negro league board game and computer simulation product released by the Strat-O-Matic Game Company in New York. I'd been the lead consultant on the project, which meant scouring over a couple thousand box scores, tabulating statistics, and untangling mysteries about league quality and ballpark effects. Strat-O-Matic wanted the most realistic product possible, and although we were only researching one hundred players, this still required a couple years worth of work. Researching blackball details (*blackball* is now commonly accepted shorthand for "Negro leagues" and "independent African American baseball") from the days before baseball was integrated, was a tough row to hoe.

Pennington, it turns out, was the only man still with us from the set. The others—Cool Papa Bell, Turkey Stearnes, Martin Dihigo, all Hall of Famers—were long gone. The reporter, fishing for a sound bite, asked Superman what it felt like to be the only one still around. Did he feel any special responsibility, speaking on behalf of these legends?

The newspaperman was probably looking for something heartfelt and inspirational, along the lines of "what an honor it was to represent these legendary African American athletes" and how he "hopes nobody forgets the unspeakable hardships these men endured during their careers." But Pennington surprised everybody in the bunker with the curveball.

"A lot of those guys drank too much, man."

Say what?

"I guess the reason I'm still here," Pennington said, as he autographed a couple trading cards on the wobbly table, "is because I didn't smoke or drink. A lot of these fellas burned the candle at both ends, and my only vice, really, was women."

After starring for the local minor league team in the 1950s, Art Pennington permanently settled in Cedar Rapids, accepting a job with a local factory. *Courtesy of Scott Simkus*

We all laughed.

The photographer snapped a couple photos.

Superman was just happy to be here among the living.

The chatter quickly drifted back to baseball.

◆ ◆ ◆

Art Pennington was born on May 18, 1923, in Memphis, Tennessee. At a very young age his parents returned to their native Arkansas (his older brother and both his parents had been born there), settling in the resort community of Hot Springs. His father, Harry, worked as an elevator man at a local medical building, while his mother, Pearl, took care of their three small children.

It was a happy childhood, with grandparents nearby, and much of Art's time was filled with school and sports. Under his father's tutelage, he became a standout ballplayer, raising eyebrows by the time he was in high school. One March morning, a gentleman showed up on the Pennington's front porch, hat in hand. Wanted to speak with the teenage boy's parents. Said his name was Jim Taylor, and he had a job offer for the youngster.

The visitor explained he was the manager of a baseball team called the Chicago American Giants, which played in the Negro American League (NAL), up north. Wanted to see if Art, who was not only a diamond star but had also been named to an all-state high school football team in Arkansas, wanted to try his hand at professional athletics.

"My mother didn't want me to go," Pennington explained to us in the bunker, nearly seventy years later. "But Jim Taylor kept working on her, insisting he'd keep me under his wing, as if I was his own son."

Taylor was more widely known around the country as "Candy Jim," and he'd already cut a wide swath through the blackball ranks, with a professional career dating back to 1903. At fifty-six years of age, Candy Jim had either played with (or against) or managed virtually every great African American and Cuban ballplayer during the first half of the twentieth century. Plus, he'd participated in a number of exhibition games versus white major and minor league stars over the years. He knew talent when he saw it.

Candy Jim pulled a roll of bills out of his pants pocket and peeled off $150 for Pearl Pennington, which according to Art "was more money than she'd ever seen at one time in her entire life." When Art's mother agreed to let her son leave with Taylor for a trial with his ballclub, the graying manager peeled off another $100 and stuffed it in the kid's shirt pocket. He was on his way to the black majors.

"He was true to his word, treating me like a son," Superman remembered with a smile. "In fact, I always called him Uncle Jim. He was never *Candy* to me, he was Uncle."

On an end table upstairs, above the bunker, was another black-and-white photo—a formal portrait—of Jim Taylor, Art Pennington, and Pearl, all dressed in their Sunday best. It was obviously one of the most cherished personal effects in the home.

♦ ♦ ♦

Although Pennington played parts of ten seasons in the Negro American League, all of them with Chicago, his baseball stories spanned two decades, bouncing from one corner of the Western Hemisphere to the other. He played ball in Venezuela, Cuba, Canada, the Dominican Republic, and Mexico. He played minor league baseball, after integration, in California, Florida, Oregon, and Iowa. He played semipro ball in North Dakota.

Superman hit a home run off an aging Dizzy Dean in an exhibition game, and batted against a young Whitey Ford. He caught fly balls hit by Josh Gibson, Roger Maris, Luis Aparicio, Buck Leonard, and Whitey Herzog. He played in two East-West All-Star games, struck out against Satchel Paige, and once topped Harvey Kuenn by nine points, winning a minor league batting championship.

He won a $100 prize for clubbing the longest home run in Manitoba-Dakota League history (a 480-footer in the mid-1950s) and easily beat future New York Yankee Elston Howard during a long-distance throwing contest held at old Municipal Stadium in Kansas City.

He got involved in some wild parties, south of the border, with a teammate named Wild Bill Wright. The details of these escapades are left to your imagination.

During his career, in and outside of organized baseball, Pennington is credited with single-season batting averages of .370, .359, .357, .349 (twice), .348, .345, .339, and .329. He played eight positions during the course of his career. In 1945, he stole 18 bases in the 70-game NAL season, second only to Sam "the Jet" Jethroe, who would later lead the American League in steals, twice.

After Pennington's career, he worked the railroad for a couple years, ran a popular night club in Cedar Rapids, and landed a day job with Rockwell Collins, which involved a cushy factory position during business hours and playing first base for the company ballclub at night. He had several children and five wives (not all at once) and survived a catastrophic flood that nearly wiped out his house and all of his baseball memorabilia in June 2008.

About the only thing Arthur David Pennington never really had an opportunity to do in his life was play in a white major league game. That phone call never came.

◆ ◆ ◆

There were five of us inside the baseball bunker. Four white dudes and a black man, and the moment of truth was upon us. We'd formed a semicircle around Art, tape recorders in hand, camera at the ready, notepads out. It was time to sink him with the big question, the $64,000 whopper.

Why don't you think you ever got a chance to play in the majors?

"Oh, I don't know for sure." Pennington stroked his jet black goatee, pondering the question. With the help of good genes, clean living, and some Grecian Formula, Superman looked at least twenty years younger than his age. And his mind was sharper than a needle. "I always thought it was because my wife was white. That type of situation didn't sit too well with folks back then. I remember bumping into Luke Easter at spring training one year in California, and we talked about that stuff." His first wife, the woman he was married to for more than ten years—during the bulk of his prime as a ballplayer—was a light-skinned Latina he'd met while playing for the Puebla Angels in the Mexican League.

"Man, she was beautiful."

When Pennington was signed by Portland in the Pacific Coast League, he reported to the team hotel, where he and his wife were denied a room. "I called the owner of the club and said 'Hey, what's going on here?' The man also happened to own the hotel, and he talked to the front-desk clerk, straightening everything out."

Art figured his age conspired against him as well. He was already twenty-nine years old when he played his first full season in the low minors (batting .349 with 20 home runs for Keokuk in the Three-I League). "We [the former Negro leaguers] helped put fans in the seats in the minors, but the big-league clubs were looking for younger guys."

Later on, I asked Art Pennington how good the Negro leagues were, in terms of talent. At Strat-O-Matic, this was really *the* biggest issue we had to contend with, trying to create a simulation product that could be accurately blended with the white major leagues.

"It was like a third major league, man," he replied, with zero hesitation. "When I got to the white minor leagues, it was *easy* for me."

◆ 2 ◆

BASEBALL'S ROSETTA STONE

TABLE 2.1 SHOWS HOW MAJOR LEAGUE TEAMS fared in exhibition games versus various minor league teams from 1901 to 1950. I've spent five years gathering these figures and categorizing them by organized baseball's classification system. These data do not cover every exhibition game ever played, but it's a meaningful sample, larger in size and scope than anything previously published.

2.1

Level	W	L	T	PCT.
Triple-A	731	394	23	.650
Double-A	517	175	17	.747
High Single-A	302	85	7	.780
Low Single-A	140	23	2	.859

Note: For most of the years prior to 1950, Triple-A was known as Class A, Double-A was known as Class B, High Single-A was known as Class C, and Low Single-A was known as Class D.

Right off the bat, unmistakable patterns emerge. The major league teams fared better against the lower minor league teams, which is exactly what our baseball instincts would expect. And when they played against the older, more experienced minor leaguers at the Double-A and Triple-A level, their winning percentage drops. This, too, is what one would expect to discover.

Now, let's take a look at another table of major league exhibition games. Table 2.2 pits the big dogs against college, semipro, military, and Negro league teams. The military teams are those from World War I and II during the war years. Those military clubs were usually loaded with men who had major and minor league experience. And again, this isn't a complete list, but it *is* the most comprehensive one ever published.

2.2

Level	W	L	T	PCT.
College	143	11	0	.938
Semipro	690	155	17	.817
Military	151	61	6	.710
Negro League	115	128	7	.473

College was clearly an easier opponent than any of the professional ranks in table 2.1. This also makes sense, as the rosters consisted of young kids, most of whom were not really blessed with anything approaching big-league ability. But the semipros? In more than eight hundred games versus major league teams, the semipros seem to be a tougher competitor than the lowest of the minor leagues. That's a little surprising. And military teams? They were almost as tough as Triple-A minor league clubs, but considering their rosters included guys like Johnny Mize, Bob Feller, and Ted Williams, this isn't really earth-shattering.

Which brings us to the Negro league teams. The white major leaguers—the highest level of professional baseball in the world—had a *losing* record versus the black teams. Historians have known this for quite some time, and there are several logical explanations. We'll explore this question from a couple of angles, using a couple of tools, throughout the book. But for now—and you'll have to take this at face value—you should know that the Negro league teams often added two or three stars from other clubs to fortify their rosters when playing white big-league teams and that the big leaguers were usually *undermanned* by two or three, filling in with Triple-A-caliber guys, or semipros, or using pitchers in the outfield or at first base during these games. Not to take too much away from the black clubs, because they were outstanding, but the way those particular matchups occurred skewers the results a touch.

Now for the final table, Table 2.3, which combines *all* levels of competition. The major league competition is listed in descending order, from most difficult to least difficult. We've also added in the average runs scored, for and against, for those readers who enjoy all the gory little details.

2.3

MLB vs. Various Levels	W	L	T	PCT.	RF	RA
Negro League	115	128	7	.473	4.10	4.29
Triple-A	731	394	23	.649	6.12	4.33
Military	151	61	5	.710	7.12	4.02
Double-A	517	175	17	.747	6.66	3.74
High Single-A	302	85	7	.780	6.99	3.61
Semiprofessional	690	155	17	.817	6.92	3.03
Low Single-A	140	23	2	.859	8.13	3.28
College	143	11	0	.938	9.88	2.57

We're going to revisit these tables later in the book; they're not just window dressing. In fact, these tables are going to be important just a couple chapters after this one, when we introduce the STARS system. I've collected nearly four thousand games and categorized them by level to illustrate something most baseball fans probably take for granted: Major League Baseball is, and probably always *was*, the best brand going, with the exception of the Negro leagues. There are easier ways to do this—shortcuts—such as examining the statistical track records of players who moved from the minor leagues to the major leagues, but I deliberately chose the long form because it shows us things other methods overlook. Getting a quick understanding of where the Negro league, white semipro, and military teams fit into the hierarchy helps guide us to where we'll cast our net as we look for hidden talent.

◆ 3 ◆

THE RISE OF THE NATIONAL LEAGUE

Hᴇʀᴇ ɪs ᴀ ʙʀɪᴇғ, ɪɴᴄᴏᴍᴘʟᴇᴛᴇ (and possibly incorrect) history of baseball before ᴀᴅ 1900.

2000 ʙᴄ—Two boys are playing along the shore of the river Nile in Egypt. One lad tosses a round stone, and the other swings at it with a wooden stick, whistling a line drive into the water. The next pitch is a fast one, up and in. Both benches empty, requiring an umpire to restore order before play resumes.

ᴀᴅ 1744—Children in Great Britain play a game called "rounders," involving a bat, ball, and several posts, which serve the same function as today's bases. The game is actually referred to as "base ball" in England's *Little Pretty Pocket-Book*, printed in 1828. This little diversion drifts over the pond and becomes popular here in the United States. It will later be determined to have nothing whatsoever to do with the evolution of the distinctly American game of baseball.

1791—No joke here: the first reference to "base ball" in the United States was a local ordinance prohibiting the play of such a game near the meeting house in Pittsfield, Massachusetts. The newly constructed building included many expensive windows, and the preference was that they *not* get shattered by wayward hits and/or throws.

1838—The Olympic Ball Club of Philadelphia played a children's game called "Town Ball." Town Ball was very similar to baseball, one of the chief differences being you could retire a base runner by plunking him in the ass (or any other body part, for that matter) with the ball. I'm going to assume the orb was softer than the one used today.

1839—Abner Doubleday was *not* playing base ball in Cooperstown, New York.

1840–1900—A bunch of other baseball stuff happened.

◆ ◆ ◆

If country club golf courses had existed in America back in the 1840s, baseball may have never evolved into an adult diversion, let alone become the mega business it is today. Seriously. It likely would have fizzled out in its original form, Town Ball, and been relegated to the juvenile domain of grade school recess activities—hopscotch, leapfrog, dodgeball, and foursquare—if clubs such as the Knickerbockers of New York hadn't begun taking the game seriously. You see, after adults finally got their grubby hands around it, early baseball served much the same function as a chamber of commerce scramble or rotary golf outing does today. Groups of white-collar businessmen with bushy mustaches and super-tight slacks gathered for exercise, fresh air, and networking. It was an *exclusive* activity. It was eccentric. It was grown men—professionals—turning a child's game into a manly diversion. They had membership dues and rules of decorum. There were penalties for arriving late, using curse words, or missing scheduled events. The men took ferries over to the Elysian Fields in New Jersey for the same reason business folks knock off early on a Friday these days and hit the golf links. They wanted to get out of the office, feel the warmth of other suns, talk about business and politics, or lie about their latest sexual conquests in a relaxed environment.

Almost immediately, there was an exclusionary element to baseball's operations. Certain gents, men from certain types of backgrounds, simply weren't going to be admitted as members of the old Knickerbocker, Olympic, or other highfalutin baseball clubs. And so these outcasts (let's call them blue-collar folks) started their own clubs. Dockworkers and factory guys and shit shovelers combined forces to play their own version of baseball, creating their own teams. And they quickly became good at it.

Inevitably, challenges were issued and match contests scheduled, sometimes pitting clubs from different social classes against one another. Soon after, people wanted to pay money to watch these Shakespearean battles between the classes. Gamblers became interested. Women began popping up in the crowd. The best players were being paid "under the table" to help clubs gain competitive advantages but then sometimes "revolving" to other rival clubs just days later to help *them* gain a competitive advantage. The crowds were getting larger, the stakes higher, and the whole enterprise murkier.

Finally, some of the highfalutin clubs began looking beyond social class, hiring ballplayers based solely on their ability to help them win games, regardless of which social circles they were part of. These clubs eventually declared themselves "professionals," and as gambling, revolving, and other things got out of hand, they realized they needed an association to govern the activities of all these various baseball clubs.

Anybody could start a baseball team, but not everybody could be a member of the National Association of Base Ball Players. Teams with black players were out. Teams who couldn't afford the annual membership dues were out. Teams who couldn't afford to travel or complete their schedules were out.

But this wasn't enough. There were still far too many clubs gaining entry.

After a few years, the very best of the association clubs wanted to distance themselves from the riffraff of the larger group. These clubs formed an even smaller, more exclusive "league" of teams, and this is when the primordial diamond dust erupted, igniting baseball's Big Bang in the 1870s and setting into motion the conditions for what would eventually become the modern structure of the game.

There was now a primitive major league and an insatiable interest in following the sport. But there was also no way to distribute this "national" baseball league to the country at large. And there was an extremely inefficient process for finding and developing talent. *These* were the conditions that precipitated the rise of an alternative professional baseball universe, beginning with independent minor leagues and rival major leagues and followed by barnstorming teams, all-black leagues, and the novelty clubs of the early twentieth century.

◆ ◆ ◆

Despite the growing pains of the Big Bang era—including player rebellions, competing leagues, rule changes, and other uprisings at the end of the nineteenth century—the National League had won the war of the insiders. They were kings of the baseball hill. It would be short-lived, of course, but for nine straight years (the longest span in history), they had a monopoly, serving as the only "major" baseball league in the country from 1892 to 1900. But was it the *best* league? Could some of the minor league teams operating at this time have held their own if given an opportunity in the big show? And just to make sure we're not giving short shrift to any lesser reservoirs of baseball talent, can we figure out how well the semiprofessional and college outfits stacked up compared to the National League?

How good were the outsiders?

We can answer just about anything by organizing data, and this includes the question of how baseball talent was distributed before 1900. Using information from retrosheet.org (much of which was compiled by researcher Walter LeConte on behalf of the website) and a sizable chunk of my own data, we can calculate the won-lost records of National League clubs against a variety of leagues and levels of amateur competition. Remember, official league games were only *part* of a team's regular summer schedule. Open dates were filled with nonleague engagements, as teams tried to make a couple extra bucks, plugging these exhibition games into their itineraries.

So here they are, the mighty National League teams *against the world*, circa 1876 to 1900 (drumroll, please). They're ranked in order from the easiest level of competition (or more precisely, the groups they had the most success against, head to head), to the most difficult.

3.1

National League Against the World (1876–1900)	W	L	T	PCT.	RF	RA
Cuba	9	0	0	1.000	115	19
Semipro teams	223	60	10	.788	2,538	1,198
Eastern Association	24	7	0	.774	216	132
College teams	9	3	0	.750	104	40
League Alliance	60	25	5	.706	418	275
International Association	55	35	5	.611	502	337
New England League	21	16	1	.568	185	175
National Association	21	20	2	.512	234	210
Eastern League	9	9	0	.500	111	106
Western League	8	10	1	.444	122	128

As in chapter two, the data are mostly what you'd expect. The National League dominated semipros, Cuban teams, and college clubs. If they didn't, there'd be a helluva baseball story here. Yet at the bottom of the list, it *does* get interesting. National League clubs managed a sub-.500, 38–39 combined record against the National Association, Eastern League, and Western League. If we're keeping score at home, that's a *losing* record, in 77 games, against minor league teams. And yeah, three other games wound up tied.

It's obvious these latter three groups weren't three run-of-the-mill base-ball operations, and they warrant a closer look. The National Association (NA), against whom the NL clubs went an uninspiring 21–20–2, was actually *the* major league before 1876. The NL clubs were defectors from the NA—the cream of the crop, really—but these reunion matchups yielded only lukewarm results. It's clear there was still some talent hovering on the NA rosters, and surely they played with something to prove.

In the 1890s, National League teams went 9–9 against Eastern League (EL) clubs. Sure, it's a small sample, but still, that's break-even baseball. Most of the EL rosters were peppered with men who had (or would get) major league experience, and by 1895 the Eastern League was classified as "A" ball, the highest minor league distinction at the time. It would eventually grow into the International League and be considered one of the top two or three minor leagues in the country for more than one hundred years. We'll talk more about the EL and its place in the hierarchy later on.

Finally, we get to the old Western League (WL). In a limited collection of games the NL comes up short once again, winning only eight, losing ten, and tying one. Under the leadership of Ban Johnson, this Midwest-based minor league boldly challenged the National League monopoly, actively recruited top talent from their rosters (Cy Young, Nap Lajoie, Mike Donlin, Joe McGin-nity), and eventually declared themselves a second major league under a new name, the American League, in 1901. Apparently, based on their head-to-head matchups with the National Leaguers, they were playing some decent baseball even before they raided the senior league of its star players.

And let's not forget there were other major challengers to the NL's claim as America's premier league aside from the top minor leagues. From 1876 to 1900, there were actually three other "major" leagues: the American Asso-ciation (1882–1891), the Union Association (1884), and the Player's League (1890). How did the NL stack up versus *these* competitors?

First of all, the Union Association of 1884 hardly deserves recognition as a major league. It lasted only one year, fewer than half its teams completed their entire schedules, and the majority of its players (70 percent, to be pre-cise) would either never play in another major league, other than their brief tour of duty in the enigmatic UA, or they would have a brief trial but fail. The St. Louis Maroons, who finished first in the one and only Union Association season, racked up a ridiculously superb 94–19 (.832) record, then transferred to the National League the very next season and finished dead last, managing to win only 36 of 108 games, even though they'd upgraded their talent at sev-eral positions. In his influential *Historical Baseball Abstract*, author Bill James eviscerates the UA's status as a major league, piece by piece, leaving only a bloody carcass at the end. No need to pile on at this point.

The Player's League of 1890 is much more intriguing. The by-product of baseball's first real struggle between labor (the ballplayers) and ownership (the wealthy old dudes), the Player's League came about when several NL veterans, led by star shortstop/attorney/president of the players' union/all-around interesting guy John Montgomery Ward, ditched their contracts and formed their own league. This was, in essence, baseball's first high-quality "outsider" baseball league. The Player's League warrants its own chapter later on. We'll have fun using the STARS system to untangle how the PL, NL, and lowly UA compared to one another.

Although unimaginable from today's vantage point, in the early 1880s there were *no* alcoholic beverages served inside National League ballparks. In 1882, a group of business magnates, many of whom owned breweries and distilleries, decided to form another major league where patrons could actually catch a little buzz at the game. Known pejoratively as the "Beer and Whiskey League," the American Association (AA) lasted from 1882 to 1891, serving as the party-time yin to the National League's puritanical yang. The two leagues formed a working relationship, and seven editions of a World Championship Series were held during the AA's ten-year history. The American Association took only one of these Fall Classics, while losing four and tying two. (Back in those days, teams were known to stop playing the World Championship Series midstream if the fans lost interest.)

So if we add up *all* the games between the Boozers and the Teetotalers— including the World Championship Series games, postseason tours, city series, and preseason and in-season exhibitions—we come up with this:

3.2

Boozers vs. Teetotalers	W	L	T	PCT.	RF**	RA
National League (Teetotalers)*	77	70	9	.523	749	614
American Association (Boozers)	70	77	9	.476	614	749

Note: *Although the National League ballparks didn't serve alcohol, its players included many world-class drinkers, such as Hall of Famers Michael "King" Kelly and "Smiling" Mickey Welch, who were sometimes pickled while on the field.

Note: ** For the obsessive reader: the runs scored haven't yet been collected for all the games. The RF and RA listed in table 3.2 are for 133 games (of 156), during which the NL went 73–54–6.

Today, exhibition games are few and far between. And thank heavens for that, really. With big-money TV contracts, lucrative merchandising arrangements, packed grandstands, and a full 162-game schedule spread out from late March to early October, there simply is neither time nor need for major league teams to squeeze in extra games against minor league clubs, let alone college or amateur groups. There are *some* of these sorts of games in spring training, yes, but big-league clubs often shuffle fifteen or twenty men into the lineup (many of them Triple-A guys) during the nine-inning affairs, and the outcomes are considered irrelevant. For that matter, when major league teams *play each other* in spring training today, the outcomes are irrelevant.

So, for many of us, it's difficult to conceptualize the past without filtering information through a modern-day lens. This means, among other things, we might have some skepticism about the significance of National League exhibition games in the 1800s. If those games don't mean much of anything today, how can we prove things were different one hundred years ago? For starters, the exhibition games were a larger part of their schedule back then, and relatively speaking, they must have been lucrative, otherwise they wouldn't have booked them. For these engagements to remain profitable, I'm assuming the major league clubs would have had to put on a good show. Losing, especially as the result of lackadaisical play, is *not* a good show. For most world-class athletes, losing doesn't sit well under any circumstances, and surely this must have applied to the mustachioed dandies from one hundred years ago.

But is there a way to analyze these exhibition games that showcases at least a patina of science? Well, yes. We can sort all the big-league exhibition games by where the clubs finished in the overall standings. We can show the exhibition records for the first-place teams, second-place clubs, third place, and so on and so forth. The hypothesis here is that the first-, second-, and third-place clubs should finish with better records in these exhibition games than the sixth-, seventh-, and eighth-place clubs. If the teams were going all out, it seems logical that the pennant winners/contenders would have fared better than the garden variety also-rans.

We'll go ahead and group the teams this way. Now keep in mind, these rankings do *not* include exhibition or World Championship Series games against other major league clubs. These are the NL teams versus minor league, amateur, college, and other nonprofessional teams.

3.3

NL Performance by Rank (1876–1900)	W	L	T	PCT.	RF	RA
First place	83	12	1	.874	946	299
Second place	60	29	2	.674	532	356
Third place	58	16	7	.784	516	270
Fourth place	70	38	7	.648	782	473
Fifth place	80	35	5	.696	818	507
Sixth place	42	25	0	.627	372	278
Seventh place	22	15	0	.595	257	198
Eighth place	14	14	1	.500	164	137
Ninth place	5	3	0	.625	61	48
Tenth place	6	6	0	.500	92	86
Eleventh place	7	3	0	.700	75	63
Twelfth place	2	3	1	.400	32	48

Note: The National League was formed with eight teams in 1876. The next season, they dropped two clubs that had failed to complete their playing schedules during the inaugural campaign, going down to only six clubs. By the 1890s, when the NL's top competitors (the American Association and Players League) folded up shop, the league ballooned to twelve franchises, where it would hold steady for most of the decade.

As you'll notice, the first-place teams did, in fact, roll up the best record in exhibition contests, going 83–12–1. At the bottom of the pile are the twelfth-place basement dwellers, who scratched out a meager 2–3–1 mark in our database. There *is* some of the usual numerical deviation here, but if you focus on the records of the first- through fifth-place finishers compared to the sixth- through twelfth-place clubs, the difference in quality is apparent. Even in these exhibition games, the better clubs separated themselves from the herd. Everybody seems to have played to their level, suggesting they took these games seriously. Or seriously enough.

Nobody likes losing.

◆ 4 ◆

ULYSSES

Ulysses Franklin "Frank" Grant was born August 1, 1865, near Pittsfield, Massachusetts. As you recall from the previous chapter, one of the earliest references to "base ball" in the American written record occurred in Pittsfield, where a village ordinance prohibited playing the game near the town's new meeting hall, owing to its several expensive (and easily shattered) glass windows. The ordinance was written in 1791, or nearly seventy-five years before Frank Grant was born.

Just four months after Frank's birth, his father, a farm worker highly regarded in the community, became seriously ill with a stomach ailment, passing away at the age of forty-four. Shortly thereafter, Frank's mother, Frances Grant, packed up her seven children and moved to the small village of Williamstown, twenty-five miles north, to accept a job as a housekeeper. To help pay the bills and care for her children, Frances, now a thirty-two-year-old widow, took in several boarders. She'd lost her husband, as well as one child during infancy, and now found herself in a crowded house, in a new town, with no choice but to soldier on, working long days to make ends meet.

Despite the hardships, Williamstown was in many ways a bucolic setting in which to raise a family, with leafy oak and hickory trees, bubbling streams, and rolling hills. It was home to a prestigious college (in fact, home to the first collegiate baseball game, in 1859); it had an outstanding library (with copies of the original Declaration of Independence and other historic documents on display) and strong community leadership. It was a slice of the old Americana some people fantasize about today, with apple pies and horses and all that stuff. It still is, actually: Williamstown hasn't changed too much since the Grants moved there nearly one hundred and fifty years ago.

By the late 1870s, Williamstown was about as baseball crazy as any other American burg at the time. The two youngest of Frances Grant's brood—Frank and his older brother Clarence—spent much of their free time on the open fields, likely emulating the stars of Harry Wright's Boston Red Stockings, who were arguably the greatest baseball club the country had ever seen. With his sure hands, extraordinary running speed, and strong stick work, Frank quickly became the envy of all the neighborhood boys. There was just something different about the way he played the game, a self-assuredness only those blessed with superior athletic gifts have.

◆ ◆ ◆

It came as no surprise when the old gang learned Frank had signed a professional contract to play with the Meriden Silvermen of the Eastern League. At age twenty, he was the youngest member on the squad, but he quickly established himself, going 4-for-5 with a double in a spring exhibition game versus the Yale University team. Despite the fact that eight of his teammates would get (or already had) major league experience, Frank's .316 batting average and .441 slugging mark were tops on the squad, by a wide margin.

Although Grant's emergence was a revelation, Meriden suffered from a lousy pitching staff and faltered in the standings. By late June, the home town's grandstands were mostly empty, save for the squirrels and bird shit. Management decided to cut their losses, closing up shop in early July, with most of the now-unemployed ballplayers signing on with other clubs in the region. Grant hooked up with the Buffalo Bisons of the International League. His new manager, Jack Chapman, was a crusty veteran from Brooklyn whose playing career dated way back to the days before professionalism. Jack had been the skipper of the old Louisville Grays, when they were charter members during the inaugural 1876 National League season.

Grant didn't miss a beat after changing uniforms. In 49 games, he batted .344 for Chapman's crew, which was easily the best mark on the Bisons. On his new team, there were twelve teammates who'd play Major League Baseball, and although Grant was clearly the top prospect of the bunch—and one of the youngest—he never got an opportunity in the big leagues. He returned to Buffalo in 1887 and batted .353 and came back in 1888 and batted a team-high .346 with 11 home runs. He'd been a member of four teams in three minor league seasons and had the highest batting average (and one of the top two slugging percentages) on every single team.

Defensively? Grant established himself as the best second baseman in the league. He was quiet but flashy in the field. Opposing sports reporters described his game as having "circus-like" qualities. One newspaper account said he could "jump three feet in the air and peg wayward throws with one hand." *Sporting Life*, a national newspaper, compared him directly to Fred Dunlap, who was considered by many to be the finest major league second baseman at the time.

Yet after three years, despite all he had accomplished as a ballplayer and all the accolades, things were less than rosy in Grant's career. To protect himself, he'd fashioned little wooden ankle guards to wear in the field because opponents went out of their way to spike him at every opportunity. At the plate, he'd become accustomed to hitting the dirt, as one or two pitches whizzed by his head during every game. Hecklers in the stands—even women and children—saved their most vile material for when Grant took the field. On road trips, he was often denied accommodations at hotels. His own *teammates* refused to be photographed with him during two of his three seasons.

So what exactly was wrong with Frank Grant? Was he arrogant? Was he a misanthrope? A drunkard? Did he play the game selfishly?

At age twenty, Frank Grant was one of the best players in the Eastern League, batting .316 with a .441 slugging percentage. *National Baseball Hall of Fame Library, Cooperstown, New York*

No, it wasn't any of those things. You see, Frank Grant was *black*. Being an African American born in 1865 was what some baseball historians have referred to as being "born too soon." As if one has a choice in such matters. If he'd been born fifty-five years later, he might have been Jackie Robinson.

But he wasn't.

Frank Grant came of age as a ballplayer when the professional game was still a boiling cauldron. The game's rules, structure, and hierarchy of power were in flux. There were labor issues simmering beneath the surface at the major league level, and in the late 1880s, it wasn't exactly clear how any of this would play out. It wouldn't be clear, actually, for another couple decades. And when it came to the color of a man's skin, things were even more trouble-some, especially for those of a darker hue.

The National Association of Base Ball Players banned black players and teams back in 1867, when Grant was still a baby, but for three decades peo-ple within the professional ranks (white owners, white managers, and white sportswriters) attempted to circumvent the segregation policy. Manager Jack Chapman, a white dude from the early days of baseball who had the guts to start Grant every day and bat him third in one of the top minor leagues in the country, is one of these forgotten pioneers.

For three years Jack Chapman tried to make it work. Actually, he attempted to sign Grant for a *fourth* campaign but gave up after learning a number of his ballplayers were considering some type of mutiny if Grant came back, even though they admitted he "was a good player." There were other teams and other managers who gave black players chances during the nine-teenth century. Moses Fleetwood Walker and his brother Welday logged some big-league playing time for skipper Charlie Morton when their club joined the American Association in 1884. At this same time, there were dozens of others who played with white teams in the minor leagues. And at every step, these little tests ultimately failed.

Eventually, all-black teams entered low-level white minor leagues and tried to make *that* work. After his tenure in Buffalo came to an abrupt end, Frank Grant played with a couple of these outfits. In terms of on-field per-formance, these little experiments were a nearly unmitigated success. The all-black Trenton Cuban Giants went 55–17 in the Middle States League in 1889, finishing second to Harrisburg, with the all-black New York Gorhams finishing third at 45–28. The York Colored Monarchs dominated the 1890 Eastern Interstate League, going 41–16 before the league collapsed midsum-mer. Finally, the Cuban Giants and a club known as the Gorhams were the prohibitive favorites in something called the Connecticut State League in 1891, but this loop fizzled out early in the season.

After the Eastern Interstate League fell apart in 1890, the York Colored Monarchs carried on as a barnstorming club, finishing the summer with an 88–27 record. After 1891, there wouldn't be any more all-black clubs perform-ing in the white minors. Often described as a "color line," it was really more like a circle, as African American baseball players and all-black teams were surrounded and then slowly penned in, excluded from pursuing opportuni-ties in what would soon be known as "organized baseball."

The years spanning roughly from 1892 to 1903 would be critical, paving the way for the insider/outsider structure of professional baseball that prevailed during the first fifty years of the twentieth century. This twelve-year period featured the following:

+ African American players and teams were completely excluded from organized baseball.

+ The players' revolt (the formation of the Players League in 1890) failed, resulting in not only the demise of their upstart circuit but also the downfall of the ten-year-old American Association as well, leaving the National League as the *only* major league in operation during the last decade of the nineteenth century. The white players were basically chattel at this point, the property of their employers, with very little wiggle room in terms of salary negotiation or the freedom to pursue job opportunities elsewhere.

+ The American League emerged as a rival to the National League in 1901. This temporarily meant better financial opportunities for those players willing to jump to the rogue operation. There was also an attempt (failed, of course) to include black players in the new "major" league, which we'll discuss in chapter twenty.

+ Peace between the rival leagues was established in 1903, resulting in the modern World Series and the two-league system that exists to this day. Also, a new version of the National Agreement was drafted, serving as the pact that governed the relationships between the various professional baseball leagues (both major and minor) and setting the rules for player contracts and other such concerns.

+ The popularity of baseball as a spectator sport exploded across the country, far outstripping organized baseball's ability to reach this vast audience or capitalize on every opportunity.

+ The first two decades of the twentieth century saw the emergence of professional baseball's shadow operation—consisting of disgruntled former major and minor leaguers, novelty baseball acts, foreigners, town teams, and black guys. Collectively, they were the *outsiders*, and on a given day, they played some of the best, most interesting baseball in the world.

◆ ◆ ◆

The legacy of Frank Grant and other African American ballplayers of his generation is that of collateral damage. They were prevented from rising to the top in organized baseball and also denied opportunities to showcase their abilities in the high-profile Negro leagues, which didn't come around until 1920, long after their playing days were over. Their careers are lost opportunities, gaps in the record, and the game's history is worse off for it.

Also lost in the fog is the legacy of men like Jack Chapman, a white manager who signed Grant and snubbed his nose at dissension from opponents, and his own ballclub, for as long as he could possibly bear, risking his own livelihood and reputation to run his team in a color-blind manner.

But as much as has been written about Branch Rickey and Jackie Robinson—and the Great Experiment—virtually nothing has been written about the white team owners, managers, and sportswriters who supported black athletes like Frank Grant in the 1880s and 1890s. These were men who tried to make integration work, in the face of four hundred years of bigoted mindsets, and that they came up short doesn't make their efforts any less admirable.

◆ 5 ◆

BASEBALL, DECODED

It does violence to common sense to suppose that, while athletes in every other sport today are measurably and vastly superior to those of fifty or seventy-five years ago, in baseball alone the quality of play has been stagnant or in decline.

—John Thorn, official historian of MLB

For several years, I've wanted to create a system for measuring league quality, where the overall talent could be presented as a single, easy-to-understand number. For example, the 1920 National League = 320. The 1934 American League = 345. The 1914 Pacific Coast League = 242. If we had a system that delivered trustworthy and tested data, in a simple format, it would enable us to research hundreds of questions that have been difficult to answer with any degree of certainty.

It's not that other people haven't worked on this problem, because they have. Prominent analysts such as Dick Cramer, Clay Davenport, David Gassko, and Nate Silver have chipped away at this issue and published various papers, articles, and books. But their findings have led to more debate than consensus. Part of this has to do with their objectives; part of it has to do with their methods.

What Dick Cramer and the analysts who came after him realized was that league quality is much more complex than the outcome of a seven-game series or midsummer exhibition game. And among other things, Cramer and crew have wanted to quantify how much baseball has improved over the years in order to evaluate players from the past versus those who populate the major leagues today.

You don't have to be a stat freak or a math whiz to understand the debate about league quality. Baseball fans have argued about this stuff dating back to the days when pitchers threw underhand and fielders didn't wear gloves. Which team was better, the Yankees or the Dodgers? Who has more great players, the National or American League? The bar bets would have to be settled by the results of the World Series or All-Star Game.

What Dick Cramer came up with in 1980, and what each subsequent generation of analysts has tinkered with, is establishing a control group of baseball players and comparing its performance from one year to the next or from one league to another league. Equivalent average (EqA) is one of the most commonly used metrics for such exercises these days because it normalizes a player's performance for ballpark and league environment.

If you compare a control group's EqA from one season to the next, you can tell things about how strong a league was in both years. For instance, if the control group's EqA gets lower or higher during the next season, one can infer whether the league is "tougher" or "easier." Same goes for minor league to major league comparisons: if you want to prove the Triple-A Pacific Coast League is a less talented environment than the major's National League, you only need to examine the performance of a control group, a group of players moving from the PCL to the NL, to see how the EqA differs. (If the control group is large enough, the EqA is always lower when moving from the PCL to the NL because the National League *is* more talented.)

Most sabermetricians agree on one thing: baseball has, indeed, become better over time, just like all other sports. What they can't agree on is how good Babe Ruth would be if he played today. Some suggest he would be nothing more than an average outfielder, while others believe he would still be an All-Star.

Because of this disagreement, sabermetricians added another mathematical component to fix the problem: regression to the mean. This was an improvement because it further normalized the data so that small adjustments didn't grow into massive distortions over the course of decades. And yet, a spirited debate still rages in the community regarding league quality.

After studying the research, I had a minor epiphany: adding my math to their thirty-plus years of hard work wasn't the right path. Not for what I wanted to learn. It was time to turn in a different direction since what I really wanted to study was how contemporary leagues measured against one another.

In short, I wanted to get away from the advanced metrics, for now, and start thinking about the characteristics of actual baseball leagues, teams, and players. What separates the great from the good and the good from the bad? Are there measurable traits that have nothing to do with their seasonal statistics? Of course there are.

◆ ◆ ◆

This is when I came up with the STARS system. I began messing around with this several years back. It's an acronym that stands for Service Time, Age, Rating System. I'll introduce the concept with a series of rhetorical baseball questions:

1. Do *most* (but not all) of the best baseball players make it to the major leagues?

2. Do the best major leaguers have longer careers than the replacement-level guys?

3. Do the very best of the long-career guys make it into the Hall of Fame?

4. Do athletes reach their peak at around twenty-eight years old?

5. Do the top seventeen men on a twenty-five-man roster have a much larger impact on their team's success than the last eight guys on the bench or in the bullpen (especially before 1950)?

6. Does it not make sense, then, that if you wanted to measure talent in a particular league (for example, the league with the best players, playing near their prime), you would want to construct a system built around points one through five?

7. Are there exceptions to points one through five?

8. Does using larger samples mitigate the exceptions?

The answer to all eight of these questions is . . . yes! So STARS is based on these eight commonsense principles. Instead of looking at a control group and examining their performance from one year to the next, we look at what we might describe as the baseball DNA of every single player in a given league. This gives us a huge control group. No stats. Basic math.

In the STARS system,

1. Players are awarded twelve points to begin with, just for playing pro ball.

2. Players are awarded one *extra* point for each season spent in the major leagues. Therefore, those who have longer careers are credited with more points.

3. Those who make it to the Hall of Fame (HOF) are awarded bonus points based on a sliding scale. For instance, inner-circle performers such as Walter Johnson, indisputably one of the greatest pitchers of all time, is credited with more HOF bonus points than players who were enshrined by the Veterans Committee, such as Joe Tinker or Johnny Evers.

4. Players are given full credit for each season of major league service (and, if applicable, full Hall of Fame bonus points) at age 28. *This is the only year they receive full credit.* For each year they move away from age 28, they lose points. For example, a player worth 20 points at age 28 is worth only 19 points at age 29, 18 points at age 30, and 17 points at age 31. His value continues to diminish as he ages. The same is true at the other end of the aging spectrum: younger players are worth less than guys in their prime. The same player is worth only 11 points at age 19, when he most likely is cutting his teeth in the minor leagues and still developing as a ballplayer.

5. The scores are tabulated for only those players who had a significant impact on their team's successes or failures. After all, when we discuss the great 1927 Yankees, we don't focus our attention on the contributions of benchwarmers Benny Bengough, Cedric Durst, and Julie Wera. We focus on the men who actually contributed. So, we choose an arbitrary number, which we hope captures each team's (and hence, each league's) most important contributors.

From 1910 through 1960, the STARS system calculates the individual points for the top 17 men on each team (or top 136 in an eight-team league).

From 1890 through 1909 (when rosters were smaller and starting pitchers completed a higher percentage of their games), this figure is reduced to 14 men. From 1876 through 1889, when teams basically went to war with their starters and a couple reserves, the number is 12.

6. You've probably picked up on this already, but STARS involves:

   ♦ calculating the scores for the top 17 men on each team;

   ♦ adding these numbers together to establish a team score;

   ♦ repeating this process for every team in the league;

   ♦ dividing this figure by the number of teams, to establish the league's STARS score.

If the eight teams in the 1908 National League totaled 2,440 points, this means the league's STARS score is 305 (2,440 divided by 8). One could then compare this score with that of the 1908 American League and have a very clear, very specific representation of how the talent level differed from one league to the other. You could also use the same system to compare one minor league to another. Obviously, any direct comparison between a major league and a minor league using this system begs the question to some extent, since the system is predicated on counting service time in the majors at a higher level than service in the minors. However, the system is exceptionally useful in comparing major and minor leagues—and teams—to each other.

7. There are several exceptions to the criteria used for grading players. Sometimes great players have short careers due to injury or death or indifference. On the other hand, there are mediocre players who have had long careers. There are bad Hall of Fame selections and men like Buzz Arlett, who spent most of his career in the minors, though he was clearly big-league timbre. All of these factors distort the STARS score a little bit.

8. The good news is we use large sample sizes, which have a tendency to cancel out the exceptions. You might argue that minor league star Buzz Arlett should have had a seventeen-year career in the major leagues, instead of the one year he actually enjoyed, and that he should be credited with all those points. But even if you give him the 16 extra points for when he was 28 years old and starring for Oakland in the Pacific Coast League, it would

only bump up the PCL's score by 2 points. Once you begin to see actual league scores, you'll understand this doesn't have a huge impact.

9. As an additional note, because a player needs to be retired before we're able to assign points to various seasons, the STARS system only works for historical comparisons and can't be used to predict anything or analyze the quality of modern leagues.

Although STARS is relatively simple on the surface, it would probably require an entire book to explain the system in detail. Understanding the basics should be sufficient for this book. There are a number of little adjustments that address issues such as time missed due to military service and novelty appearances in the big leagues. Should a veteran be credited with a full season of MLB service if he happened to have pinch-hit once when he was a fifty-four-year-old third-base coach? Of course not.

Let's put these ideas into action, using one of the most famous seasons from baseball history: 1927. And I'm going to begin with Lou Gehrig and the New York Yankees.

Lou Gehrig gets his initial 12 points and service time credit for 15 qualifying seasons, meaning he starts with 27 STARS points. He actually appeared in 17 different seasons, but we only give partial credit for years where position players logged fewer than 50 plate appearances, of which Gehrig had 3.

Gehrig was only 24 years old in 1927, meaning we have to deduct a few points because he's not at the peak performance age of 28. We subtract 4 points from his score, the difference between being 28 and 24, which leaves us with 23 STARS points.

Next, because he's an inner-circle Hall of Famer, Gehrig is awarded 11 bonus points. We reduce this figure as well, due to his age, leaving us with 7 HOF bonus points. This gives Lou Gehrig a final STARS score of 30 points.

We go through the same process for Babe Ruth. He gets 12 points, plus service time and Hall of Fame bonus points, adjusted by age, for a score of 37 points. This is massive. You get individual player scores higher than 30, and you're talking about guys with significant major league careers.

Then we work through the rest of the team, calculating figures for the top seventeen participants on the club, which usually means ten position players and seven pitchers. Catcher Pat Collins gets 19 STARS, shortstop Mark Koenig gets 18, and so on. The 1927 New York Yankees players' scores add up to a team total of 391.

After working through all the steps, we then repeat the process for the top seventeen players for the second-place Philadelphia Athletics, the third-place Washington Senators, and right on down the line to the last-place Boston Red Sox. The 1927 American League standings (with STARS scores) look like this:

5.1

1927 American League	STARS Score	W	L	PCT.
New York Yankees	391	110	54	.714
Philadelphia Athletics	387	91	63	.591
Washington Senators	384	85	69	.552
Detroit Tigers	366	82	71	.536
Chicago White Sox	346	70	83	.458
Cleveland Indians	337	66	87	.431
St. Louis Browns	324	59	94	.386
Boston Red Sox	295	51	103	.331

After adding all the team scores and dividing by eight, the 1927 American League finishes with an average STARS score of 354 per team. We call this the *league's* STARS score.

Notice that the STARS scores for the American League line up perfectly, with the first-place team having the highest mark and the last-place team the lowest. Everybody else in the middle lines up in an orderly, descending manner. I want to acknowledge this and dismiss its importance a little bit at the same time. Although there is a strong correlation between a higher STARS score and a better finish in the standings, the yearly totals aren't always going to line up as perfectly as the 1927 American League season.

The 1927 American League has a STARS score of 354. This gives us one data point. Without something to compare it to, that single score is meaningless. To find a comparison we can stay in the same year and use the same process for the 1927 National League, beginning with the first-place Pittsburgh Pirates (who were swept in the World Series by Gehrig, Ruth, and Co.). The Pirates have a score of 355. The second-place St. Louis Cardinals finish with 362. John McGraw's New York Giants had the best score in the NL (385) but finished third overall in a tight race. The Chicago Cubs, with Hall of Famers Hack Wilson and Gabby Hartnett, had 370. Rounding out the standings were the Reds (365), Dodgers (289), Braves (306), and last-place Phillies (297). This adds up to 2,729 total STARS points for the National League, which when divided by eight teams gives the senior circuit a STARS score of 341.

Here's the league comparison in table 5.2:

5.2

League	STARS Score
1927 American League	354
1927 National League	341

The American League gets a slight edge over the National League in 1927, which we can say translates to it being 3 or 4 percent more talented.

Now let's add one of the top minor leagues of 1927, the Pacific Coast League, whose STARS score is only 194:

5.3

League	STARS Score
1927 American League	354
1927 National League	341
1927 Pacific Coast League	194

There's a huge drop-off, naturally, as the STARS system is predicated on the fact that the major leagues are better than the minors. But there were some very good players in the PCL. Buzz Arlett was on the first-place Oakland Oaks, yet the highest team score was 216 for the second-place San Francisco Seals. They featured future Hall of Famer Earl Averill, a young slugger named Dolf Camilli, and Lefty O'Doul, who'd finish his big-league career with a .349 batting average. The Seals had several other decent major leaguers in their lineup but lacked pitching. They would have gotten clobbered at the major league level over the course of a long schedule.

I want to dig deeper into the minor leagues for some additional context. We'll calculate the STARS scores for the Cotton States League of 1927. If you've never heard of the Cotton States League, you're not alone. The league was part of what was known as Class D baseball back then, roughly the equivalent of today's low Single-A. Bottom of the pile. The best team in the 1927 Cotton States League was the Jackson (Mississippi) Senators, who featured future Hall of Fame catcher Bill Dickey and a handful of other guys who'd get cups of coffee in the majors. Most of these men were young; so the Jackson Senators team score was 134.

Let's compare the Cotton States League to the higher-level PCL:

5.4

League	STARS Score
1927 Pacific Coast League	194
1927 Cotton States League	108

Hopefully, what we understand now is the size of baseball's professional tent in 1927. We know the very best teams approached a score of near 400, and the major leagues *overall* had a score around 350. We know the high minors penciled in around 200 while the low minors scored closer to 100.

But what exactly does any of this have to do with outsider baseball and this book in particular? Quite a bit, actually. One of the major themes of this book is the distribution of talent. It's about how, before 1950, a number of the best professional baseball players in the world plied their trade outside the domain of organized baseball. There have been other books and articles written about the outsiders—the Negro leaguers, white semipros, and barnstorming foreign clubs from our game's past—but there's never been a framework for quantifying how talented these teams and leagues were.

STARS offers a precise view of how talent was distributed and reveals differences in ability obscured by the classification system used by organized baseball at the time. But because it is based on a player's age and service time, it can be used to measure any minor league against another, even if it's a league of teams who were not part of baseball's official professional system.

The system becomes one of the tools used in this book to answer questions that have persisted for decades. A white semipro team called the House of David became famous after defeating a number of major league teams during spring training games in the 1930s. We can examine their roster and use the STARS system to figure out how good they were relative to the rest of semiprofessional baseball. The Pittsburgh Crawfords of the Negro National League are often touted as one of the greatest teams of all time. A specially modified version of STARS (explained later in this book) reveals the truth about the team and its league. We'll also use the STARS system to look at clubs inside organized baseball's tent, putting the spotlight on several legendary minor league teams from the game's past. What this reveals may surprise you.

◆ 6 ◆

THE STARRY-EYED UNION ASSOCIATION

WHAT CAN THE STARS SYSTEM TELL US about baseball in 1884? This was the year the Union Association (UA) emerged, declaring itself a third major league. In his *Historical Baseball Abstract*, author Bill James wrote at length about the UA's merits as a major: "When I sat down to take a hard look at that issue, I was astonished to discover how weak the Union Association's argument to be considered a major league actually is." James went on to methodically take down the UA, piece by piece. But the most damning bit of evidence, in my opinion, was the fact that the UA's championship club, the St. Louis Maroons (who *dominated* the UA, winning 83 percent of their games), transferred to the National League the very next year and finished dead last.

Let's look at the situation using STARS. For context, we'll include the average STARS scores for the top three professional baseball leagues in the country: the National League, American Association, and Union Association. All Union Association players are given credit as if the UA was a major league in Table 6.1.

6.1

1884 Major Leagues	STARS Score
National League	239
American Association	191
Union Association	168

The work of Bill James, and others, has called into question the UA's designation as a major league. What if we took away the STARS credit from the UA teams, then lined the league up with two of the top minor leagues of 1884 in an apples-to-apples STARS table?

6.2

1884 Minor Leagues	STARS Score
Union Association	155
Northwestern League	110
Eastern League	107

Looking at this problem from two different angles, it seems the Union Association was clearly inferior to the two established major leagues in 1884 but head and shoulders above the two highest minor leagues, occupying the void between the two top levels of competition.

◆ ◆ ◆

At the end of the season, the Providence Grays (250 STARS), champions of the National League, played the AA Champion New York Metropolitans (233) in the first official interleague World Championship Series, sweeping them in three straight games. They outscored their opponents 21–3, winning the crown in dominating fashion.

The Union Association was actually much closer to the Northwestern and Eastern leagues than it was to the National League. If we ranked the teams by STARS scores, then divided them into descending groups of eight, with each subset representing the hierarchy of talent in 1884, this is how things shake out: of the best eight teams on paper in 1884, six are from the National League, with the other two representing the American Association. In the second group of eight, six of the clubs are from the American Association, with one National League team and one club from the Union Association. The third tier has the final NL club, two AA clubs, two UA teams, one Eastern League team, and one Northwestern League team. The fourth tier (and I don't think we'll need to go any further after this) is represented by two AA clubs, three UA teams, two NW clubs, and one EL outfit.

In summary, the Union Association obviously doesn't merit its major league classification. We've known this since Bill James shredded it apart years ago, but we now know the Union Association certainly appears to have been better than the Northwestern and Eastern leagues.

◆ 7 ◆

A LEAGUE OF THEIR OWN

IMAGINE BACK IN 1994 if, instead of hitting the picket lines, Greg Maddux, Tony Gwynn, Barry Bonds, Mike Piazza, and another couple hundred National League players had simply walked out on their contracts and started their own league, playing on newly formed ballclubs in the same cities where they normally plied their trade. This is exactly what occurred in 1890, when the National League nearly came unglued, and the future of Major League Baseball hung in the balance.

In 1885, something called the Brotherhood of Professional Base Ball Players (BPBBP) was organized, with Monte Ward, star shortstop of the New York Giants (and recent Columbia Law School graduate), assuming its presidency. The Brotherhood was the first professional sports union of note, and in the beginning, aside from slowly building their membership, they concerned themselves with fraternal and charitable activities.

By 1887, ninety National League players had joined the organization, and each city had its own BPBBP chapter. There was power in numbers, and Ward began speaking out on behalf of the group against the biggest labor issue of the day: baseball's reserve clause.

In order to curb escalating salaries, big-league owners formally adopted the first official version of the reserve clause in December 1879. During this era, all players signed one-year contracts, but under the new clause, teams were able to "reserve" the services of a certain number of players for the upcoming season, even after their contracts had expired. By 1885, the reserve clause was expanded to include *everybody*. Players were forbidden from shopping their services to other clubs or leagues and therefore had almost zero leverage when negotiating compensation issues with their employers. About the only thing players could do, when dickering over contract details, was threaten to hold out. At the time, it was either shut up and sign the contract or hunker down in a nerve-racking, one-man player strike. Many men chose the latter; others simply walked away—played in outlaw leagues—or pursued work in other professions. Such was baseball at the time.

Under Monte Ward's leadership, the Brotherhood won some small, temporary concessions from the National League ownership group. Most notable was the reserved player's "right" to shop his services to other clubs when his contract offer was for *less* money than the previous season. This was all well and good, assuming the owners weren't in collusion with one another.

Star player John Montgomery Ward spearheaded baseball's first important players' union. They not only battled the establishment but started their own league. *National Baseball Hall of Fame Library, Cooperstown, New York*

Before the beginning of the 1889 season, John T. Brush, owner of the National League's Indianapolis franchise, proposed a salary cap for players. Known as the "Brush Classification System," the other owners quickly adopted this five-tier program, setting *all* salaries from a range of $1,500 to $2,500 annually, depending on a player's "habits, earnestness, and special qualifications," as demonstrated the previous season.

This was the last straw. In June 1889, members of the Brotherhood gathered in secret to brainstorm a formal response to what Monte Ward would later refer to as an "utter failure to consider the rights of the players." Unconfirmed rumors circulated that the players planned to strike during the first week of July, which included the lucrative Independence Day doubleheaders, a tradition at the time.

Nothing came of the strike, but at another clandestine meeting held in mid-July, at the Fifth Avenue Hotel in New York, Ward and his cohorts decided to explore the feasibility of starting their own league. Specifically, they wanted to see if they could recruit financial backers who could help get their league—the Players League—off the ground in 1890.

In short order, several money men were rounded up and convinced of the idea's viability. Included in the mix were New York real estate speculators, streetcar entrepreneurs, contractors, and a couple "old money" boys from Philadelphia who ran a large meat processing business. Some of the players, including Brotherhood president Ward, agreed to invest some of their own money in the venture.

With financing in place, the Players League began the 1890 season with eight solid franchises in place, each of whom would complete their 130-odd-game schedule. Thanks to the appeal of its numerous stars, the PL did well at the gates, and although accurate figures are elusive (teams from both leagues were fudging attendance numbers throughout their summer-long publicity war), most historians believe the upstart organization actually outdrew the older, more established National League.

While all of this was occurring, the original "second" major league—the American Association—was still in operation, meaning there were no fewer than twenty-four big-league clubs competing for patrons in 1890. The AA rosters weren't hurt by the emergence of the contracting-raiding Players League as much as the NL had been, but they had other issues to contend with. Their top club from 1889, the champion Brooklyn Bridegrooms, jumped to the National League in 1890, weakening the AA's faith in the National Agreement, which had fostered peace between the two major leagues for nearly a decade.

In their preseason promotional publication, Monte Ward wrote, "The Players League stands brightly forth as the strongest eight clubs in playing talent and general personnel ever gathered together."

Let's pause right here. Organized baseball, at its very top level, was on the verge of imploding in 1890. Although the PL did well at the gates, compared to the National League, attendance figures for both leagues combined were severely down. Two American Association teams went bankrupt during the season. The talent was being spread thinly across three leagues, just as it had been back in 1884. But let's look at Ward's claim: was the upstart Players League *really* the most talented of the bunch?

Let's go ahead and use the STARS system at this point, so we can line up the three major leagues from 1890 in an easy-to-understand table, giving us a quick answer:

7.1

1890 Professional Leagues	STARS Score
Players League	299
National League	274
American Association	226

In one fell swoop, the players had indeed created the most talented league in the country.

◆ ◆ ◆

In 1889, the Baltimore Orioles finished 70–65 (.519) in the American Association, good for fifth place in the eight-team major league. The next season, they moved down to the Atlantic Association, a minor that had aspirations of becoming a *fourth* major league. Although the Orioles suffered a number of roster defections (apparently their best players weren't too keen about playing in a lower league), they were still good, dominating the Atlantic Association. By late summer they had rolled up a ridiculous 77–24 (.762) mark, by far the best in the league.

But with the lack of competition, attendance at the ballpark suffered. Finally, in an act to salvage the final six weeks of the summer, the Baltimore Orioles rejoined the major leagues, becoming a member of the American Association again. In 34 games, they went 15–19 (.441). I'm not sure how many fans returned to the ballyard to watch their men lose to stiffer competition. But the Orioles provide a glimpse of how each league related to one another at the time.

At the end of the season, with animosity at a fever pitch, manager King Kelly of the Players League–champion Boston Reds offered to participate in a three-way World Championship Series with the Brooklyn Bridegrooms and Louisville Colonels, the pennant winners in the NL and AA, respectively. Kelly's overture was simply ignored.

Instead, Brooklyn and Louisville embarked on a best-of-seven series to determine the "champion of the world." The series went back and forth, each team winning three games (with one tie) before interest simply fizzled out and both clubs returned home without ever playing the deciding contest. The season ended as it began—in limbo.

It's sort of fitting, really. The 1890 World Championship Series marks the first time the best teams from the best league in the country weren't part of the program. For one summer, the Players League teams were the outsiders, and yet they were kings of the baseball diamond.

In 1968, Major League Baseball's records committee determined the Players League met its criteria as a big league and added its statistics to the official record.

◆ 8 ◆

INHERIT THE WIND

ALL THREE MAJOR LEAGUES HEMORRHAGED MONEY in 1890. The National League reportedly lost from $300,000 to $500,000 during the season. Although kept secret at the time, one of their most important franchises, the New York Giants, needed an $80,000 midsummer loan from the other league magnates to keep from going bankrupt during the campaign. The American Association was even worse off, as two of their franchises (Philadelphia and Brooklyn) *did* file for bankruptcy during the campaign. Brooklyn, in fact, finished the season playing in a minor league.

At the end of the year, the upstart Players League actually held the advantage. Their rosters had most of the star players, and during the season they had higher attendance figures than the other two leagues. Although they'd also lost money, their operational deficit at the end of the year was said to be only $125,000. Their players had resisted lucrative offers to defect back to the National League, and it appeared everything was in order for a second season. In fact, a group of owners from the National and Players leagues met in New York to discuss a peace proposal.

Although the details are lost to time, what occurred was akin to a poker game. The financial backers of the Players League were naïve in the ways of the baseball business and had no idea they were sitting at the table with the upper hand. Instead, National League magnate Albert Spalding convinced the PL ambassadors to reveal the specifics of their financial situation early in the negotiations while remaining mum on the National League's troublesome disposition. The men from the Players League were led to believe their investment was in dire straits and, according to some historians, they may have thought they were the only league to have lost money during the season.

It was an unexpected turn in the conversation, and Spalding seized the opportunity to shift the tone from compromise to liquidation. With the fear of losing their investments, the Players League representatives turned their backs on the Brotherhood (the players' union) and surrendered to the National League. They were holding a royal flush but simply panicked while sitting across the table from experienced baseball men.

The shocking demise of the Players League set into motion a number of cataclysmic events in the upper echelon of the baseball universe. After a truce was called, most of the rogue manpower from the PL was reabsorbed by the older, more established National League. Rival teams from the same cities were consolidated. Ownership groups bought and sold franchises to one another. One club—the PL-champion Boston Reds—jumped to the American Association, which was bloodied but still considered a major league at the time. And one year later, after the 1891 season, the entire American Association fell apart, with *its* remnants gobbled up by the gravitational pull of the National League.

By 1892, the National League was a monopoly—the last major league standing. Just eight years earlier, there had been three leagues and thirty-four "major" league franchises. In 1890, there were twenty-five big-league teams. In 1891, after the collapse of the Players League, there were only seventeen clubs. In 1892, the National League fielded twelve teams. By 1900, when they were still the only game in town, the National League had contracted to eight clubs.

In astrophysics, the prevailing theory of black holes—stellar masses whose gravitational pull is so strong not even light can escape—is that they will continue to absorb the energy of other fallen stars, growing larger and more powerful over time. The exact *opposite* seems to be true of the National League at the end of the nineteenth century. They not only went from twelve teams down to eight, but attendance figures shriveled. An economic recession and a lack of competition were killing the game.

The rough-and-tumble Baltimore Orioles of the John McGraw and Wee Willie Keeler era, clearly the most famous team of the 1890s (and winners of three straight pennants), lost nearly 65 percent of their gate receipts from 1894 to 1899 before becoming one of four clubs *contracted* out of the league following the regular season. Overall, the National League attendance figures were down a more modest 3 percent.

◆ ◆ ◆

Although they probably wouldn't have understood this, the National League actually *needed* competition, and by the mid-1890s, just as things were turning for the worse at the game's highest level, a man named Ban Johnson had something brewing in the Midwest.

◆ 9 ◆

SORRY, CHARLIE

A T THE DAWN OF THE TWENTIETH CENTURY, Art "Superman" Pennington's grandfather, Elmer J. Walker, worked as a drayman in Hot Springs,
Arkansas. A resort town, it's likely Walker's delivery route included a number
of the luxurious hotels within the small community, as they were (and still are)
the lifeblood of the area.

When Superman grew up in Hot Springs during the 1930s and '40s, it
was, he remembered, a "friendly" place for African Americans to live. The
town had more than doubled in size since the time his grandfather lived and
worked there, but at twenty thousand full-time residents, it still maintained
the intimacy of a close-knit community. The fact that the Pennington/Walker
family, with various branches of aunts and uncles and cousins, stayed there for
more than five decades, gainfully employed, is certainly a testament to their
comfort level and the opportunities available within this integrated southern
town.

Although now known more for its therapeutic springs and its legacy as
a gilded-age getaway (as well as the hometown of President Bill Clinton), the
small Arkansas village also has a fascinating baseball history. It was there, of
course, that blackball impresario Candy Jim Taylor showed up on the Pennington's front porch in the late 1930s, asking for permission to sign their
teenage son to a professional baseball contract to play for an all-black team
called the Chicago American Giants.

More than fifty years earlier, another Chicago baseball team made history in Hot Springs. In 1886, the National League powerhouse Chicago White
Stockings (predecessor to the Cubs) traveled south, setting up camp in what
would later be recognized as the first modern spring training. By the time

Grandpa Walker was delivering various merchandise and sundries around town, it seemed as though *everybody* in big-league baseball was converging on little Hot Springs during the month of March. Eventually, nearly half of all major league teams would use the community as their home base for training camp, and nearly every big-name player in baseball history, from Ty Cobb to Walter Johnson to Dizzy Dean, would limber up (and enjoy the restorative powers of the "magical" spring waters there) at some point during their careers.

In fact, on St. Patrick's Day in 1918, the great Babe Ruth himself launched an epic Hot Springs home run that cleared the right-field fence, landing inside a pond at an enclosed alligator zoo. Because the place is still there, unchanged for nearly one hundred years, modern investigators used GPS and other tools (interviewed the older alligators?) to estimate the distance of Ruth's Arkansas bomb. Their best guess ranges from 500 to 570 feet.

The man who first brought the Chicago White Stockings to Arkansas for spring training was one Adrian Constantine Anson of Marshalltown, Iowa.

Known affectionately as "Cap," Anson was arguably the greatest player of the nineteenth century and manager of the era's best team. Under his leadership, Anson's clubs won five pennants and finished second four times in twenty-one seasons. Overall, they won 58 percent of their games from 1875 to 1898. As the starting first baseman for most of these teams, Anson racked up 3,425 hits (the first man to collect 3,000 hits in a career) and compiled a fine .334 career batting average. He also led the National League in RBI eight times. For comparison's sake, the big guy who slugged the massive alligator pond home run led the American League in RBI on only six occasions.

Perhaps the greatest player of the nineteenth century, Adrian "Cap" Anson has become baseball's symbol of **bigotry**. *National Baseball Hall of Fame Library, Cooperstown, New York*

Yet today, among serious fans of the game's history, Cap Anson is widely known for something other than his career batting records and managerial excellence: he's known for his bigotry. Just a year after their first trip to Hot Springs, Anson and the Chicago White Stockings became the principals in an incident that would reverse the flow of racial integration at baseball's highest level.

A close examination of the facts suggests that prior to the Anson affair, the currents of racial harmony on the baseball diamond were turbulent but gradually flowing in a positive direction. African American brothers Fleetwood and Welday Walker made brief appearances in the major leagues as teammates on the American Association's Toledo Blue Stockings. Frank Grant, our old friend from Pittsfield, Massachusetts, was starring for the all-white Buffalo Bisons in the International League. A number of other African Americans had earlier played minor league baseball with established white clubs, including Bud Fowler, who batted .308 in ten professional seasons, and pitcher George Stovey, who won 60 percent of his ballgames in the white minor leagues.

On July 14, 1887, Cap Anson and the Chicago White Stockings traveled to Newark, New Jersey, to play an exhibition game versus the Little Giants of the International Association. Before the game, Anson announced his team would refuse to take the field if the Little Giants' black battery of George Stovey and Fleet Walker were penciled into what was otherwise an all-white lineup. Stovey, for what it's worth, was in the midst of an astonishing season, eventually finishing with a 34–14 record and an excellent 2.48 ERA for Newark. There were rumors the New York Giants of the National League were interested in his services.

Little Giants skipper Charlie Hackett acquiesced, permitting the game (and the promise of a large gate receipt) to proceed. Stovey didn't pitch and Walker didn't catch, both having come down with some type of last-minute illness. Although they didn't field their top battery, the Newark Little Giants actually defeated Anson's mighty men anyway, 9–4.

That evening, just hours after the game, executives from the International Association met to discuss various issues, including Sunday baseball (forbidden in certain cities) and what newspapers referred to as the troublesome increase of the "colored element" within the league. Specifically, at least one owner suggested the league's top white players were "threatening to leave" if the issue of race wasn't addressed—and by *addressed*, they meant they didn't want any more nonwhite players in the league. There was some sort of motion passed preventing the signing of additional "colored" players, effective immediately.

The existing black players, including Stovey and Walker, were grand-fathered in and thus permitted to continue playing in the International Association.

A couple additional facts add to the complexity of the issue being raised at the International Association's meeting: Newark was in first place when the White Stockings visited town, playing .700 ball behind the leadership of African American George Stovey, who happened to be the most dominant pitcher in the league. Fleet Walker, the black catcher and former major leaguer, didn't hurt their cause with his excellent defense and respectable .264 batting average. In second place were the Buffalo Bisons, who featured Frank Grant from Pittsfield (yes, him again) and his stellar .353 batting average and league-high 11 home runs. Not to be outdone, the Syracuse Stars had a black pitcher named Bob Higgins, who rolled up an impressive 20–7 mark with a 2.90 ERA. The next year, despite vocal opposition from several teammates, Higgins returned to Syracuse, going 17–7 with a 2.76 ERA. It's likely that some of the opposition to a *complete* ban on black athletes in the IA was due to the simple fact that these athletes could *play*.

There was one final wrinkle: on the same day Anson's White Stockings refused to take the field against a team featuring black players, the Indianapolis Hoosiers (who'd finish dead last in the National League, six spots behind Cap's team) were just fifty miles away, getting their butts kicked by an all-black club called the Trenton Cuban Giants. Clearly, not all major league managers shared Anson's views.

◆ ◆ ◆

So, exactly how *did* Cap Anson become the unofficial figurehead of baseball's color line? Why is this former star, idol to thousands of nineteenth-century lads, now the mustachioed face of hatred?

Anson was dead for nearly fifty years before authors Robert Peterson (*Only the Ball Was White*) and Art Rust began untangling the knotted history of baseball's segregated past. The rediscovery of the incident at Newark and the revelations from Anson's own autobiography, published in 1900 and later excerpted as a series of nationally syndicated newspaper articles in 1911 (both peppered with painfully racist commentary), proved damning.

But it was actually another book, published in 1907, that first exposed the Chicago manager's role in the development of baseball's so-called color line. *Sol White's History of Colored Base Ball, With Other Documents on the Early Black Game, 1886–1936* was (to my knowledge) the first *specific* reference to Cap Anson and the 1887 incident in Newark. White was an African American ballplayer who starred for many seasons during the integrated minor league era. An erudite man and natural leader, he'd later organize one of the greatest black teams ever, during the first decade of the twentieth century. He probably crossed paths with Anson during his career and certainly knew other black players who had had interactions with the man. In fact, Sol was teammates with George Stovey for many seasons *after* the incident in Newark, and it's a pretty good assumption that they would have discussed the Anson affair at some point.

In White's book, we have perhaps the closest thing we'll ever get to a primary-source account of the Newark incident, from the perspective of the black athletes. The George Stovey situation wasn't the first time Anson refused to field his club against a black opponent (a couple other times it involved Fleet Walker), but it became the most famous because Cap was something the other baseball bigots weren't: he was powerful. He was somebody big enough to retroactively attach all of the rage and indignation and exasperation of an entire generation to.

The controversial title of Art Rust's book, *"Get That Nigger Off the Field!" A Sparkling, Informal History of the Black Man in Baseball* (1976), was supposedly a direct quote from Cap Anson himself. It was shouted from the bench, some believe, during an 1883 encounter versus the Toledo Mud Hens, who had Fleetwood Walker at catcher. It's vile. It's hateful. It's certainly the type of language Anson (and many people) used in everyday conversation back then. But when modern researchers traced the origins of that specific quote, it doesn't appear to go back much further than Rust's book. We're simply not sure Anson ever really uttered that specific phrase back in 1883, yet the stench of it lingers like a skunk.

◆ ◆ ◆

The cruel irony is that as African Americans were being denied opportunities in organized baseball here in the States, the game itself was being introduced abroad to myriad cultures. Cap Anson's boss, Albert Spalding (who owned both the Chicago White Stockings and a growing chain of sporting goods stores), organized a world tour in 1888–1889, bringing baseball to several foreign countries, including New Zealand, Australia, Egypt, France, and the United Kingdom.

In 1890, John McGraw and an obscure minor league pitcher named Al Lawson organized the first American baseball tour of Cuba, mopping up the competition. At around this same time, academics and ex-patriots were organizing ballgames in Japan. The seeds of both globalization and winter baseball were being planted.

By the end of the nineteenth century, the white players in the States were more pissed off than ever over the reserve clause (which limited their negotiating leverage), and they looked to create a new union. The black players had been virtually eliminated from every corner of organized baseball. And the National League (although the *only* big league in business) was eliminating teams and watching its gate receipts diminish during the country's economic recession.

Recognizing a moment of weakness, Ban Johnson, a former reporter from Cincinnati, assumed control of the Western League (said to be the top minor circuit in the country) and secretly hatched a plan to convert it into a major league. One of his managers would go rogue, launching a scheme to include black guys in the new circuit.

◆ ◆ ◆

The Western League was formed during the mid-1880s, and although its rosters were filled with a number of former and future big leaguers, the Midwest-based minor league had a series of sputters and starts, with franchises coming and going from one year to the next. A couple times, the entire circuit collapsed, disappearing for a season or two before a new crop of delusional entrepreneurs decided to throw some more money at it, starting it up all over again.

When Cincinnati Reds manager Charlie Comiskey's contract wasn't renewed following the 1894 season, he decided to leave the National League and purchase a minor league team. Comiskey bought the Western League's Sioux City franchise and promptly moved it to St. Paul, Minnesota. Comiskey was already good friends with Western League president Ban Johnson, whom he knew from his managerial days back in Cincinnati, where Johnson had covered the Reds while working as a reporter for the Cincinnati *Commercial-Gazette*. It's been suggested that Comiskey actually *helped* Johnson land the administrative job in the struggling minor league in 1893, then joined the circuit a year later himself as part of what was already a grand scheme to create a second major league. Indeed, by 1896 Ban Johnson was already suggesting his league was "ready to go on its own." And by the end of the decade, the Western League was considered the finest minor league in the country.

Following the 1896 season, Connie Mack, player-manager of the Pittsburgh Pirates (and a Players League alum), vacated his National League post, moving to the Western League's Milwaukee Brewers, where he'd manage, play catcher on occasion, and own 25 percent of the ballclub. A couple years later, young John McGraw (pioneer of the first American baseball trips to Cuba) was hired to manage the Western League's new Baltimore franchise.

In Comiskey, Johnson, Mack, and McGraw (all later elected to the Hall of Fame in Cooperstown, based on their track record as managers/administrators), the Western League had four of the shrewdest baseball minds of a generation under one tent. The pieces were in place for a bold move. Meanwhile, over in the National League, disgruntled reps from the players' union met with ownership, proposing new reforms to the standard contract and reserve clause, but were basically laughed out of the room. And with this opening, the well-funded Western League prepared its attack.

◆ ◆ ◆

At the same time Ban Johnson and Charlie Comiskey were leaving Cincinnati for the Western League, another Queen City resident named Charlie Grant was venturing off to pursue *his* baseball dreams. Born the son of an Ohio horse trainer in 1877, Charlie Grant was an African American second baseman known for his slick fielding and steady work at the plate. In 1896, at just eighteen years of age, Charlie joined the Page Fence Giants of Adrian, Michigan, the so-called "Colored Champions of the West."

Founded one year earlier as a promotional vehicle for a white-owned wire fence company in Adrian, the Page Fence Giants were spearheaded by Bud Fowler, who back in the 1870s became one of the first black men to play professional baseball in the white leagues. Fowler helped construct the Giants' roster by recruiting several established players from the Chicago Unions, the best black professional team in the Windy City. During their inaugural campaign, the Page Fence Giants went 118–36–2, prompting manager A. S. Parsons to suggest his team was "of Western League quality" by the end of the season.

Incidentally, the club actually got off to a rocky start in 1895, going 5–13 in April while playing against such teams as the National League's Cincinnati Reds (Comiskey's old club) and several outfits from Ban Johnson's upstart Western League. Perhaps fearing the worst, Bud Fowler, architect of the Page Fence Giants, jumped from his own team early on to play for Adrian's white team in the Class B Michigan State League, where he batted .331. Parsons was installed as manager, and although the club now had a void at second base, they rattled off a remarkable 113–23 (.831) record after Fowler was gone.

The next spring, Parsons secured the services of the teenage phenom from Cincinnati. With young Charlie Grant at second base and twenty-three-year-old Grant "Home Run" Johnson at shortstop, the Page Fence Giants boasted perhaps the best middle infield in black professional baseball. Home Run Johnson had cracked 60 home runs while a member of the semipro Findley

(Ohio) Sluggers in 1894, then batted .471 during his first season with the Page Fence Giants.

By 1896, the two best second basemen in black baseball were teenager Charlie Grant in Michigan, and thirty-one-year-old Frank Grant of New York. Frank, of course, was the veteran who had for many seasons dominated the nearly all-white International League, hitting for both average and power and playing flashy defense, raising the eyebrows of the opposition and sports reporters alike. By the end of the '90s, as opportunities for blacks in white baseball became few and far between, Frank had signed on with one of the great all-black East Coast powerhouses, the Cuban Giants.

By the end of the nineteenth century, Western League president Ban Johnson was ready to challenge the established National League. *National Baseball Hall of Fame Library, Cooperstown, New York*

So, in the burgeoning world of all-black, independent professional teams, three of the biggest stars were Charlie Grant, Frank Grant, and Grant "Home Run" Johnson. The top clubs were the Page Fence Giants, Cuban Giants (sometimes called the "Genuine" Cuban Giants), and the Cuban X-Giants (who were often simply referred to as the Cuban Giants, without the *X*). There were *no* actual Cubans performing on any of these Giants teams, mind you, but John McGraw (manager of the Western League Baltimore franchise and eventual skipper of the New York Giants) had already traveled to the island a couple times with minor league all-star clubs, playing the real *Cubanos* in what would come to be known as the "American Series."

Confused? You should be, as things weren't really any less murky at the time. In fact, the convergence of all these befuddling details would play a small role in the sabotage of Major League Baseball's last attempt to employ an African American, decades before Jackie Robinson and Branch Rickey concocted their Great Experiment.

◆ ◆ ◆

It's impossible to know for sure, but Art "Superman" Pennington's grandfather, Elmer J. Walker, may have been making a delivery to the Eastman Hotel in Hot Springs, Arkansas, just as Baltimore skipper John McGraw met with a skinny black kid out front. If Walker *had* passed by on that fateful March afternoon in 1901, it's likely he would have recognized Charlie, the new kid, who was working as a bellhop at the hotel over the winter.

Even if Grandpa Walker didn't visit the Eastman that day, he probably would have heard about what was happening later on. There were about nine thousand people living in Hot Springs at the time, of which only a couple hundred were African American. It was a small, insular community, and certainly those blacks who worked in connection with the hotel industry (say, delivery men and bellhops) would have gotten to know one another.

The new kid at the Eastman was a twenty-three-year-old African American baseball player/bellhop named Charlie Grant. People said he had played a little ball up north, with a team called the Page Fence Giants, and was working at the hotel during the off-season. John McGraw, manager of the Baltimore Orioles, wanted to speak with the second baseman about the possibility of playing some *major league* baseball in the freshly minted American League. McGraw's team was going to need some talent, he explained, if they were going to compete with the National League monopoly.

◆ ◆ ◆

Ban Johnson's Recipe for Building His Own Major League:

1. Purchase a minor league.

2. Declare your intentions to become a major league.

3. Secure the backing of a financier with deep pockets. In Johnson's case, the primary money man was coal industry executive Charles Somers, who lived in Cleveland. During the early years of the American League, at one point or another, Somers's cash helped keep at least five of the eight franchises afloat.

4. Lure other ambitious, strong-willed baseball minds into the enterprise, offering partial ownership of clubs, if needed.

5. Expand the scope of your minor league's appeal by moving its franchises from smaller burgs into larger, major league markets. Change the name from Western League (which had only a regional appeal) to the much more illustrious-sounding "American League."

6. Offer the best ballplayers in the world better salaries and more favorable treatment.

7. Proceed with a directness of purpose, fearing nothing from the National League and focusing on what is good for the American League *as a whole* above all other concerns. If this meant reprimanding your own troops for getting out of line, so be it.

Downfall of the National League Empire (in Eight Simple Steps):

1. Withstand a player revolt, crush your competition, become a monopoly.

2. Install a powerless figurehead named Nick Young as league president.

3. Quickly expand the number of league franchises, while ignoring the importance of competitive balance.

4. Allow multiple ownership groups to have their fingers (and dollars) invested in multiple league franchises at one time, further undermining the league's competitive integrity.

5. Witness ownership groups splitting into two distinct cliques, not only at odds with one another over smaller issues but engaged in nefarious behavior (including gate receipt fraud and secret revenue-sharing schemes), threatening the league as a whole.

6. Ignore the rising tide of discontent among the players.

7. Pay little mind to the decreasing attendance figures at league games.

8. Miscalculate who your real challengers are. At the end of the decade, the NL arrogantly believed their biggest threat would be a newly constructed version of the old American Association, when in fact it was Ban Johnson's Western League.

It wasn't as if Ban Johnson had kept his league's intentions secret. Ultimately, there wasn't anything anyone could do to stop him, but Johnson had had conversations with the National League to see if the Western could become a second major with their consent. Ultimately, these overtures were rebuffed, then met with legal action, as the National League scrambled to keep its most valuable assets (its players), who were jumping to the new league in droves.

❖ ❖ ❖

John McGraw was Ban Johnson's personal choice to manage the new Baltimore franchise in the American League. McGraw, of course, had been a star performer for the National League powerhouse Orioles (recently contracted out of the senior circuit) and was eager to stay in the city. At twenty-eight years old, McGraw would become the youngest skipper in the league. He was also the most pugnacious, known for battling opponents, umpires, and teammates alike. Almost immediately, this drove a wedge between him and Johnson.

McGraw would eventually go on to manage the New York Giants for thirty-one years, winning ten pennants and three world championships. An innovator in exploiting untapped resources of talent, he was always complimentary of African American players; during the course of his career, he hired Cubans, Jewish players, and Native Americans when other managers and owners shied away from certain ethnic groups. In the late 1920s, McGraw even invited Buck Lai, a third baseman of Chinese descent, to spring training.

And in 1901, at the dawning of the American League, he tried to sign his first black guy.

According to 1880 census records, Charlie Grant's parents, Charles Sr. and Mary, were of mixed race. Their son had light skin, high cheek bones, and wavy-straight hair. At first glance, it wasn't particularly easy to determine his ethnicity. The meeting between McGraw and Grant was probably arranged by another black player named David Wyatt. Like Grant, Wyatt was working at the Eastman during the off-season, and he used his connections to facilitate a conference between the Baltimore skipper and the good-looking, light-skinned second baseman.

At some point during the first two weeks of March, McGraw and Chicago White Sox manager/

A star pitcher before becoming owner of the Washington Senators, Clark Griffith pitched batting practice to Charlie Grant in 1901, during an elaborate scheme to sign an African American ballplayer. *National Baseball Hall of Fame Library, Cooperstown, New York* pitcher Clark Griffith ran Charlie Grant through the baseball gauntlet, giving him a tryout near the grounds of the Eastman Hotel. The former Page Fence Giant star impressed both men during his fielding drills and batting practice session. Shortly thereafter, wire stories sizzled across the nation's newspapers, announcing John McGraw was preparing to sign an "Indian" named "Tokohama" to play second base and right field for the Orioles.

By this time, there were no longer any black men playing inside organized baseball. The door had been shut for African Americans, but just a couple years earlier, in 1897, Louis "Chief" Sockalexis of the Penobscot tribe became the first Native American to play major league ball, batting .338 for Cleveland in the National League. Apparently McGraw, Grant, and Wyatt agreed to use subterfuge to break the color line—they'd claim Grant was an American Indian named Tokohama, or "Tokie" for short.

How they cooked up the fictional name is the subject of some debate. The late baseball historian Lee Allen suggested McGraw came up with the name after examining a large map in the lobby of the Eastman Hotel. There was supposedly a creek named Tokohama, which inspired the moniker. Turns out, modern baseball nerds haven't been able to verify the existence of a Tokohama Creek in Arkansas—or anywhere else, for that matter.

My own theory is the name is simply a lazy twist on the Japanese city of Yokohama. The second largest municipality in Japan, *Yokohama* was a name that appeared almost daily in American newspapers at the time of the McGraw/Tokohama affair, especially in regard to international business and political news. My guess is they were sitting around the lobby one morning, reading newspapers, when the real inspiration struck.

Ultimately, how and why they settled on Tokohama isn't nearly as important as Charlie's real surname: Grant. The fact he had this in common with a very well-known black player from years earlier—a man who played the same exact position—would unwittingly contribute to the scheme's sabotage.

Frank Grant, the man from Pittsfield, Massachusetts, was thirty-six years old and still playing high-quality ball for the Cuban Giants in and around New York. He had been a tremendous minor league star in the International League during the late 1880s and had been written about extensively in newspapers throughout the region. He was widely known by baseball fans, both black and white, around the country.

Prior to his tryout with Baltimore, twenty-three-year-old *Charlie* Grant (our Chief Tokohama) played for the Chicago Columbia Giants. The Page Fence Giants had disbanded after the 1898 season, and Charlie was becoming rather well known in Chicago. In retrospect, it's easy to see now the stars had no chance of lining up in favor of John McGraw's little scheme. Grant's last name would work against him, and the fact he played second base and that he had moved to the Chicago-based Columbia Giants would cut the legs out from beneath the effort just as it got started.

◆ ◆ ◆

The *Baltimore Sun* was the first to report the story, initially referring to McGraw's recruit as the "Cherokee ballplayer Grant." But just five days later, "Grant" had disappeared, and the "full-blooded Cherokee" was known simply as "Tokohama." By this time the *Chicago Tribune*, and numerous other national papers, had picked up on the story, giving the man's height and weight, describing his ball-playing attributes, and even running some photographs of the aspiring Oriole. This was the height of popularity for diversions like Buffalo Bill's Wild West Show. The nation had a seemingly unquenchable thirst for cowboy and Indian stuff, a fetish that would persist well into the 1950s and '60s. Louis Sockalexis had boozed his way out of the big leagues in 1899, and the prospect of another talented "Indian" ballplayer emerging was exhilarating.

And then it happened.

It slipped out that Tokohama might actually be black. If there had been a sound associated with this revelation, I guess it would have been the fart noise of air fluttering violently from a balloon nozzle. Indians were pretty cool, but having *blacks* play big-league ball was *not* an exhilarating proposition.

Two weeks after John McGraw announced his intensions to sign Grant/ Tokohama, a widely distributed wire story reported the controversy:

> Just why he should be called "Grant" is a mystery and tends to arouse suspicion. It is openly asserted that "Tokie" is none other than Grant, a negro second baseman known as the "colored Dunlap," who played with the Cuban Giants. McGraw has fixed him up with an Indian name and an aboriginal pedigree. The manager knows that a negro baseball player would be unpopular in Baltimore, and so the wily official concocted his scheme of a redskin phenomenon. Truly the modern baseball sharp is wiser than his generation.

Obviously, some eastern reporters were confusing the youngster Charlie with the more widely known Frank. In Chicago, where Charlie Grant had actually played the previous couple seasons with the Columbia Giants, things became even more dicey. Charlie Comiskey, owner of the upstart White Sox (he'd moved his St. Paul franchise to Chicago in 1900, to compete directly with the Cubs) caught wind of the plan, possibly from his own club's manager, Clark Griffith, who threw batting practice to Grant during the Hot Springs tryout.

On March 16, the *St. Louis Republic* ran a very interesting article, under the headline McGRAW'S INDIAN IS A NEGRO:

COMISKEY SAYS HE IS GRANT, THE CRACK MAN OF THE PAGE-FENCE GIANTS

CHICAGO, MARCH 15—Comiskey came forward with a declaration to the effect that he could not stand for Muggsy McGraw bringing in Indians on the Baltimore team. "If Muggsy really keeps this Indian I will get a Chinaman of my acquaintance and put him on third. Possibly I might whitewash a colored man. Somebody said this Cherokee of McGraw's is really Grant, the crack negro second baseman, fixed up with war paint and a bunch of feathers."

Grant is an A-1 ball player, good enough for any company, but for his color. According to the records there has not been a negro player in the National League since 1877. Along in those times, there was a capable negro infielder on one of the teams, but he was driven out by the Southern players of the clubs. It is an open secret, however, that two men of the National League both fairly prominent, who are now out of the game, were negroes, who simply tended to their work like quiet gentlemen, never had a word to say, and played three seasons without having the slightest trouble.

So within the first week, Comiskey (arguably the second most powerful figure in the new American League) put his foot down. Charlie Grant and the Page Fence Giants had played many, many times versus Western League clubs, as had Grant's new club, the Chicago Columbia Giants. McGraw, who'd spent

The swanky Eastman Hotel in Hot Springs, Arkansas, where Charlie Grant tried out for John McGraw's Baltimore Orioles. *Courtesy of Scott Simkus*

most of his career on the East Coast, probably didn't anticipate the confusion that would arise with the well-known veteran Frank Grant and how easily recognizable Charlie Grant would be in Chicago and around the Great Lakes.

If Grant had a different last name and played a different position, might things have worked out differently for McGraw's little experiment? It's possible.

As an aside, it's worth noting that Clark Griffith, Comiskey's manager with the White Sox, apparently wouldn't have had any personal issues with Grant playing in the league. Griffith, who had been a star pitcher for Cap Anson's teams in the 1890s, would eventually move on to become owner of the Washington Senators, where he became a pioneer in recruiting Cuban talent (real Cubans, some with African heritage) before Jackie Robinson broke the color line. And during the 1930s and '40s, Griffith would work directly with the famous Homestead Grays, renting his facility to the Negro league powerhouse in what was a long-term, mutually lucrative arrangement.

This event was one instance in what would become a series of disputes between John McGraw and American League president Ban Johnson. In fact, it may have been the first. Mac would be suspended several times (mostly for upbraiding umpires) and after only a season and a half would orchestrate a plan to leave Baltimore, rejoining the National League as manager of the New York Giants.

Although peace had been forged between the two leagues, McGraw and his 1904 National League–champion New York Giants refused to participate in a World Series with Boston, pennant winners in Ban Johnson's American League. The bad blood lingered.

◆ 10 ◆

VICTORIAN FACT OR FICTION

THE YEARS 1890 TO 1900 were about as crazy as any decade in professional baseball history. There had to be some moments of doubt regarding how everything would shake out. The game went from having three "major" leagues to just one. The pitching distance was lengthened to the modern 60'6", and rules were adjusted so that foul bunts were now counted as strikes. The infield fly rule was instituted. Almost every catcher and first baseman wore fielding gloves by this time, and by the mid-1890s, many of the other position players were sporting the leather as well. Permanent "Ladies Days" were employed as marketing tools targeting the fairer sex, yet there were regular incidents of violence and drunkenness on the field. Several international, off-season baseball tours were held. There were serious debates about serving alcohol at ballgames, scheduling games on Sundays, appropriate ticket prices, and the role of gambling. Attendance slowly dipped at the highest level, as the country entered an economic recession. A handful of Native Americans emerged as major league prospects, while African Americans (hundreds of whom were being paid to play professionally) were completely excluded from organized baseball. White players protested being treated "like chattel" under the reserve clause and twice formed unions to fight the power.

Considering all the chaos associated with baseball and race relations at the end of the nineteenth century, I've often wondered how much talent was getting pushed to the fringe. Surely, the National League didn't have *all* the best players in the world at this time, did they?

Focusing on two pools of "outsider" talent—Ban Johnson's Western League and the all-black professional teams of the era—we'll use the STARS system, some new research, and a few other baseball tools to see if we can get some answers.

◆ ◆ ◆

A couple years after taking over the helm of the Western League, Ban Johnson suggested his minor league might be ready "to go out on its own." This was a rather bold statement. In effect, he was saying they might be able to leave the National Agreement (which was the legal structure binding the major and high minor leagues with respect to things like player contracts, the reserve rule, draft procedures, and salary limits) and strike out on their own as an independent major league.

The Western clubs were certainly talented. By the end of the 1890s, independent observers were in agreement that Ban Johnson's circuit was "the best minor league" in the country. In a limited sample of in-season exhibition games, the Western League clubs actually beat the National League teams ten out of nineteen games, with one tie, outscoring the major leaguers 128–122. Now, sometimes the NL teams didn't use their number-one pitcher during these exhibition games. I wouldn't want to dismiss the evidence entirely, but we need something more substantial. We need to look at the STARS scores of the two leagues to see how their rosters actually compared to one another, from one season to the next.

10.1

1895 Western League Standings	W	L	PCT.	STARS Score
Indianapolis Hoosiers	78	43	.645	229
St. Paul Apostles	74	50	.597	198
Kansas City Blues	73	52	.584	187
Minneapolis Millers	64	59	.520	204
Detroit Tigers	59	66	.472	188
Milwaukee Brewers	57	67	.460	185
Toledo Swamp Angels*	52	72	.419	169
Grand Rapids Gold Bugs	38	86	.306	170

Note: *As an aside, the Western League's "Toledo Swamp Angels" is a pretty cool nickname, right? It's a better team nickname than *anything* in the National League in 1895, in my opinion.

The 1895 season is a good place to start as this was right around the time Ban Johnson began hinting at the Western League's big-league ambitions, suggesting they were almost ready to go out "on their own." Let's first look at the 1895 Western League standings, with each team's STARS score listed in the last column. For table 10.1, we'll add service time credit for the Western League:

Remember, STARS measures talent on paper, assigning points for players who have the longest careers and are closest to their prime seasons as athletes. In general terms, the higher the STARS score, the better the ballplayer, club, or league. Indianapolis had the highest score, and they finished in first place. The Grand Rapids Gold Bugs had the second lowest STARS score and finished in last place. The 1895 Western League's STARS score (as a whole) was 160.

Now for the 1895 National League, the only big league at the time. (Western League alum have service time added in, so both 1895 charts are apples-to-apples.)

10.2

1895 National League Standings	W	L	PCT.	STARS Score
Baltimore Orioles	87	43	.669	310
Cleveland Spiders	84	46	.646	316
Philadelphia Phillies	78	53	.595	316
Chicago Cubs	72	58	.554	287
Brooklyn Grooms	71	60	.542	296
Boston Beaneaters	71	60	.542	320
Pittsburgh Pirates	71	61	.538	288
Cincinnati Reds	66	64	.508	284
New York Giants	66	65	.504	309
Washington Senators	43	85	.336	236
St. Louis Browns	39	92	.298	287
Louisville Colonels	35	96	.267	271

Other than the superiority of the Swamp Angels team name, there's really not much of an argument regarding which was the better of the two circuits. The National League STARS score is 293, compared to the Western League's meager 191. This is a huge gap. It's significantly wider, for instance, than the difference between the 1884 National League and the 1884 Union Association. If you recall, we came to the conclusion that the 1884 UA has no business being considered a major league. The National League's last-place Louisville Colonels would have *dominated* Ban Johnson's clubs, if they'd transferred to his minor league in 1895.

Johnson may have believed his group was "ready to go out on its own" at that point, but looking at this from a new point of view, we can see they would have been nothing more than a mediocre, outlaw minor league with a team in Grand Rapids, for cripes sakes. They weren't ready to *do* anything, really, but the ambition was there. The seeds of moving up had been planted.

It all starts with an idea.

Let's jump ahead to 1900. Johnson has renamed his aggregation the "American League." St. Paul, Toledo, and Grand Rapids are out; Chicago, Cleveland, and Buffalo are in, as the old Western League takes massive steps toward becoming a major league. At this point, they're still technically a minor league (although some of the later *Spalding Base Ball Guides* lumped them in with the annals of major league history), but reporters at the time considered them the "strongest" of the lesser loops.

Running both leagues through the STARS meat grinder (we'll give AL rosters major league credit for 1900), this is what we come up with:

1900 National League: 322 STARS

1900 American League: 207 STARS (technically still a minor league)

A couple important things have happened. First, the National League contracts from twelve teams down to eight, with many of the best players of the dormant franchises being absorbed by its other teams. The league is more talented, from top to bottom, than it was in 1895. In the Western League (rebranded as the "American League" for 1900), they've upgraded their rosters with what today we would call "replacement level" major leaguers. It's a much better league than it had been in 1895; they've constructed a foundation of average professional ballplayers from which they can build upward, but the gap between the AL and NL is almost identical to what it had been five years earlier. The National League is still the best league in the world, and it's not really close.

After the 1900 season, all hell breaks loose. Ban Johnson's American League declares itself a second major, and they open up their wallets, actively seeking out the services of superstar players from the senior circuit. War is now raging between ownership groups of the two leagues. By spring, the upstart American League has Cy Young, Napolean Lajoie, Hugh Duffy, and Iron Man McGinnity, all studs from the National League (and all future Hall of Famers), under contract.

Let's take a look at how the two "major" leagues compared in 1901, after the first real wave of player raids:

1901 National League: 301 STARS

1901 American League: 251 STARS

As expected, the American League has made a significant leap forward in terms of its talent on the field. It's a major league but still not as good as its archrival. The National League has lost a number of all-star-caliber guys and slides backward in its talent level. The top four clubs in the AL would probably be competitive in the NL, finishing somewhere in the second division. The bottom four American League clubs would have had a hard time finishing ahead of the National League's last-place club.

Let's cut to the chase and look at how the two leagues' STARS scores compare from 1900 to 1905:

10.3

League	1900	1901	1902	1903	1904	1905
National League	322	301	270	270	266	269
American League	207	251	288	288	282	279

Before Ban Johnson assumed the helm in 1893, the Western League limped from season to season, struggling to survive. When Johnson took over, he came with a vision for the league's future, implementing a major course correction. By 1895, his was the top minor league in the country. By 1900, they were knocking on the door of major league classification. By 1902, they were, from the top down, the *best* professional baseball league in the nation. This entire process took about eight years, forging the two-league structure that is still in use to this day.

In 1903, after two years of bitter fighting, the National and American leagues signed a new National Agreement, ushering in an era of peace between the two major leagues. At about the same time, the minor leagues were going through their own version of reorganization. Although true farm systems were thirty years off in the future, the independent minor leagues became aligned by a classification system similar to today's arrangement. The top minor leagues were called Class A, which would be the equivalent of today's Triple-A. This top classification had two leagues in 1895, expanded to three in 1901, then jumped to five in 1903. Eventually, things would cool down. After the creation of the modern farm systems, where the minor leagues were used specifically to develop talent for the major leagues instead of operating as independent baseball businesses, the top classification would be reduced from five, down to two or three leagues, maximum, which is the structure in effect today.

If the color line was drawn in the 1880s, the other invisible line—the barrier between baseball's "insiders" and "outsiders"—was being forged at the beginning of the twentieth century. As the popularity of the game surged once again, and the structure of Major League Baseball became rigid, opportunities to exploit supply and demand (sometimes born of necessity) emerged on the fringe.

◆ ◆ ◆

By the time Ban Johnson set his sights on turning the Western League into a second major, perhaps a half dozen or so all-black professional teams were playing as independents, mostly on the East Coast and in the Midwest. Among these clubs were the previously mentioned Page Fence Giants of Adrian, Michigan, as well as the Cuban Giants, the Unions of Chicago, the Cuban X-Giants, the Acme Giants, and the Gorhams, who all performed during the late 1880s or 1890s and beyond.

Most of these clubs played more than 100 games per summer, usually as barnstorming outfits. As we saw in their debut campaign, the 1895 Page Fence Giants rolled up an impressive 118–36–2 record. In 1897, they compiled an astonishing 125–12 record.

Meanwhile on the East Coast, the Cuban Giants defeated several National League teams, including the Cincinnati Reds and New York Metropolitans, and held their own in a number of hotly contested games with top minor league squads.

3

Let's pause the narrative right here and ask a couple very direct questions. How *good* were these black professional teams? Could they have actually challenged for championship pennants in the major or minor leagues?

To find some answers, I've assembled perhaps the largest collection ever of nineteenth-century games that pitted black professional teams against white major league and minor league clubs. By looking at how they *actually fared* in a large collection of games, as opposed to focusing on a couple key triumphs (or defeats), we get a better sense of how they truly fit into the larger scheme of things.

Let's start this little exercise by listing each team's record against white clubs from organized baseball (1885–99):

10.4

Black Clubs vs. White Professional Teams (1885–1899)	W	L	PCT.
Chicago Columbia Giants*	2	2	.500
Page Fence Giants	31	35	.470
Cuban Giants	21	40	.344
Cuban X-Giants**	4	14	.222

Black Clubs vs. White Professional Teams (1885–1899) *continued*	W	L	PCT.
Unions of Chicago	1	7	.125
Gorhams	0	1	.000
Acme Giants	0	2	.000

Note: *The Page Fence Giants folded after 1898 with most of their star players transferring to Chicago, where they formed the new Columbia Giants. **A number of key players defected from the Cuban Giants to form the rival "Cuban X-Giants."

The early returns aren't great. Combined, the top black clubs were only 59–101 against white pro clubs, and they were outscored by their opponents 1,554 to 1,109. When you consider most of these games were against *minor* league opponents, things actually go from bad to worse. But before we rush to judgment, let's combine these 160 games, sorting them by level of competition and separating the major league, high minor league, and low minor league contests.

10.5

Black Clubs vs. White Professional Teams (1885–1899)	W	L	PCT.
Major league teams	5	17	.227
High minor league teams	7	23	.233
Low minor league teams	47	61	.435

Combined, these black clubs won only 23 percent of their games against white major league teams. Against the high minors (basically the Eastern/International and Western leagues) they were only slightly better, copping seven of thirty ballgames. Against the low minor league clubs, they found their comfort zone, winning a respectable (but far from awe-inspiring) 44 percent of their games. And what about manager Gus Parson's Page Fence Giants, whom he believed could have held their own in the powerful Western League? In eighteen games versus Ban Johnson's soon-to-be second major league, the Giants managed an abysmal 3–15 record and were outscored 210 to 109.

Okay, I think we can rush to judgment now.

These were good ballclubs, but we would have to be delusional to suggest the black clubs could have held their own in anything higher than the lowest-level minor leagues. There were some major league–caliber position players on these squads. Guys like Frank Grant, Charlie Grant, and Home Run

Johnson spearheaded offenses that scored nearly 7 runs per game—any one of these men might have been stars in the bigs—and one of them is in the Hall of Fame. But their pitching staffs were atrocious. In 161 games (there was one tie), they coughed up a mind-boggling 9.65 runs per game.

From a purely baseball standpoint, pitching depth was the Achilles' heel of the professional black teams. This criticism would persist over the next six decades. The pioneering black clubs of the nineteenth century never had all of the best available talent on their top one or two teams. For instance, during the 1880s, many of the very best black players were still in the white minor leagues and *not* on the Cuban Giants. And during the 1890s, the top players were split between the Page Fence Giants and the other clubs on the East Coast.

After the turn of the century, Sol White, the African American player/ manager who later became the first historian to chronicle Cap Anson's role in "creating" baseball's color line, assembled a team in Philadelphia that changed all of this. With his Philadelphia Giants, we'd finally see a black club that *may* have had the pitching depth to compete at the major league level.

◆ 11 ◆

ANY GIVEN SUNDAY

THICK BLACK SMOKE BILLOWED from the top floor of a downtown Washington, DC building in 1904.

Folks returning home from their Sunday morning church services noticed the small fire near an eave at the top of the building, and by the time the first horse-drawn hook-and-ladder company was on location, the fourth story of the wooden facility was a roaring furnace. A second alarm was quickly sounded, summoning *all* fire companies from the nation's capital to the scene.

Trapped inside the William F. & B. J. Downey's Livery Stable, located in the 1600 block of L Street Northwest, were more than one hundred forty horses and several hundred carriages, most belonging to politicians, foreign diplomats, and the capital city's business elite.

There were some notable acts of heroism early on. Truck No. 16 was the first to throw its ladder up against the front wall. Private Heimath, of Engine No. 6, scaled halfway up and twisted the nozzle on the heavy hose, unleashing a powerful stream into the blaze that shot from several broken windows. The crowd of civilians who'd gathered in the streets below roared their approval.

On the other side of the building, things weren't going so well. There were a number of dangling electrical wires, and until engineers could be ushered to the scene to cut the power and safely remove the cords, the firefighters would be kept at bay. In the meantime, the stable's gigantic steel elevator—used to transport carriages up and down—collapsed with a loud, dusty thud, nearly crushing three firefighters stationed at the bottom. By the time ladders were finally hoisted up, part of the fourth-story roof had caved in, and shortly thereafter, the entire top floor collapsed, crushing dozens of carriages and reigniting the blaze.

Meanwhile, on the north side of the building, Private Heimath had been joined by numerous reinforcements. Several hoses were now dousing the building, stifling the progress of the fire. According to the *Washington Post*, the sea of gapers circling the building had swelled to nearly seven thousand people, forcing the police department to marshal all of its resources within the city, many of whom arrived by bicycle to help with crowd control.

At the building's main entrance, on the side where Private Heimath and his compatriots were beginning to get an upper hand, the people lining the sidewalks witnessed a most unusual act of heroism. A tall civilian, with a handkerchief tied around his face like a bandit, emerged from the smoke with several horses in tow. He released them to bystanders, then quickly reentered the building, rescuing a few more. Several firemen—and some police officers—joined the mystery man, entering the smoky first floor and eventually emerging with more horses and expensive leather harnesses, which had been stored on the ground level.

All told, the mystery man and city employees saved the lives of one hundred forty horses, plus thousands of dollars in other materials. With the animals safely outside (mulling about the streets "pell-mell," according to newspaper accounts), the man with the handkerchief obscuring his identity reentered the building, side by side with the firefighters, helping to hose back the flames and saving half the building.

The French embassy lost a handsome carriage in the blaze, as did Senators Wetmore, Dryden, and Fairbanks; Representative Hitt; and the Westinghouse family (of the Westinghouse electrical empire). More than two hundred carriages were destroyed on the fourth floor, and another couple hundred were damaged on the level below. Estimates of the total losses exceeded $100,000.

After the grueling three-hour battle was over, the fire chief ordered sandwiches and drinks for the men, which he jokingly said he'd pay for "with the coffee fund." Joining the men as they rested along the sidewalks and cobblestone streets was the handkerchief fire bandit. He removed his mask and introduced himself to the fellas. Said his name was Rube Waddell, was in town on business, played some ball for a club from Philadelphia.

The man who helped save some horses and beat back the flames was arguably the greatest, most famous pitcher in the world at that time.

The very next day—Monday, October 10, 1904—Rube started the second game of a doubleheader versus the Washington Senators. It was the last game of the year for both teams, and although his club lost, 4–3, Rube struck out 6 men in 5 innings, raising his season total to an all-time modern record of 349. Rube's strikeout mark would last more than sixty years until it was finally broken by Hall of Famer Sandy Koufax in 1965.

◆ ◆ ◆

In the early days of Ban Johnson's American League, George Edward "Rube" Waddell was the best pitcher in the league, the Randy Johnson or Sandy Koufax of his generation. Working for Connie Mack's Philadelphia Athletics, the left-hander won more than 20 games in four consecutive seasons, leading the league in strikeouts six straight times. His best season was probably 1905, when he went 27–10 with a 1.48 ERA and a career-best 0.90 WHIP (walks plus hits per inning pitched).

Waddell was an alcoholic whose eccentricities entertained (and infuriated) friends, foes, and spectators alike. His managers, including his most compassionate supporter in Connie Mack, had a long-standing, love-hate relationship with the fireballer. He was suspended for both insubordination and inebriation several times during his career. And although Hall of Fame shortstop Honus Wagner considered Rube a friend, and socialized with him during the off-season, he remembered Waddell as being a mooch who, despite earning a handsome salary, was always broke.

Rube was married three times, the first two wives filing for divorce after being abandoned by the big, overgrown kid. During his seventeen-year career (cut short at the major league level, due mostly to his alcoholism and erratic behavior), Waddell pitched for five major league teams and six minor league clubs, eleven outfits in total, in an era where a star's career was typically much more stable. On several occasions, the lefty jumped his contract midseason, playing for semipro outfits in Wisconsin, Pennsylvania, and California.

◆ ◆ ◆

Andrew Foster was born on September 17, 1879, and grew up in Calvert, Texas, a small, predominantly African American plantation community. His father (also known as Andrew) was the local preacher. The younger Foster had five siblings, three of whom survived beyond infancy.

As a child, young Andrew was attracted more to the pitching mound than the pulpit. By the time he was in his early teens, Foster quit school and began his baseball career with the Waco Yellow Jackets, a well-known all-black regional powerhouse. In 1898, the big right-hander helped the Texas juggernaut roll to a reported 94–10 mark on the season. A couple years later, at the age of twenty-two, Foster traveled north, signing with Chicago's Union Giants. The next season, 1903, he went to the East Coast, pitching for the Cuban X-Giants. He'd made the big time.

◆ ◆ ◆

The year before playing hero in the Washington, DC fire, Rube Waddell had perhaps the most tumultuous season in a string of tumultuous campaigns. In June, he met a young lady named May Wynne Skinner and, after a courtship of exactly three days, dragged her to the altar, where they were married. This was his second marriage and would prove to be no more successful than the first, with Ms. Skinner filing for divorce several years later, after the couple had been estranged for nearly as long as they had been married. Waddell, who struggled with his money, hadn't provided for his wife for quite a long time.

In July, in the middle of a twelve-strikeout gem versus the St. Louis Browns, Rube Waddell jumped into the grandstands and beat the shit out of a heckler named Maurice Blau. Blau was said to be a well-known gambling figure in Philadelphia, and when it became apparent there would be some losses over the game's outcome, he began verbally accosting Waddell from the box seats. Things turned personal, and Rube lost his cool.

After leaping over the railing, Waddell shattered Blau's nose with one punch, then proceeded to rip the man's jacket, shirt, and collar off. Grabbing the dude by the neck, Waddell dragged Blau down the steps, toward the

Rube Waddell enjoyed baseball, beer, and fires, but not necessarily in that order. *Courtesy of Scott Simkus*

playing field. Finally, six police officers intervened, escorting the bloodied and battered Blau from the ballpark. After a several-minute break, Waddell dusted himself off, returned to the mound, and shut down the Browns in a complete-game victory.

The next day, Ban Johnson, former Western League–turned–American League head honcho, suspended the big lefty for five games. In August, Connie Mack, manager of the Athletics, released his star pitcher after Waddell failed to show up at the train station as the club departed for a road trip. Rube was later found tending bar somewhere, happy as a clam.

Hall of Famer Sam Crawford, who played with Waddell in the minors, said, "Baseball was just a game to Rube. He'd pitch one day and we wouldn't see him for three or four days after. He'd just disappear, go fishing or something, or be off playing ball with a bunch of twelve-year-olds in an empty lot somewhere."

◆ ◆ ◆

Rube Waddell was the yin to Andrew Foster's yang. Waddell was a lefty with a big fastball, sharp breaking ball, and an out-curve (what today would be known as a "screwball"). Foster was a righty with a big fastball, sharp breaking ball, and an out-curve. Waddell was tall, with a sinewy build. Foster was a bit shorter, with a pudgy (soon-to-be fat) physicality. Waddell was white and aloof, Foster black and serious. Waddell was often intoxicated, wild, and terrible with money. Foster was sober, disciplined, and excellent with finances.

On Sunday, August 2, 1903, these two pitchers from two different worlds opposed one another on the baseball diamond for the very first time. Foster took the mound as a member of the Cuban X-Giants, while Waddell made a spot start for a semipro team from New York City called the Murray Hills.

Here, in the midst of Rube Waddell's troublesome summer, two future Hall of Famers went head-to-head as the worlds of insider and outsider baseball converged.

◆ ◆ ◆

After leaving Texas, Andrew Foster's ascent up the professional ranks was almost as rapid as his blazing fastball. In just two short years, he went from beating the bushes with the Waco Yellow Jackets to playing for the Cuban X-Giants, who were one of the best-known black ballclubs on the East Coast. Among Foster's new teammates were former members of the Page Fence Giants (the club having fallen apart after the 1898 season) and the original Cuban Giants, whose history dated back to 1885 when blacks were still allowed to play in the white minor leagues.

When Andrew Foster took the mound against the great Rube Waddell, he was backed by second baseman Charlie "Tokohama" Grant, who'd met with John McGraw in Hot Springs, Arkansas just two years earlier, when they attempted to use an "Indian" identity to integrate the new American League. At shortstop was Grant "Home Run" Johnson, the premier home-run hitter in black baseball at the time and another alumnus of the Page Fence Giants.

The showdown between these two great pitchers occurred just two weeks after Rube's fracas in the Philadelphia grandstands. Waddell and the Philadelphia A's were being sued by Blau. Rube's new wife, May Wynne Skinner Waddell, had already approached John Shibe, owner of the Athletics, about getting some of her husband's salary advanced because after only three weeks of matrimony he had abandoned her and was in arrears on most of their bills. She was on the verge of being evicted from their boarding house less than two months into their marriage. According to newspaper reports, Waddell had already been advanced most of his salary for the season, and the club's attorney was contemplating suing their star pitcher.

◆ ◆ ◆

The details involving the encounter between Rube Waddell and Andrew Foster are sketchy, but we know this much: Philadelphia was in New York City for a series with the Highlanders (Yankees). Sunday baseball was still illegal at this point, so on his off-day, Waddell hired himself out to Nat Strong's Murray Hills club of Manhattan. It wasn't unheard of for big leaguers to do this sort of thing at the time to make a couple extra bucks playing Sunday ball for semipro clubs, but it was certainly less common for *stars* to do this, especially midseason. But of course we now know Waddell was in desperate need of cash.

With both men unloading their best stuff, the score remained knotted at 0–0 through 3 innings. In the top of the fourth, the Cuban X-Giants strung together a few hits, pushing across the first two runs of the game. Murray Hills countered with one tally in the fifth inning, but the X-Giants tacked on four more runs through the seventh. Waddell's club made a desperate comeback attempt in the bottom of the ninth but came up short against Andrew Foster and his mates, 6–3.

All told, Waddell struck out 12 Cuban X-Giants, allowing 11 hits and 6 runs, all of them earned. Foster allowed 7 hits and 3 earned runs. Years later, Andrew Foster explained that this victory over the mighty Waddell was how he had first earned his nickname.

Forever thereafter, he'd be known to one and all as Andrew "Rube" Foster, and seventeen years later, he'd usher in a new era of black professional baseball by founding the first Negro National League in 1920. This is how some of the baseball legends were made back then, on any given Sunday, at semipro diamonds around the country.

◆ ◆ ◆

Waddell eventually patched things up with the Philadelphia Athletics and had several extremely effective seasons before his demons once more got the best of him. During his last seven seasons of professional baseball, he pitched for two big-league clubs and three minor league outfits. I'm not sure how many fires he helped put out, saloons he tended bar at, or semipro teams he moonlighted for during this span.

In 1913, Waddell became seriously ill with what was later diagnosed as tuberculosis. The once-mighty pitcher lost a tremendous amount of weight in a short span of time, and by early 1914, word spread that the former A's star hurler was on his last legs. On April Fools' Day that year, George Edward "Rube" Waddell passed away at the age of thirty-seven, in the company of his parents and sister.

In an odd twist of baseball serendipity, Waddell's last days were spent at a sanitarium in Texas, the home state of his onetime nemesis, Andrew "Rube" Foster.

◆ 12 ◆

IF YOU CAN'T BEAT 'EM, STEAL 'EM

FIVE WEEKS AFTER BEATING RUBE WADDELL and the Murray Hills team in New York City, Andrew "Rube" Foster scaled the mound once again for the Cuban X-Giants, this time facing the vaunted Philadelphia Giants in Game 1 of the first modern "colored world championship."

Sol White and a booking agent named Walter Schlichter had formed the Philadelphia Giants just one year earlier, quickly establishing themselves as an eastern powerhouse and finishing their inaugural campaign with a 81–43–2 record. Although the Giants were a new franchise, their 1903 roster was loaded with veterans such as Frank Grant (now thirty-seven years old), Bill Binga (thirty-four), Pat Patterson (thirty-one), and Harry Buckner (thirty-one). White, who played middle infield in addition to running the club, was already thirty-five and graying a bit. They were a new team built from refurbished parts.

On the other hand, Rube Foster was only twenty-four years old, and the nucleus of the Cuban X-Giants was decidedly youthful. Second baseman Charlie "Tokohama" Grant and up-and-coming pitching star Danny McClellan were both just twenty-five, and hot prospect Andrew "Jap" Payne was just a baby, at twenty-three. Their best hitter, shortstop Grant "Home Run" Johnson, was the veteran presence in the lineup, at thirty years old.

The series was rather anticlimactic, as the younger X-Giants easily whipped the older Philadelphia club, 5 games to 2, outscoring them 31–15 in the process. Rube Foster was a one-man wrecking crew, going 4–0 during the series, while allowing only 19 hits and 6 runs in 36 innings pitched.

Instead of cowering after the setback, Sol White and Walter Schlichter shifted their strategy during the off-season, changing the Philadelphia Giants' recruitment process into one of piracy. Over the course of the next two years, they dumped their aging core and acquired no fewer than six former Cuban X-Giants, including Foster, Charlie Grant, Home Run Johnson, and McClellan. By 1905, White and the Philadelphia Giants had also added three of the best-looking youngsters in black baseball: future Hall of Famer Pete Hill (twenty-three), Pete Booker (nineteen), and Emmett Bowman (twenty). The team was loaded with a mix of vets, stars in their prime, and a handful of young hot shots. And unlike the Page Fence Giants and Cuban Giants of the 1890s, they had the pitching ace (Foster)—and enough depth—to warrant serious consideration as a major league–caliber club.

Sol White helmed one of the greatest black teams of the early twentieth century, the Philadelphia Giants. But were they *really* major league caliber? *National Baseball Hall of Fame Library, Cooperstown, New York*

In 1905, the new and improved Philadelphia Giants made national headlines, compiling a 134–21–3 (.848) record versus all levels of competition. Baseball historian Phil S. Dixon has collected nearly 90 percent of the team's box scores from their historic season and has credited the club with three 30-win pitchers: Rube Foster (36–5), Emmett Bowman (35–7), and Danny McClellan (31–7). In the fall, Philadelphia squared off with another upstart black club, the Brooklyn Royal Giants, smoking them in three straight games, their three pitching aces each credited with complete-game victories.

They were the undisputed black champions of the world, and the "Cuban" brand—the one where African American dudes played ball while pretending to be from the islands—would slowly fade away, to soon be replaced by something more *auténtico*.

◆ ◆ ◆

In 1905, the Philadelphia Giants were the best outsider baseball team on the East Coast, regardless of color, and certainly the top black club in the country. But is there any measurable difference between this Philly team, which won 85 percent of their games, and, say, the 1895 Page Fence Giants, who went 118–36 (.766)? Or, what about the old Cuban Giants of the 1880s, who beat some major league clubs?

I ask this question because some historians believe the 1905 Philadelphia Giants should be considered one of the greatest teams of all time, regardless of color. If we already exposed the Page Fence Giants (the 1890s "colored champions of the world") as a bit of a fraud in an earlier chapter, who's to say we won't fall into the same snake pit with the 1905 Philadelphia Giants?

I've studied the question for several years and believe the Philly Giants would have crushed any edition of the Page Fence or "Cuban" clubs of the nineteenth century, based mostly on leadership, starting lineup, and pitching staff.

Other than that, it was close.

Because this book is largely about the distribution of talent, it's important to use some baseball forensics to distinguish the best of the black teams and give credit where credit is warranted. Otherwise, treating all "colored world champions" equally turns this into another vehicle for race-themed hagiography instead of a book about the truly skilled men on the field. Let's do the due diligence.

Before illustrating my point, let's simplify the argument by eliminating the Cuban Giants straight away. In 61 games versus white professional clubs (both minor and major league), they were 20–41 (.328), hardly the world beaters some historians have suggested. Sure, they played under crappy conditions, but so did every black barnstorming team over the next sixty years. The Cuban's best clubs were those of the late 1880s, but even at that point the best black players on the East Coast (Frank Grant, George Stovey, and Bob Higgins, among others) were starring in the *white* minor leagues. By the 1890s, the second generation of "Cuban" branded clubs had split into two competing factions (the original version and the "X-Giants"), which diluted their talent base. Grant and Stovey were now in the mix but past their primes. And in a couple head-to-head championship series, Michigan's Page Fence Giants held a decided edge over the Cuban clubs, and we know just how good the Page Fence team was.

This narrows down the argument to just two teams: the Page Fence Giants of the 1890s versus the Philadelphia Giants of 1905. We'll start with leadership.

Just a couple months after founding the Page Fence Giants in 1895, manager Bud Fowler, whose career dated back to the 1870s, jumped ship to play for a white minor league team. A white hotelier named A. S. "Gus" Parsons took over the helm, running the club until they folded after the 1898 season.

Not much is known about Parsons other than he doesn't appear to have much of a baseball resume, running a semipro club out of Adrian, Michigan, for a year or two before his four-year tenure at the wheel of the Page

Fence Giants. His brother, George Parsons, was a fairly well-known actor who made a name for himself in Chicago's theatre district, then later appeared in several silent films. Gus appears to have gotten out of baseball entirely after the Page Fence team disbanded. He later shows up as a hotel impresario in Chicago, after that as a sales agent representing a steel firm in Detroit, and then enmeshed in various entrepreneurial schemes with his ambitious, more famous sibling.

Truth is, the players were probably "managing" themselves and doing a rather fine job of it, running up an impressive won-lost record over the years, against inferior competition. Grant "Home Run" Johnson was the on-field captain and probably deserves some credit for his efforts. Parsons was responsible for the business affairs more than anything else—booking games, keeping the team's private train car operational, selling tickets, and paying salaries. Considering the club folded after 1898 due to financial difficulties—not their performance on the field—we could probably give Parsons a subpar grade in this job, as well.

The Philadelphia Giants, on the other hand, were captained by Sol White, who had a lengthy track record in professional baseball. Born King Solomon White on June 12, 1868, Sol first broke into baseball with a white team in his hometown of Bellaire, Ohio. He used to hang around the park as a teenager, and when one of the hometown players broke his finger, the men—who knew and liked young Solomon—pressed him into service in a game versus an all-white group from Marietta.

In an article published in the *Pittsburgh Courier* in 1927, White said he would never forget that day because the second baseman and captain of their opponent was none other than Byron Bancroft "Ban" Johnson, later destined to turn the fledgling Western League into a second major, becoming the long-time president of the American League.

White broke into professional baseball with the all-black Pittsburgh Keystones in the National Colored Baseball League (NCBL) in 1887, then later transferred to the Wheeling (West Virginia) Green Stockings in the white Ohio State League after the NCBL disbanded. He batted .370 in 52 games as a nineteen-year-old rookie. During five seasons in organized minor league baseball, Sol compiled an impressive lifetime .359 batting average. Later, when the doors to white baseball shut, White spent a number of seasons with both the Cuban Giants and Cuban X-Giants. He even had a brief stint with Gus Parsons's original Page Fence Giants, batting .404 in 12 games, before moving on to greener pastures.

By the time the 1905 edition of the Philadelphia Giants was assembled, Sol White had nearly twenty years of experience in the pro game, both in and out of organized baseball. Plus, he was in his fourth season as player-manager of the club, a stretch during which they would win more games than they had the previous season every single year. In 2006, in honor of his accomplishments as a manager, ballplayer, and historian (as you'll recall, the Wilberforce University alum later wrote the earliest history of black professional baseball, detailing, among other things, Cap Anson's role in the creation of the color line), Sol White was posthumously elected to the Baseball Hall of Fame in Cooperstown, New York.

We'd have to take Solomon White over Gus Parsons—in a landslide.

◆ ◆ ◆

Interestingly, the two top hitters in the Page Fence Giants batting order were probably Grant "Home Run" Johnson and Charlie Grant, both of whom also started for the 1905 Philadelphia Giants. Setting aside Sol White's brief fling with Parsons's team in 1895, Johnson and Grant are the only two Page Fence regulars who also starred for Philly. But even this isn't comparing apples to apples; it's more a case of comparing green apples to ripe ones.

Charlie Grant was just eighteen years old when he joined the Page Fence team in 1896, an age when most mere mortals are just getting their start in the lowest levels of professional baseball. Home Run Johnson was just a couple years older, at twenty-two, when he signed with Parsons for the '95 season.

By 1905, when they formed the middle infield for the Philly Giants, Charlie was twenty-seven and in his athletic prime, while Home Run Johnson was an experienced superstar at thirty-two. Yes, their STARS scores would be higher. Both of these ballplayers were men in full, with more than 1,000 games of professional experience under their belts, and their documented playing record reflects this.

Any sentient being would take the mature version of Charlie Grant and Home Run Johnson over the raw, extremely young prospects first getting their start in the late 1890s. If they were the two best hitters in both the Page Fence Giants lineup *and* the Philly team, we could simply move on.

But they weren't.

In 1905, Grant Johnson tied for the team-high with 10 home runs in 117 games, and Charlie Grant was third in homers (8), second in doubles (29), and third in stolen bases (27), but there were a slew of other men with similar production. Bill Monroe, a cocky, slick-fielding twenty-seven-year-old third baseman, led the Philly Giants with 35 stolen bases and 15 triples and tied Charlie Grant with 8 round-trippers. Outfielder Harry Moore, who'd started his career with the Chicago Unions in the 1890s before going east, had 20 doubles, 7 triples, 7 homers, and 27 stolen bases in 126 games. Even Rube Foster, who played in the field when not pitching, could swing the stick a bit, pounding out 29 doubles, 4 triples, and 5 homers, while stealing 12 bases.

This core of five men was certainly good enough to win a lot of ballgames, and was probably in and of itself better than the Page Fence Giants team, but the presentation of evidence doesn't end here. In the middle of their talented batting order was one more huge weapon—a young outfielder named Pete Hill.

◆ ◆ ◆

Born on October 12, 1882, near Buena, Virginia, Pete Hill moved north to play professional baseball, first making a name for himself with Sol White's Philadelphia Giants in 1904. By 1905, this son of former slaves was the top slugger on the Giants. At just twenty-two years of age, he quickly passed up Grant "Home Run" Johnson, becoming the premier African American hitter in the country.

In 128 games played, Hill led the team in hits (192), doubles (37), and total bases (281). He tied Johnson for the lead in home runs with 10 and was second in stolen bases (32) and sacrifice hits (12). In addition to his work at the plate, Hill anchored the outfield with outstanding range and an extremely powerful throwing arm. He was described at the time as a "natural" ballplayer, one who looked good doing everything. Today we'd call him a "five-tool guy."

In a handful of games against white minor league teams in 1905, Hill led the club with a .389 batting average. Hitting well against clubs from organized baseball would become a trend during the left-handed batter's long career. When playing against major league teams in Cuba, Hill cracked out an impressive .347 mark in 23 games, a figure that seems even more impressive when you consider it was accomplished in a huge ballpark where the league-wide offensive environment was an abysmal .235/.304/.291 (AVG/OBP/SLG). Against white minor league teams here in the states (mostly Pacific Coast League outfits), Pete piled up a .384 mark in 164 at-bats, cracking out 11 doubles and 9 home runs while stealing 11 bases.

All told, in 70 games versus white professional teams, Hill went 96-for-257 (.374), with 17 doubles, 3 triples, and 10 home runs. He stole 16 bases. His slugging percentage was .580. And remember, this was an era when 10 home runs and a slugging percentage of more than .550 in a full season was usually more than enough to lead *any* league, and Hill did it in less than half a season's worth of games.

How good was Pete Hill? He was elected to the Baseball Hall of Fame in 2006, for whatever that's worth. During the winter of 1910, playing in a

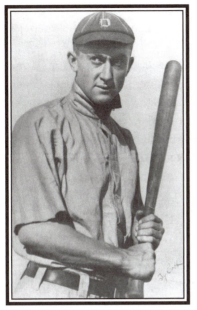

During the winter of 1910, Ty Cobb (left) played in the same Cuban winter league as African American star Pete Hill (right). Cobb batted .350, Hill batted .342. Both men are now enshrined in Cooperstown.
Images courtesy of National Baseball Hall of Fame Library, Cooperstown, New York

four-team, integrated short season in Cuba (featuring the Detroit Tigers and Philadelphia Athletics, of the American League, and Habana and Almendares from the Cuban League), Ty Cobb batted .350 for Detroit while Pete Hill batted .342 playing left field for Habana.

Overall, I don't know that Hill was really at Cobb's level. Nobody was, right? But to sandwich him in the conversation somewhere between Tris Speaker and Sam Crawford seems realistic at this point. He was a hell of a ballplayer, lost among the outsiders.

And when you figure he was in the middle of the Philadelphia Giants lineup in 1905, this speaks volumes about their firepower. There's little doubt they had a better offense than the Page Fence Giants.

◆ ◆ ◆

Pitching is 90 percent of the game, and the other half is mental, at least according to the great Yogi Berra. Nowadays, we realize it's really pitching *and* defense that make the difference.

When it came to pitching and defense, the Page Fence Giants were young (pitching) and bad (defense)—at least compared to the top competition. It wasn't that they didn't have talent; it was just raw and undeveloped. Their two best pitchers, southpaws Billy Holland and George Wilson, were twenty-one and nineteen years old, respectively, when they signed on with the Michigan barnstorming outfit.

During their first trial against top-level competition, going against Charlie Comiskey's St. Paul team in the Western League, the Page Fence Giants were besieged, 15–2 and 9–2, in two games. Across town, versus Minneapolis, it got even worse. They lost 25–2, 17–1, and 18–7. Their best pitcher, the nineteen-year-old Wilson, lost four of these games but didn't get much support in the field, either, as the Page Fence Giants averaged nearly 10 errors per contest.

Wilson actually pitched well in the 9–2 loss to Comiskey's bunch. He allowed only 8 hits in 9 innings of work, walked 3, and struck out a game-high 6. Thanks to his mates' 8 miscues, only 2 of the Saints' runs were earned.

For some reason, Wilson left the 1895 Page Fence Giants shortly after the spring debacle, signing on with the white Adrian club in the Michigan State League, where he'd right the ship, going 29–4 during the summer. Apparently he had better defensive support with Adrian. For about a month, his teammate was none other than future Hall of Famer Honus Wagner, one of the greatest shortstops of all time. Wilson would re-sign with the Page Fence bunch after the season, serving as their ace the next three years.

The difference here is elementary: Rube Foster, pitching stud of the Philadelphia Giants, was entering the prime of a career that would eventually land him in Cooperstown. He'd held his own against Rube Waddell, beating him in their head-to-head encounter. He'd later pitch admirably against Ed Reulbach and the great Chicago Cubs. George Wilson was just a kid getting started in pro ball, backed up by other youngsters just getting *their* starts. The veteran Philadelphia Giants pitching and defense allowed only 4.07 runs per game when playing minor league outfits, while the Page Fence Giants coughed up a whopping 8.61.

Overall, the Page Fence Giants went 31–35 versus *all* white professional teams (1895–1898), including two losses against the National League's Cincinnati Reds. Versus the Western League, which we previously demonstrated was the best minor league in the 1890s, they were an anemic 3–15. When pitted against the lower-level minor league clubs, they were rather impressive, actually, rolling up a 28–18 record.

The 1905 Philadelphia Giants dominated white professional teams, going 13–1 against minor league clubs (they weren't given an opportunity to play any major league teams that year), including a perfect four straight wins versus Eastern Leaguers, the top minor league at the time.

But the question still stands: could Sol White's 1905 aggregation have challenged for a National or American League pennant? Should they, as some hagiographers have suggested, be considered one of the greatest baseball teams of all time, black or white?

The beauty of this book is we're allowed to look at things objectively. We're not using baseball history as a tool to discuss America's well-known, well-documented difficulties (and associated atrocities) with racial prejudice. Those kinds of baseball books have become, frankly, platitudinous at this point. Everybody already knows racism is bad.

We're using baseball tools to talk about *baseball history*, and we discuss skin color openly, if only to sharpen the narrative and provide context. This allows us to comment on the all-black Philadelphia Giants (and all other subjects) honestly, without worrying about hurting anybody's feelings.

Or at least I think so.

That being said, when folks spent twenty-five cents to see Sol White's club during the summer of 1905, I believe they *were* watching a major league–caliber team in action. With Home Run Johnson and Charlie Grant in the middle infield, and Pete Hill anchored in left, they had a core that matched up well with any team in the country. In Rube Foster, Danny McClellan, and Emmett Bowman, they had three workhorses who held their own against the very best competition available. The Giants were 13–1 against minor league teams. For comparison, during exhibition games in 1905 versus minor leaguers, white *major league teams* went 32–15–1.

No doubt the Philadelphia Giants could have beaten big-league teams head-to-head had they been given opportunities. After all, the Cuban Giants beat a couple major league outfits in the late 1880s, and I doubt the "Cubans" were even as good as the low-minor-league-caliber Page Fence team. Indeed, Sol White's men could have probably held their own in a short series versus the big league's very best, maybe even hung around for a couple weeks or a month. But after that, I become skeptical.

My problem with the Philly Giants as a legitimate pennant contender over the course of a full big-league campaign has nothing to do with what they had but rather with what they were *missing*. In short, they were short a couple players. Literally. Their pitching staff was only three deep in an era when every single big-league team was distributing the workload among five men, sometimes six. Plus Philadelphia's best pitcher, Rube Foster, also doubled as their starting right fielder when he wasn't on the hill. There were no longer any full-time, two-way guys in the major leagues by 1905.

The big-league rosters were small in those days: they carried only seventeen or eighteen men. But the Philadelphia Giants were downright Spartan by comparison. Although twenty-six guys appeared in games for Sol White's team, only fourteen played in more than ten games, and it appears they were actually traveling with only twelve men at any given time. There's just no way this would hold up in a 154-game season, when every opponent (even the last-place clubs) presented a serious challenge.

If the Philly Giants could have cherry-picked three pitchers and another position player from the other top black teams—heck, if they could have cherry-picked a couple *white* minor leaguers from the Eastern League or Pacific Coast League—I think they could have given Rube Waddell's American League–champion Philadelphia Athletics a run for its money.

The next year, in 1906, the Philadelphia Giants did play Connie Mack's Athletics in a two-game postseason series, and despite the loss of Grant "Home Run" Johnson, who'd defected to the Brooklyn Royal Giants earlier in the year, they hung tough. Very tough. The Philadelphia Athletics' future Hall of Famer Eddie Plank nipped twenty-one-year-old Emmett Bowman in the first contest, 5–4. In the second game, none other than Rube Waddell himself exacted a measure of revenge from the Murray Hills game back in 1903, shutting out the Giants on 2 hits—while striking out 18—as the A's beat Danny McClellan, 5–0.

Just a few days earlier, Waddell had made national headlines by striking out 16 Washington Senators in an exhibition game played in Hartford, Connecticut. A portion of the gate receipts was donated to the "workingman's free bed" at the local tuberculosis hospital. In two consecutive starts, the hard-throwing lefty had punched out 34 batters in 18 innings pitched. Two years later, he'd set a modern American League record with 16 strikeouts in an official game.

Unfortunately, the two Rubes (Foster and Waddell) didn't face each other in a rematch. Foster was preparing to leave for the winter league in Cuba and didn't appear in the series.

◆ 13 ◆

FUGITIVES AND REFUGEES

UP NEAR THE CEILING, orange Victorian paper curled in the corners, peeling slowly away from the wall, while on the kitchen table, droplets of condensation streamed down a tall glass of sarsaparilla. Several house-flies danced around a half-eaten slice of breakfast pork, and although it was midday, the front parlor was almost pitch-black, as shades had been drawn and windows closed in defense against the oppressive southwesterly summer breeze. A heavyset woman, her perspiration-drenched blouse clinging snug to her back, shuffled around, sweeping the hardwood floor.

Outside, a Model T backfired, then accelerated quickly around a horse-drawn ice truck. The Jefferson Ice Company had dispatched twice the number of wagons this week to keep up with the demand. The car sounded its horn as it passed, kicking up brown dust and startling the horses a bit. The man driving the wagon, an older feller with a white beard, cursed in German, shaking his fist at the automobile, but by this time the car had already jerked into an alley, the sound of its engine fading as it sped away.

The man with the white beard muttered something in broken English to his black assistant and wiped his brow with a handkerchief before pulling on the reins. And with that, things were back to normal: late July, hooves clapping over cobblestone, cicadas buzzing high up in the elms, and the rustle of paper-dry leaves fluttering in the wind.

A young postal worker approached a gentleman standing at the street corner. "Hear you got the Giants today, Nixey."

"S'right, keed. Supposed to throw the tall one, the Cyclone, at us. Should be good."

"I'll be there."

"Glad to hear it. Tell your pals. We're gonna have a man out there with Coca-Cola soda fountains on a dray this afternoon. Plenty of shaved ice, too, to beat the heat."

The Jefferson wagon passed through the intersection, and the two men walked their separate directions. Nixey wore a straw boater hat and a white shirt with the sleeves rolled up. Strapped over his shoulder was a brown leather satchel stuffed with metal tools that rustled around a bit, cling-clanging with every stride. Three teenage boys waited for Nixey across the street. He was a bit of a celebrity in this neighborhood.

◆ ◆ ◆

The reports of tuberculosis had slowed down quite a bit. Happened every summer it seemed, but nobody understood why. Most people ventured out into the world, defiant. Despite the heat and looming specter of an incurable disease that had already cut down one classmate and two older members of the Lutheran church, residents of Logan Square, Illinois were intent on stealing a few minutes of bliss when and where they could. You had to work, and you had to eat, and you had to live, and Logan Square folks were as hungry for fun as anybody, becoming consumers and connoisseurs of the finer things.

When it came to capturing the entertainment dollar of the locals, Nixey Callahan's ballpark had some serious competition. Within a five-block radius, there were at least half a dozen theaters offering a variety of live shows. You could even see George Parsons, whose brother once ran the Page Fence Giants, sing and dance there if you wanted. If people preferred the outside, they could reach Lincoln Park Beach in less than 15 minutes. If they wanted to shop, they could take the elevated train downtown.

Jimmy Callahan
Outfield/Manager

Logan Squares
★

Former Chicago White Sox manager Nixey Callahan quit the American League in 1906 to start his own semipro team. Five years later he'd return to the big leagues without having missed a beat. *Courtesy of Scott Simkus*

◆ ◆ ◆

Nixey flicked a cigarette out of the oldest kid's mouth.

"Told you no smokin' till you're eighteen, lad. That's the rules. Makes yer balls shrink, and then nobody'll marry ya."

The other kids laughed.

"Ah right, we don't got time to putz around. Stosh, you're gonna come with me to Schmitt's. We need to get some parts. Gotta fix one of the commodes at the field before game time. Freckles, you go rake the infield and chalk the lines. Straight this time, see."

Callahan handed the redheaded kid a key, then pulled out a roll of blue tickets from his satchel.

"Fin, we're gonna try something new this week. Want you to hit every pub up and down Milwaukee Avenue and pass out these blue freebies. Remind everybody we got a hot ballgame with the colored Chicago Giants at 3:15 today. They can get in free, of course, but we'll make it up in beer sales and soda pop. And every blue ticket we collect, I'll give ya a penny."

◆ ◆ ◆

There were theaters, beaches, and Chicago's Loop to contend with, but by far Callahan's fiercest competition was the Riverview Amusement Park. Opened in 1904, the seventy-four-acre facility was just ten minutes away from the Logan Square ballpark and replete with the latest in thrill rides and attractions, many inspired by ideas the ownership group picked up in Europe. Indeed, the park's famous seventy-horse carousel was carved by a team of Swiss-Italian craftsman and installed in 1908.

The park was billed as "the world's largest amusement park" during its sixty-four years of operation. Riverview's carousel, Old Mill Tunnel of Love, Toboggan Slide, and Aerostat Swing attracted thousands of patrons daily during the ragtime era. The Scenic Railway Coaster, tame by today's standards, was perhaps the most popular ride. One of the more popular games was the "Dunk the Nigger" tank, where a colored barker would heckle, cajole, and convince passersby to try to sink him by hitting a target with a baseball—for a penny or a nickel.

Fact is, Callahan's club really couldn't compete with Riverview, which had broad appeal. He just hoped to capture some of the runoff, the folks sick of eating cotton candy and making out in the Old Mill tunnel. He had his niche audience, and they were baseball fans.

◆ ◆ ◆

After leaving Comiskey's Chicago White Sox in 1906, Callahan claimed he had earned more than $12,000 running his semipro team during their inaugural season. This was, he pointed out, much more than his previous salary with the Sox. Twelve grand is close to $300,000 in today's money, if that helps you calibrate the size and scope of an outsider baseball business. By 1910, things began changing in the semipro game. Nixey noticed he needed to work a little harder to attract the crowds, and this had little to do with Lincoln Park Beach, the Toboggan Slide, or shopping at Marshall Field's downtown. This had to do with the niche. This was a baseball issue.

With the Cubs and Sox still operating on the near west and south sides of the city, respectively, Callahan and the other semipro impresarios still held a monopoly on Chicago's north side, but it was beginning to crumble.

Nixie's old employer, Charles Comiskey, had just opened a state-of-the-art steel and concrete ballpark. The White Sox attendance jumped from fifth in the American League in 1909 to third in 1910, despite a sixth-place ballclub. By 1912, after Callahan returned to the White Sox as player-manager of the team, the Sox would lead the AL in attendance, attracting more than 600,000 patrons.

Callahan was long gone as a full-time participant in the semipro scene, but in 1914, the Chicago Federal League team moved into Weegham Park on the city's north side. By 1916, after the Federal League disbanded, the Chicago Cubs moved into the abandoned ballyard (later rechristened Wrigley Field), and the semipro monopoly of north-side baseball was effectively finished.

There were a couple outstanding gate attractions left during Nixey's final season in outsider baseball. The first was a tall African American named Joseph Williams. Known as "Cyclone" at the time, the big, hard-throwing Texan would later wind up in Cooperstown under the more familiar moniker of Smokey Joe.

The other big draw was a team called the Leland Giants, managed by Andrew "Rube" Foster and featuring Pete Hill in center field, Grant "Home Run" Johnson at second, and John Henry Lloyd as a young shortstop. After a couple seasons of dominating diamonds out east under the Philadelphia Giants moniker, Foster had grabbed several star players, setting up shop in Chicago and putting together a club that may have been superior to Sol White's 1905 "colored world champions."

◆ ◆ ◆

Fin walked past three or four taverns before making a beeline toward the local playground. Later on, just about every kid in the neighborhood would show up at Callahan's ballyard with a blue ticket. Nixey was too busy fixing the chalk lines Freckles had messed up (again) to work the front gate. Fin made an extra sixty cents that day for his efforts, beer sales stayed flat, and it would be weeks before Callahan caught wind of what was really happening with the blue freebies.

Sitting up in the wooden bleachers, still wearing his postal worker uniform, was the stocky twenty-two-year-old who'd encountered Nixey earlier in the day. His name was Knute Rockne. In the fall, this Logan Square kid would enroll as a freshman at Notre Dame to study pharmacy, run track, and play college football.

An hour before the gates opened, Callahan and Stosh got the toilet fixed. As a teenager, before getting the courage to pursue baseball in the professional ranks, Nixey had worked as a plumber's apprentice in Massachusetts, but that didn't necessarily mean he enjoyed troubleshooting leaky pipes and water pressure issues.

Back in 1903, twenty-nine-year-old Callahan had been named player-manager of the Chicago White Sox. He'd originally jumped across town from the Cubs in 1901, when Ban Johnson and Comiskey turned their minor league into a second major, inducing talent with the promise of bigger bucks. In 1904, with the team off to a good 23–18 start, Callahan stepped away from the managerial duties, explaining in the local papers that playing second base and managing the team was too much. He wanted to move back to the outfield and concentrate on being a ballplayer.

There was apparently something else in the works. After a peace accord was reached between the American and National leagues, salaries flattened a bit and the structure of baseball at the highest level returned to the status quo. The reserve clause was still in effect. Players had little wiggle room when it came to negotiations or plotting their own career paths. And the black guys, the Charlie "Tokohama" Grants of the world, whom John McGraw had once tried to sneak into the big time, were surging forward with their own plans, building powerhouse baseball franchises that dominated the professional game's fringe. When Callahan first jumped to the White Sox, he was looking for greener pastures, and he apparently found them—to the tune of his $12,000 income—during an era when the game's best all-around players, Honus Wagner and Ty Cobb, were earning roughly $10,000 ($257,000 in the modern world).

But by the end of his five-year stint in the semipros, Callahan wasn't just managing and playing at the same time: he was fixing toilets, chalking lines, selling tickets, bringing box scores and game stories to the local papers, negotiating with vendors, scheduling doubleheaders, and playing psychologist to the various egos on his baseball team. And as the workload increased, the money was somehow dwindling.

Callahan longed for a return to the relative simplicity of the major leagues. Even being a player-manager seemed relatively easy compared to being everything for the Logan Squares.

◆ ◆ ◆

The biggest attraction in the 1910 Chicago City League was young Cyclone Joe Williams of the Chicago Giants. He'd been a star in San Antonio, Texas, but would face much stiffer competition in the Windy City's fast, integrated semi-pro league, which had become a lucrative alternative for disgruntled major leaguers, disenfranchised minor leaguers, and prospects who still harbored dreams of moving up in the organized game. One year, to gain leverage with the Detroit Tigers during contract negotiations, Ty Cobb threatened to join Callahan's team rather than report to spring training.

Like the Philly Giants and Page Fence teams before them, the majority of the Chicago Giants' schedule consisted of white opponents, and from the fact that most of their pitching competitors in the City League had professional experience, we get a rare glimpse of how future Hall of Famer Cyclone Joe Williams stacked up against men with verifiable track records.

Before getting to the near-complete pitching records from 1910, rebuilt from box scores, we'll provide profiles of six pitchers who participated in the league.

Cyclone "Smokey" Joe Williams: A twenty-four-year-old rookie from Texas, Williams was getting his first taste of big-time baseball in 1910. He started slowly, splitting his first eight decisions before things started clicking. He struck out 17 batters in one game, late in the season. In the fall, Williams traveled west with the Giants and continued his rapid ascent in the California Winter League. According to William F. McNeil's *The California Winter League*, Williams compiled a 4–1 record with 78 strikeouts in only 60 innings pitched against mostly Pacific Coast League athletes. He was well on his way to becoming the top African American pitcher during the dead-ball era.

Charles "Chick" Fraser: Thirty-six-year-old Chick Fraser won 175 games during his major league career. He pitched with the Chicago Cubs in 1907 and '08, and with their outstanding defense behind him, he compiled a 19–14 record with a 2.27 ERA. After pitching just one game in 1909, he walked out on the team and joined the semipro ranks in his hometown of Chicago. He was clearly still a major league–caliber pitcher and, along with Cyclone Joe, was one of the two best hurlers in the league.

PETE HENNING: Indiana native Pete Henning was a little bit like Cyclone Joe—a young prospect getting his first taste of big-time independent baseball. He'd go on to pitch two seasons for the Kansas City Packers in the Federal League, compiling a 14–25 record and a 3.83 ERA at the major league level. He'd later pitch in the American Association.

WALTER BALL: Ball was teammates with Joe Williams on the Chicago Giants. The right-handed veteran had been playing independent black professional baseball since the mid-1890s and would continue pitching professionally into the early 1920s, a span of more than twenty-five years.

PERCY SKILLEN: Percy was the Stephen Strasburg of his era. A college star at Dartmouth, several of his pitching records still stand near the top at the institution. He was offered $4,000 to sign with the Boston Red Sox but turned it down to pursue an opportunity with his hometown Chicago White Sox. The Sox offer didn't pan out, and Skillen went into business in Chicago, playing semipro ball in the summer. He was so successful in non-baseball affairs that by the time he was in his mid-twenties, he was able to build a large mansion in Winnetka, on Chicago's north shore.

NIXEY CALLAHAN: After a five-year hiatus, Callahan returned to Comiskey's White Sox club in 1911, stringing together several of his best offensive seasons ever. It's worth noting that he had been a very solid major league pitcher before switching to outfield and second base. He won 99 games in the big leagues, including two 20-win seasons for the Chicago Cubs, in 1898 and 1899.

13.1

1910 Chicago Pitchers	W	L	ERA	G	GS	CG	IP	H	BB	K
Cyclone Joe Williams	13	4	1.09	21	17	16	156.0	101	44	132
Rube Foster*	12	1	1.89	16	15	13	138.0	138	18	69
Chick Fraser	9	4	0.94	18	14	12	124.1	92	32	103
Walter Ball	8	5	2.23	16	14	10	121.0	120	37	69
Pete Henning	5	9	2.82	18	15	10	130.2	99	24	67
Percy Skillen	3	11	3.60	14	14	13	120.0	111	31	61
Nixey Callahan	0	1	9.00	1	1	0	7.0	6	2	5

Note: *We've tossed Rube Foster in here as a bonus. Cyclone Joe Williams played for Frank Leland's "Chicago Giants"; Rube Foster pitched for a different Chicago outfit, called the "Leland Giants." Prior to the season, there had been a legal brouhaha (Rube had served as player/manager of Frank Leland's team the previous three seasons), ending with Rube owning the rights to the Leland Giants team name and Frank running a different outfit—but unable to legally use his own last name. Think "Cuban Giants" and "Cuban X-Giants" from the 1890s or *Kramer vs. Kramer*, if you're a late '70s movie buff. And if this seems utterly confusing, you have nothing to worry about. It's supposed to be confusing. It's outsider baseball.

As a result of these shenanigans, Rube Foster's Leland Giants weren't allowed entry into the Chicago City League in 1910, but they *did* eventually play some unsanctioned games against the league clubs, as well as some other city league–caliber teams, such as the Gunthers. Rube's statistics are a combination of outings versus these clubs, plus major black teams and white minor league teams. They don't represent his entire season, of course, but provide a nice glimpse into the type of pitcher he was, for those who enjoy the language communicated by baseball statistics.

Cyclone Joe Williams, Chick Fraser, and Rube Foster were three of the top semipro pitchers in Chicago in 1910. Williams, as previously mentioned, was a rookie. Fraser was a major league veteran who'd just ended his career. And Rube Foster was a thirty-year-old player midway through his prime. His ambitions as a club owner and league magnate were already beginning to dominate his activities, chief among them eating—his weight had ballooned from 230 pounds in 1905 to perhaps 275 by this time. His won-lost record was more the result of an incredible supporting cast behind him rather than overpowering stuff. He got by on guile and pinpoint control, issuing far fewer walks per 9 innings than anybody on the list.

At the end of the 1910 season, Foster began publicly exploring the possibility of starting a major league for African American baseball teams. This was reported in both black and white papers across the country. Over the next four or five years, he'd pitch less and less, focusing much more on the business end with each subsequent season. Foster had no idea of knowing it at the time, but it would be another ten years before his dream of an all-black major league would come true.

◆ ◆ ◆

Nixey Callahan put down the wrench and grabbed his glove. It wasn't until he was actually on the diamond, playing, that he could finally relax. His Logan Squares club was one of the very best semipro teams in Chicago, and the colored Chicago Giants were perhaps their biggest rival. The game against

Cyclone Joe Williams was a rematch; back in May, the big righty had shut down Callahan's men on five singles, beating them 4–1. Nixey had gone hitless in the contest.

In the blistering late-afternoon sun, Callahan sent Pete Henning to the mound, and the kid appeared to have his good stuff, painting the corners with fastballs and buckling the Chicago Giants batters' knees with a sharp curve. But through the first three innings, Cyclone matched the white boy pitch for pitch, striking out several men with a wicked heater that seemed to rise as it approached home plate.

In the bottom of the fourth inning, Cyclone blinked. Manager/outfielder/ plumber Nixey Callahan lined a single into center field, then advanced to second on a sacrifice bunt. The next batter fanned, bringing up a fellow named Brown, who was filling in at second base because the Logan Squares' regular starter, Dutch Meier (who'd played briefly with the Pittsburgh Pirates), couldn't get off work in time for the game. Brown had struck out his first time up and fell behind in the count, 0–2, with Callahan in scoring position.

Cyclone Joe Williams made a mistake, hanging a nickel curve over the plate, and the Logan Square batter fisted a Texas Leaguer over the Giants' second baseman's head, scoring Callahan. It would prove to be the only run of the game. Williams recovered his bearings and shut down the Logan Squares the rest of the way, striking out 10 in the process. But Pete Henning, the future Federal League pitcher, was a touch better, shutting out the all-black lineup on just 3 hits, while striking out 3 men.

Two weeks later, these two clubs would be at it again. This time Williams and his Chicago Giants teammates got the upper hand, winning 3–1, as Cyclone Joe held Callahan hitless, while striking out another 7 batters. The future Hall of Famer would finish the season 2–1 versus the Logan Squares, with an earned-run average of 1.00. He struck out 24 batters in 26 innings pitched.

This was the world of outsider baseball in Chicago, circa 1910.

◆ 14 ◆

1911 MINNEAPOLIS MILLERS

"Quit it, asshole, or I'll blow your fucking brains out."

Mrs. Reinsmith, the unassuming landlady at 3635 Dodier Street, had a revolver pointed directly at the man's head. The thumping noise and crash of broken glass were what had startled her in the first place, and the ear-piercing screams of a woman in distress were what made her grab the pistol and run upstairs.

When she first opened her tenant's door, Mrs. Reinsmith saw the man had his wife by the ankle and was spinning her in a circle, as if trying to rip her limb off. He was in a drunken rage, cursing. It was 2:00 AM. This wasn't unusual, as the man had been laid off by his employer a few weeks earlier due to his problems with the bottle. He was *always* inebriated, day and night.

The man's name was George "Rube" Waddell. The year was 1910, and his tenure with the St. Louis Browns (indeed, his entire big-league career) was coming to a close.

He and his young bride, Madge McGuire Waddell, were newlyweds. This was the third (and final) trip to the altar for the big left-hander.

Rube's first divorce, from Florence L. Waddell, had been granted back in April 1902. His second split, from May Waddell, was announced just before Valentine's Day in 1910, although they had been separated for several years. Less than two months after officially dumping May, he went to the Grand Avenue Methodist Church in St. Louis and tied the knot with twenty-five-year-old Madge McGuire, who'd been raised in New Orleans.

The thirty-two-year-old was coming off his worst season ever at the big-league level, having finished 11–14 in 31 appearances for the seventh-place Browns. With an earned-run average of 2.37 and a K/9 rate of 5.8, the man still had incredible physical talent, but he missed a few starts and was unable to pitch in relief as often as he had in the past, as his drinking spiraled out of control.

"My marriage to Miss McGuire will make a man out of me," Waddell had said as he left the church. "I have stopped drinking and am in better condition than I have been for years. We will live in St. Louis, and I think the happy part of my life has just begun. I have had a great deal of trouble lately, but it is all over now."

The "new and improved" Waddell lasted a couple weeks, maybe. His salary the previous season had been only $1,200 in an era when the top players, such as Christy Mathewson, were earning $10,000 and up. Rube was making just a fraction more than the average working man, spending the majority of it on suds and hard liquor, and by summer he was selling his wife's clothes just to pay for room and board.

According to the census records, just before her marriage to Rube, Madge was working as a saleslady for a "dry goods" company. In actuality, the attractive, petite brunette worked as a "pajama girl," modeling silk PJs at trade shows and local events. She was like an old-time version of a Victoria's Secret model. The Waddells were clearly two people who enjoyed being the centers of attention.

The problem was, Madge quickly became the eye of Waddell's personal storm, just as his previous two brides had been. According to testimony that emerged later, Rube was fond of hurling empty bottles at his wife when the mood struck or pounding her with his fists.

"Aw, she's my wife," he explained upon being released from prison one day after blackening Mrs. Waddell's eye. "And I can do as I please with her."

Waddell was of unsound mind, according to his wife. "He's crazy," she explained, "and I intend to have him examined mentally by the court and put away. I'll be crazy myself if I live with him another day. He says he simply can't live without excitement, but I'm tired of furnishing the excitement. We've been fighting every night for a week.

"When he can't find any other way to start a roughhouse, as he calls it, he comes home and shows me letters and pictures of other women to arouse my jealousy. I'm done with him, and I'll enter suit for a divorce along with the suit to have him examined to his sanity."

But marriage is a weird thing. She'd still be married to the brute a year later, in 1911, after he'd become a member of the minor league Minneapolis Millers.

The 1910 season was a total disaster for Rube, both personally and professionally. In addition to his marital woes, Waddell faltered on the mound, making only two starts and pitching just 33 innings before St. Louis dumped him. He was thrown in jail at least once, maybe twice, for domestic abuse.

He finished the year with Newark of the Eastern League, pitched well, reconciled with his wife, and prepared for a course correction in 1911. Joe Cantillon, who'd been relieved of his managerial duties after leading the Washington Senators to a last-place finish in '09, accepted a job with Minneapolis in the American Association the next year. Cantillon convinced Rube to come along in '11, as he was assembling what was going to be a historically great minor league ball club.

◆ ◆ ◆

The minor leagues at that time were the link between the two major leagues at the top and professional baseball's outsider clubs on the periphery. Although participants in the National Agreement, most minor league teams were independently owned, and at this point, none of them were part of any organized farm system.

They didn't exist specifically to develop talent for the major leagues. They existed to make money, and if they didn't do well at the box office, or by selling players on the open market, they folded. There were basically two ways for minor league clubs to generate revenue before the modern farm systems were established: sell lots of tickets and concessions during games, and sell players to the major leagues, either via the draft or on the open market. Oh, there was a third revenue stream if the club owned its own ballpark: they could lease it out when they were on the road, for scholastic sporting events, theatre troupes, Negro league games, circuses, whatever.

Greenlee Field, which was Pittsburgh's main blackball venue in the 1930s, rented out its park for boxing matches, car races, and football games—*during the season*—which makes one wonder what sort of condition the playing surface was in at any given time.

Bill Veeck, who owned the minor league Milwaukee Brewers franchise during the 1940s, explained in his autobiography that he didn't really make any money during the season. It wasn't until afterward, when he sold prospects to major league clubs, that he was able to pay his debts and bank a couple dollars during the off-season.

Joe Cantillon, who in addition to being manager of the team was also a part owner, was probably targeting option one: build a great club, win games, contend for the league pennant, and sell lots of tickets and concessions at the ballpark. If you operated in a big enough city, such as Los Angeles, Baltimore, or, say, Minneapolis, you had a fighting chance to earn a baseball living the old-fashioned way: through the loyalty and box office support of your local fan base.

In 1911, Cantillon had a solid nucleus in the field. Thirty-year-old Claude Rossman, who had appeared in two World Series as the starting first baseman for the Detroit Tigers, was in the mix, hitting .356. Otis Clymer, who had five years of service time in the majors, batted .342 for the Millers, then would later return to the big leagues for one more stint. Jimmy Williams, who had started for eleven seasons in the show and had once batted .354 with 27 triples (tied for seventh all time) for the 1899 Pittsburgh Pirates, anchored second base for Minneapolis, hitting .332.

But the centerpiece of the lineup was a thirty-year-old outfielder named Gavvy Cravath. The right-handed hitter had played for three major league teams over the course of two unsuccessful tours in the American League. He'd batted only .240 with 2 home runs before being handed his walking papers.

In Minneapolis, playing in cozy Nicollet Park, Cravath found his stride. His first year there, he batted .291. His second season, he jumped to .327 with a team-high 14 home runs. Then in 1911, he exploded for 53 doubles, 13 triples, and a league-best .363 batting mark. To top that off, he pounded an astonishing 29 home runs in an era where the game was still dominated by the bunt, steal, and hit-and-run and he drove in enough men to win the American Association's Triple Crown. No minor league fluke, the next year Gavvy Cravath found himself in the Philadelphia Phillies outfield, where he led the National League in home runs six out of seven years, with a high of 24 in 1915, which was remarkable in the pre-Ruthian days of the dead ball. He also batted .341 on two separate occasions. Over the course of his last nine years in the big leagues, Cravath batted .291, topping 100 RBI three times, before retiring at the age of forty.

But it was in the pitching core where Cantillon made his most significant changes in 1911. Long Tom Hughes, a 31-game winner for the 1910 Millers, was on his way back to the major leagues. Nick Altrock, who won 19 games in '10 with a fine 2.28 ERA, was traded to the Kansas City Blues midseason.

In their place, Cantillon brought in Pug Cavet, who'd gone 18–15 in the Three-I League one year earlier; Rube Peters, who'd compiled a 19–12 record in two different minor leagues in 1910; Jack Gilligan, who'd apparently escaped the island to spend some time with the St. Louis Browns the previous summer; and thirty-nine-year-old major league veteran Sam Leever, who'd gone 6–5 with the Pirates in 1910, closing out a big-league career during which he'd won more than 20 games four times.

But the belle of the ball was Rube Waddell. Yeah, he was battling a pandemic of personal demons, but when sober, he was still capable of throwing fastballs past any hitter in the country. If they could keep Rube relatively healthy, and in uniform, Cantillon must have figured the turnstiles were going to click. Publicly, the manager boasted the big lefty was going to be the cornerstone of their staff.

◆ ◆ ◆

In late spring of 1911, Ohio's headline stories turned bizarre.

"She brought a butcher knife into our bed and threatened to cut my heart out," the man explained to the judge. "She'd thrown a frying pan at me, splashed a pitcher of beer in my face, and once, she knocked me unconscious for twenty minutes with a jar of cold cream or something like that."

"She was terribly and unreasonably jealous," the man continued. "One time, I didn't get home to dinner until about 8:30. My wife was in a rage, and when I sat down at the table she jerked the tablecloth from the table and everything on it fell to the floor. Then she went upstairs and brought down my best suit and another light suit. She put both in the kitchen stove and burned them. Then she took the poker and threatened to brain me."

Couple days later, the judge granted these two a divorce. Turns out the man was having an affair. "Whatever she has done in annoying her husband he brought on himself. Women are almost always the product of their husband."

No, this wasn't Mr. and Mrs. Waddell; apparently other folks had marital problems in the old days, too. This was the scandalous case of Mr. and Mrs. H. K. Ferry of Cleveland, Ohio. Mr. Ferry was a reasonably well-known political figure in the city, serving as the longtime director of Cleveland's Humane Society. Among other things, he was responsible for detaining stray dogs, ensuring all horses were properly shod, and breaking up illegal cockfighting rings. He worked long hours, belonged to a cycling club in the summer, served as the director of a bowling league in the winter, and allegedly had a girlfriend for all four seasons. He was busy.

Although I doubt there was any connection whatsoever, a couple weeks prior to the Ferrys' marital collapse in Cleveland, a small wire story hit the papers from Columbus. Rube Waddell, pitcher for the Minneapolis Millers, had caused quite a ruckus at the Northern Hotel. Joe Cantillon's bunch was in town for a series with their American Association rivals, the Columbus Senators. Apparently the former Miss Madge McGuire was traveling with her husband on the road trip, and the two became embroiled in another knock-down, drag-'em-out fight. This one resulted in Rube locking the former underwear model (described as "one-third his size") in their hotel room for several hours, raising the ire of his teammates, who came to the young lady's defense.

Joe Cantillon tried to serve as peacemaker. For some reason, despite the protests of several Minneapolis players, the hotel felt compelled to share this dirty laundry with the newspapers. The story seems to have died out before gaining serious traction on the wires. (Searching historical digital newspaper archives is sometimes like monitoring a one-hundred-year-old Twitter feed; you're looking to see what was trending back then.)

Up north, in Cleveland, there was one more odd detail that emerged from the divorce proceedings of Mr. and Mrs. Ferry. According to the husband, a few years earlier his wife "went to Boston on a visit. On her return she said she had met [Rube] Waddell and Doc Powers, late catcher with the Athletics."

"The next time Philadelphia came here to play," Mr. Ferry testified, "Waddell came to our house. He was there every day and every night, until midnight." Mr. Ferry was implying there had been a tryst between his wife and the big left-hander (probably during their first meeting in Boston), and he was in some way damaged by the audacity of this man visiting his home for several straight evenings, after the indiscretion had occurred.

◆ ◆ ◆

Joe Cantillon's men won their first couple games of the season, then steamrolled through the remainder of the April schedule. They were 18–9 and in first place around the time Rube Waddell and his wife got into the squabble in their Columbus hotel room. Waddell had pitched well, winning two games versus Toledo in the days leading up to the hotel-room brawl. After this, the Millers went through a nasty spell. Despite having the most talented roster in the American Association, they'd lose 27 of their next 45 games. On July 1, nearing the midway point of the season, the club was dead even in the won-lost column at 36–36.

But then something clicked. Big Gavvy Cravath kept pounding home runs. Roy Patterson surprised on the mound, winning game after game en route to a 24–10 campaign. And Rube Waddell, who was now permanently estranged from his third wife but still battling his demons, muscled his way to a team-high 300 innings pitched, 20–17 record, and a 2.79 ERA while leading the American Association in strikeouts.

The Minneapolis Millers won the 1911 American Association pennant with room to spare, compiling a 99–66 record, five games ahead of Kansas City in the win column. In their last game of the year, versus Kansas City, Waddell played right field, at one point dragging a chair and a keg of beer out to his position. With the pennant a foregone conclusion, the game was a clownish affair, and Rube was the center of attention, hamming it up with teammates, opponents, and fans. It was a happy day for Waddell, the last day of the last great season in Waddell's professional career.

Rube Waddell and Madge would be officially divorced in August 1912. In less than a year and a half after that, the big left-hander would be dead from tuberculosis. When he was pitching well, spending his off-days on the sandlots with amateurs, or helping the local fire department battle blazes, he was called "colorful."

The rest of the time, he was pretty much a monster.

◆ ◆ ◆

Baseball historian Bill James, in his seminal work *The New Historical Baseball Abstract*, suggested the 1911 Minneapolis Millers were the best minor league team of the decade. In Rube Waddell, they had *the* most dominant strikeout pitcher of his generation. In Gavvy Cravath, they had a slugger who'd become the premier home run hitter in the National League during the dead-ball era. Almost everybody else on the roster had a major league pedigree.

Turning our attention away from the personal dirt for a moment and redirecting our attention to the diamond dust, the question needs to be asked. How good were the Millers? Could this minor league team have held their own in the major leagues?

Let's use the STARS system to help sharpen our understanding of where they fit into the hierarchy of professional baseball. We'll begin with the final American Association standings for 1911, with each club's corresponding STARS score:

14.1

1911 American Association	W	L	PCT.	STARS Score
Minneapolis Millers	99	66	.600	240
Kansas City Blues	94	70	.573	207
Columbus Senators	87	78	.527	204
St. Paul Saints	79	85	.482	205
Milwaukee Brewers	79	87	.476	186
Toledo Mud Hens	78	86	.476	205
Indianapolis Indians	78	88	.470	191
Louisville Colonels	67	101	.399	178

In 2001, in celebration of the 100th Anniversary of the National Association of Professional Baseball Clubs (the NAPBC was the umbrella organization for minor league ball), the NAPBC hired a couple historians to write a series of articles about the 100 greatest minor league teams of the twentieth century. They came up with an entertaining (albeit misleading) list, covering a broad cross section of minor league levels, eras, and teams.

Instead of relying entirely on subjective measures, the men in charge of the project wisely created a formula for ranking the teams. First off, they assigned a point system for the level of competition. The Triple-A-caliber league clubs (similar to the 1911 American Association) received 100 points, with the lower levels—e.g., Double-A, Single-A, Rookie ball—being assigned points on a sliding scale of reduced value. The lowest level league teams, for instance, were credited with 20 points.

Then they added two more categories: winning percentage and total number of victories. This is where things fall off the tracks a bit. Their system became biased in favor of great teams playing in bad leagues, or leagues where the talent was poorly distributed, and teams who played in leagues with very long schedules, such as the Pacific Coast League, where they sometimes played 200 games in a year.

Not surprisingly, the 1911 Minneapolis Millers, who played .600 ball in a league that had tremendous balance and an average Triple-A-length schedule, didn't make the list. They had that rough stretch after the Waddell hotel incident, when they went 18–27, effectively killing their chances of winning 100-plus games. They recovered well enough but fought to prevail in a league where seven out of the eight teams won at least 47 percent of their games. The only truly *bad* team in the league was the Louisville Colonels, and they just missed playing .400 baseball, which isn't atrocious.

When Bill James tabbed the Millers as *his* choice for the top minor league team from 1910 to 1919, I suspect he was focusing on the actual talent on the roster and envisioning how they fit into the larger world of professional baseball. This is more in line with what my objectives are, figuring out how all the pieces in baseball history fit together, in terms of actual talent.

There was only one team from 1911 that made the official "Top 100 Minor League Teams of the 20th Century" list and that was the Denver Grizzlies of the Western League. The Grizz had an awesome summer, going 111–54 (.673) and running away with the league crown. They finished a full 18 games ahead of their nearest competitor, the St. Joseph Drummers, who went 93–72. They ranked high on the all-time minor league list, coming in as the twenty-second greatest minor league club of all time.

The problem, as I demonstrate here in a moment, is that the Minneapolis Millers would have *crushed* the Denver Grizzlies in head-to-head competition. Denver's roster was peppered with a bunch of nobodies, and although the Western League was technically the same level as the American Association, it was at least a couple notches down in terms of actual talent. In the American Association, forty-six of the top fifty most productive batters appeared in the major leagues at some point. In the Western League, only twenty-nine of their top hitters ever made the show. Same thing with the pitchers, where there's a similarly huge gap.

So, before figuring out how the Millers might fit in at the major league level, let's look at the so-called twenty-second greatest minor league team of all time, the 1911 Western League–champion Denver Grizzlies, and try to gauge how they would have fared had they played in the American Association. Using the STARS system, let's go ahead and squeeze them into the AA's final standings:

14.2

1911 American Association	W	L	PCT.	STARS Score
Minneapolis Millers	99	66	.600	240
Kansas City Blues	94	70	.573	207
Columbus Senators	87	78	.527	204
St. Paul Saints	79	85	.482	205
Milwaukee Brewers	79	87	.476	186
Toledo Mud Hens	78	86	.476	205
Indianapolis Indians	78	88	.470	191
Louisville Colonels	67	101	.399	178
Denver Grizzlies (!)	*111*	*54*	*.673*	*166*

That's not a typo. The Grizzlies grade out at just 166 STARS points. I'm guessing this legendary 111-win team would not only have had a difficult time handling the Minneapolis Millers, they probably would have finished dead last had they simply switched minor leagues in 1911.

◆ ◆ ◆

The American League was the better of the two majors in 1911—trust me on this. Connie Mack's Philadelphia Athletics (without their old ace, Rube Waddell, who was up in Minneapolis) rolled to a 101–50 mark, finishing 13½ games ahead of Ty Cobb's Detroit Tigers. Afterward, they smoked John McGraw's New York Giants 4–2, winning the World Series in impressive fashion.

Now back to the Minneapolis Millers. How might they have fared in the major leagues? For the sake of fairness, we'll adjust the STARS system to *include* American Association service time. That is, for all teams, all seasons in the AA will be considered to have a value of 1 point, same as the major leagues.

14.3

Team	STARS Score	League	Finish
Philadelphia Athletics	377	AL	1st place
Chicago Cubs	368	NL	2nd place
New York Giants	367	NL	1st place
Detroit Tigers	362	AL	2nd place
Pittsburgh Pirates	357	NL	3rd place
Philadelphia Athletics	353	NL	4th place
New York Yankees	351	AL	6th place
Boston Red Sox	348	AL	4th place
Minneapolis Millers	339	AA	1st place (American Assoc.)
Cincinnati Reds	330	NL	6th place
Cleveland Indians	329	AL	3rd place
Chicago White Sox	320	AL	5th place
St. Louis Browns	320	AL	8th place
Washington Senators	314	AL	7th place
St. Louis Cardinals	300	NL	5th place
Brooklyn Dodgers	294	NL	7th place
Boston Braves	292	NL	8th place

Since each player is credited for service time in the American Association (if they happened to have played there at some point during their careers), this might distort the ranking of the Millers. But even if we adjusted the AA credit to reflect the lesser competition level, it doesn't make a large difference. In fact, a value reduction of 20 percent for American Association service time doesn't affect the Millers' ranking at all. They'd still be ninth on the list.

With the presence of Rube Waddell and Gavvy Cravath, it seems the Minneapolis Millers really could have been a middle-of-the-pack major league team. This opens up a series of new questions about legendary minor league clubs of the past, such as the Baltimore Orioles of the early 1920s and the Los Angeles Angels of the 1930s: would putting them under the STARS microscope provide new insight, revealing truths or debunking long-held assumptions? I'm guessing it would.

And what of those vaunted Denver Grizzlies, who won an astonishing 111 games in the 1911 Western League? Considering the talent gap between them and Minneapolis, I don't think they'd have a very realistic chance of competing in the big leagues. Anybody who thinks otherwise might want to join ol' Rube and get their head examined.

◆ 15 ◆

MONO AMARILLO

AFTER LOSING TWO OF THEIR FIRST THREE GAMES, John McGraw assembled his players at the Hotel Plaza and gave them a severe dressing
down. "Either you start playing ball, or you take the next steamer home," Mac
shouted. "I didn't fucking come down here to let a lot of coffee-colored Cubans
show me up, and I don't intend to have the Giants' reputation ruined by bur-
lesque baseball. I'm not going to be the goat
for a joy trip. You'll beat these clowns, or I'll
know the reason why."

With two days off until their next
game with the Cubans, McGraw called
for an unscheduled workout at Havana's
Almendares Park before the club ventured
off on a sightseeing expedition arranged
by the tour's promoter, Eugenio Jimenez. A
couple players seriously considered going
home on their own, since they weren't
technically playing under their contract
as employees of the New York National
League ballclub.

Going back to the World Series, which
had ended just a month earlier, the Giants
had now lost six of their last eight games
with McGraw at the helm. Losing to Connie Mack's supremely talented Philadelphia
Athletics club was one thing, but screwing

John McGraw and Christy Mathewson visited Cuba in 1911 with one
objective in mind: to win baseball
games. *National Baseball Hall of Fame Library,
Cooperstown, New York*

the pooch on the islands, against a bunch of colored amateurs, would be an indignity of the highest order.

For the first time ever, there was some actual anxiety associated with a Cuban tour. As a player, McGraw had visited Havana twenty years earlier, in 1891, with a group called the All-Americans. They had crushed the locals in five straight games, outscoring them 66 to 8. Nixey Callahan, the man who would later run the Logan Squares team in the integrated Chicago City League, had visited Cuba with the Brooklyn Dodgers in 1900, and *they* had exhibited a similar dominance, winning all four games while outscoring their opponents, 49–11. Lumping those two tours together, the Cubans had been clobbered, 115 to 20, by the visiting Americans. Despite their enthusiasm for the game, the Cuban teams were still in their primordial form, amateur in every respect. But a sports culture evolves rather quickly, and things had certainly changed since the first American baseball tours.

Jose Mendez, a lithe fireballer with wicked movement on his fastball, helped put Cuban baseball on the map for good in 1908. In his first start against a major league team, the twenty-four-year-old came within one out of no-hitting the Cincinnati Reds, settling instead for a 1-hit, 1–0 victory, with 9 strikeouts to his credit. He'd throw 25 consecutive scoreless innings during the series, allowing only 8 base hits, while fanning 24, as his Almendares club went 5–1–1 against the National Leaguers.

Cuban star Jose Mendez tossed a one-hitter versus the Cincinnati Reds in 1908. *Courtesy of Scott Simkus*

The next fall, Mendez's teammate, Eustaquio "Bombin" Pedroso, made even bigger noise, throwing an eleven-inning no-hitter versus the Detroit Tigers. In the three fall tours prior to the New York Giants visit in 1911, the Reds, Tigers, Athletics, and an All-Star club featuring future Hall of Famers Three Finger Brown and Addie Joss had managed only a sub-.500, 23–28–2 record against the Cuban teams. Things had definitely evolved in the tropical baseball paradise.

The reaction to this was a lot like Team USA basketball losing to Puerto Rico, Lithuania, and Argentina back in 2004, when they settled for bronze medals in the Summer Olympic Games. Baseball back then, like basketball today, was a huge part of our country's athletic identity. We were arrogant, confident in our superiority on the diamond, and the Cubans were pricking holes in our egotistical little bubble.

John McGraw became the first big-league manager to accompany his team during the fall tour, and he insisted the team's ace, Christy Mathewson, come along. The Giants had some serious business to attend to.

◆ ◆ ◆

Flocks of buzzards circled the air, high above the ballpark. In the farthest reaches of the huge arena, lush palm trees dangled beyond the outfield walls, fluttering in the humid, tropical breeze. On the field itself, mounted police galloped on plunging steeds, armed with huge revolvers, patrolling the perimeter as if the ballplayers were foreign dignitaries.

The *Fortaleza el Principe*, the main prison in Havana, sat next to Almendares Park, a constant reminder to rowdy patrons (and players, for that matter) that justice was just a couple hundred yards away. A folk band roamed the grandstand, playing rumba music and filling the atmosphere with crisp guitar licks, sensual bongo rhythms, and maracas. There was cigar smoke, of course, plus the smell of fried pork.

This was all well and good, McGraw thought, *But can we get the goddamn game rolling?*

With the crush of folks entering the ballpark, the first pitch had been delayed by more than an hour and a half before the Havana club casually strolled onto the field. Punctuality was a little less stringent in this Castilian culture, but the delay probably had more to do with the frenetic mob of last-minute wagering taking place in the stands than anything else. Gambling was as big a part of baseball on the islands as it was with cockfights, horse racing, or the matadors.

Whoever had their cash on the Giants in Game 1 ended up in good shape, as Christy Mathewson started the lid-lifter, winning 4–1 over Havana. In Game 2, Almendares started Bombin Pedroso, the man who had no-hit the Tigers two years earlier. This time, although much less dominating, he led his club to a 6–4 victory

Bombin Pedroso, who tossed a no-hitter versus the Detroit Tigers in 1909, beat John McGraw's Giants, 6–4, in 1911. *Courtesy of Scott Simkus*

over Doc Crandall and Hooks Wiltse. Game 3, twenty-year-old rookie Adolfo Luque, who would later go on to win 194 games in the major leagues, bested McGraw's men, 3–2.

And this is when Mac exploded at the hotel.

Young Giants outfielder Josh Devore was fined twenty-five dollars for, apparently, not playing well. Although the kid had been hitless in the first three games, McGraw may have still had the nasty taste in his mouth from the World Series one month earlier, when Devore (after having a spectacular regular season) had batted only .167, striking out a team-high 8 times in six games.

The players, possibly led by Devore, fired back at the skipper, pointing out that they were in Cuba on their own jurisdiction, as "private individual attractions," and that they "were not subject to strict discipline inasmuch as the New York club [was] not paying salaries to them at present."

"All right," said McGraw, possibly fearing mutiny, "I came down here for two reasons. One was because Mr. Brush [John T., owner of the Giants] refused to allow the team to make the trip unless I came along and because Mr. Jimenez has risked more than $10,000 on the project. If I say so, the trip ends today and you go home. I'll stay, but you must cut out the fooling and play ball."

Not exactly Vince Lombardi stuff, but it was enough to close the argument. Two days later, the matchup everybody had been waiting for, Christy Mathewson versus Jose Mendez, took place. Before the game, the Giants pooled their money and bet $800 on themselves. Jumping on Mendez for 3 runs in the first, the New Yorkers never looked back, winning behind Matty, 4–0. Mendez settled down, giving up only 5 hits in 9 innings, but Mathewson was better, shutting the Cubans down on just 3 safeties.

Two weeks later, Pedroso and Mendez would combine

When twenty-year old Cuban Adolfo Luque beat McGraw's team, 3–2, the skipper's temper erupted at the team hotel, where he threatened to send everybody home if they didn't perform better. *National Baseball Hall of Fame Library, Cooperstown, New York*

their efforts, defeating Mathewson and the Giants 7–4. But that would prove to be the only highlight of the tour's remainder, as the Giants finished the series by rattling off eight victories in their last nine games. They were champions of the so-called "American Series," restoring some measure of whatever athletic pride had been lost the previous couple years.

◆ ◆ ◆

McGraw was chatty as he and his wife got off the boat in Key West. He planned to remain in Florida for another month before returning to New York City.

"These Cubans are only fair players," explained McGraw, when asked to comment on the tour. "They are fast as lightning on the bases, and they can throw to beat the band. They have picked up all the knacks of fielding, but they cannot bat.

"They know nothing about 'inside ball,' and we were able to out-trick them most of the time. In an opposing pitcher they look for speed and usually hit the ball, but when they try to solve the mysteries of a curve they churn the air."

Interestingly, Sol White, manager of the African American powerhouse Philadelphia Giants, had some similar observations of the Cuban ballplayers, written five years *before* McGraw's interview.

"The Cuban players gave everything that constitute good ball playing with the exception of inside work," wrote White in his *History of Colored Baseball*. "They are wonderful fielders, strong throwers and fast runners. They lack the baseball nerve or staying qualities, which shows so prominently in the American player and many games are deliberately thrown away by the Cubans when they think the umpire has made a mistake or when one of their number is guilty of a misplay."

Christy Mathewson, who returned directly to New York after the last game of the tour, was amazed at how much grief the Cuban players gave the umpires and shocked at the partisanship of the local fans, who actively rooted *against* the Americans. This was unusual. Here in the states, big-league stars were accustomed to being treated like royalty during postseason barnstorming tours. But overall, Matty was impressed with the experience.

"This fellow Mendez is a great pitcher," Matty said. "It's too bad he is a negro, as his color bars him from the big leagues up here in the states. If he was a white man or an Indian, he'd be the star of leagues up here in no time."

◆ ◆ ◆

The Philadelphia Phillies, who played a series of games in Cuba at the same time as the New York Giants, accorded themselves well, going 5–4. Combining the Giants' and Phillies' records, the major league teams were now finally over .500 (barely) versus the Cubans, at 37–35–2, in games played from 1908 to 1911.

During this same period, the best black teams in America visited Havana, playing games against the same exact clubs as the big leaguers. Rube Foster, who had conquered Rube Waddell back in 1903, then later pitched for Sol White's Philadelphia Giants, brought his Chicago Leland Giants to Cuba in the fall of 1910, to face Mendez, Pedroso, and the boys. The Brooklyn Royal Giants, a rising black power in the East, also visited the island, going 9–8 in 1908, including a victory over the touring Cincinnati Reds.

If we add together all the American Series games played from 1908 to 1911, then sort the standings by team, we get a pretty good thumbnail sketch of where professional baseball was at this point. In Havana's Almendares Park, fans were literally witnessing the convergence of baseball as played at the highest level, with whites, blacks, and foreign teams going head to head.

15.1

Cuba (1908–1911) vs. Various Levels	W	L	T	PCT.
New York Giants	9	3	0	.750
Chicago Leland Giants	7	5	1	.583
Almendares Blues	28	22	1	.560
Philadelphia Phillies	5	4	0	.556
Brooklyn Royal Giants	9	8	0	.529
Detroit Tigers	11	12	1	.478
Cincinnati Reds	6	7	1	.462
Philadelphia Athletics	4	6	0	.400
Major League All-Stars	2	3	0	.400
Habana	19	30	0	.388

The major league teams weren't necessarily at full strength, but with Cobb, Crawford, Mathewson, Brown, Joss, and other stars onboard, they weren't bush league outfits either. It must have been a tough environment to play in, with hostile fans, a poorly maintained field, and a culture very different from the one back home. But once they were on the diamond, those exterior things should have evened out a bit. Both teams were battling grounders off the same rocky infield, for instance, and a 93-mph fastball was the same speed in Havana as it was in the Polo Grounds. When you boiled it down, it was just baseball. Some big leaguers fared well (Cobb hit .350 during his five games there; Christy Mathewson went 3–1 with a 2.31 ERA), while others didn't.

So few games were played that you have to take all this with a grain of salt. But the small sample size notwithstanding, one thing is undeniable: these Cuban teams and black American teams were better than the old Cuban Giants of the 1880s or the Page Fence Giants of the 1890s. It seems reasonable to suggest these clubs were already hovering somewhere between the Triple-A and major league levels.

◆ ◆ ◆

Not everyone was convinced, though. Hugh H. Fullerton, an influential, nationally known sports columnist (he later founded the Baseball Writers' Association of America and was instrumental in blowing the whistle during the World Series fix of 1919), wrote a column after the series, echoing many of McGraw's opinions of the Cuban players and teams while interjecting many of his own racist opinions.

Fullerton believed an "embargo" should immediately be placed on importing *all* Cuban players to the states. Rafael Almeida and Armando Marsans, two white Cubans who had played against big-league clubs in the American Series, had just completed their inaugural major league campaigns in 1911, having been reserves for Clark Griffith's Cincinnati Reds. The recent successes on the islands had opened doors Hugh preferred remained closed.

But Fullerton's objections weren't so much with the Almeidas or Marsans of the world, they were with the other "three fourths of the players on the first class teams in Havana" who were either "negroes or part negro," according to his eyeballing of the situation.

He felt compelled to explain his position: "Notwithstanding the alleged American sentiment for equality of the races, the baseball public would not stand for the introduction of negroes into the major leagues."

End of argument, as far as he was concerned.

But the columnist had one more gem of an observation, before signing off: "Put the twenty best Cuban players in a class B [minor] league in America and they wouldn't win."

Okay, now.

Here we go . . .

◆ ◆ ◆

One of the many fun things about writing baseball history is that you sometimes get an opportunity to look in the rearview mirror, check the facts, and make dead people eat their words. A little more than a year after he wrote his column, an all-Cuban team did, in fact, come to America to play in the Class D New York–New Jersey League.

You know where this one is headed, but stick with me. It's worth dragging it out.

No, the Cuban team didn't consist of the "twenty best players" from the island. Far from it. As Fullerton himself would have understood, three-fourths of the best players were "negroes," so they wouldn't be permitted to join a club in organized baseball. Jose Mendez and Bombin Pedroso, arguably the two best Cuban pitchers at the time, were out. Big Julian Castillo, a slugging first baseman, and Gervasio Gonzalez, a rifle-armed catcher whom many of the visiting major leaguers believed was big-league timber, were out. We'll go ahead and agree with Hugh S. Fullerton and establish that fifteen of the best twenty Cuban players in the world were ineligible due to their "coffee-hued" skin color.

This leaves us with just the *white* Cubans.

Joining the Long Branch (New Jersey) team in 1913 was a triumvirate of twenty-two-year-olds: Dolf Luque, Mike Gonzalez, and Angel Aragon. Luque had beaten McGraw's Giants in the fall of '11 and would go on to a successful twenty years in Major League Baseball. Near the end of both their careers, John McGraw signed the crafty right-hander to a Giants contract in 1932. Gonzalez would spend 17 years in the big leagues (including three seasons playing for McGraw) and, along with Luque, later became one of the immortals of Cuban baseball history, a legacy he enjoyed well into the Castro years. Aragon, who batted a team-high .358 for the Long Branch team in 1913, would bat .300 during his twelve-year minor league career, earning a couple coffee cup appearances with the New York Yankees. Rounding out the core of this club was nineteen-year-old Jack Calvo, who'd play a little bit with the Washington Senators, batting .299 during his minor league career, and a thirty-five-year-old veteran named Luis Padrón.

Padrón is an almost completely forgotten star from baseball's past. Best known as an outfielder and third baseman, Luis played with both Cuban *and* white clubs in the Chicago City League, mixing it up with Nixey Callahan, Smokey Joe Williams, and Rube Foster on the city's north side. Like Aragon and Calvo, Luis compiled a career minor league batting average hovering around .300. At least two big-league teams, Charles Comiskey's White Sox (seriously) and the Boston Braves, attempted to sign him before the offers were pulled off the table.

The problem with Padrón was he was part black. He was one of those "three-fourths" Fullerton referred to—a star with mixed blood. Yes, he played organized baseball after the color barrier had been drawn completely, but his story is largely unknown today.

So the 1913 Long Branch Cubans had perhaps five of the top Cuban ballplayers in the world, but certainly no more than that. Their core group of Luque, Gonzalez, Aragon, Calvo, and Padrón were augmented by a cast of fringe performers.

Did they win any games, playing on American soil?

During the regular season, the Long Branch Cubans went 65–29 (.691) in the New York–New Jersey League, winning the pennant by 18½ games. Frankly, this Class D league didn't provide much competition for this group of players.

On off-days, given their drawing power and proximity to New York City, the Cubans were able to schedule many exhibition games with big-league clubs. From 1913 to 1915, when the roster was almost 100 percent Cuban, the team beat several Triple-A clubs and went 12–10 in exhibition games against major league teams. Against McGraw's New York Giants, the Cubans went 4–6 on neutral grounds.

Even without their top black players, rumba bands, and home cooking, the Cubans somehow managed to do well in the states. To my knowledge, Fullerton never wrote about the progress of this team, or the fact that he was flat wrong.

American blacks were completely shut out of the program, of course. Cubans (even those with some African blood) were now trickling into organized baseball. And the best white players in the world were once again becoming disenchanted with the tightfisted major league owners and restrictive policies of the reserve system.

Something big was about to rock the apple cart.

◆ 16 ◆

BLOOMERS AND BLOOPERS

T HE FIRST CLUE SOMETHING WAS AWRY occurred before the game even started, when the long-haired center fielder from the visiting team launched a cannon throw all the way to home plate without so much as a bounce. Then, when the visiting team's female pitcher was observed chewing tobacco in the second inning, the fans' suspicions were sufficiently aroused. The Bloomer Girls played a respectable brand of baseball, to be sure, but they didn't throw 350-foot laser beams from deep center, or chew Red Man during ballgames.

A small boy was instructed to sneak up behind the muscular blonde girl cavorting about third base, where he snatched the wig from "her" head, revealing short-cropped black hair. But it wasn't just the third baseman, center fielder, and pitcher. *Everybody* in the Bloomer Girls lineup happened to be of the male persuasion. Four or five of them had donned wigs to help perpetuate the ruse.

This was fraud, shouted someone from the grandstand. There were boos and hisses, and the fans seated behind third base began chanting, "THIEVES! THIEVES! THIEVES!" Word spread throughout Washington, DC's Union League Grounds, and soon thereafter the nearly 4,000 people in attendance began shouting in unison: "WE WANT OUR MONEY BACK! WE WANT OUR MONEY BACK!"

It was Sunday, July 20, 1913, and with the hometown Washington Senators off battling the White Sox in Chicago, the appearance of the Bloomer Girls seemed like the perfect anecdote to the District of Columbia's baseball void. The booking of a team billing itself as the "Chicago Bloomer Baseball Girls" had been a last-minute, hastily arranged affair, but to get a sense of their drawing power, the four thousand walk-up customers in attendance was roughly the same number of fans who regularly attended Senators games that very same summer. This was a large crowd.

The chanting became louder, and debris was tossed onto the diamond. Captain Daley and six of his police officers from the Ninth precinct circled the diamond and tried to calm the increasingly agitated congregation. When it became apparent there weren't going to be any refunds, all hell broke loose.

According to the *Washington Post*, "Captain Daley of the Ninth precinct and six of his men were swept away like chaff before the surging rush of the crowd, which made for the gate in one swiftly moving mass, with the bloomered players, warned in time, dashing ahead."

Kid Carsey, promoter of the event, slipped out a side entrance, unnoticed, with $700 in gate receipts.

The team made it safely through the narrow gates amid a shower of soda pop bottles, bricks, and other dangerous projectiles, then barricaded themselves inside a small clubhouse across the street. Captain Daley and his patrolmen positioned themselves in front of the structure and prevented the mob from storming the door, although bottles and debris continued to fly.

The people didn't necessarily want to *kill* anybody, they simply wanted their admission fees refunded. Captain Daley announced to the crowd it would be impossible to comply with their requests, as "the manager of the team had already left the city with the gate receipts in tow."

Probably not the most tactful approach at the time. The mob spun in unison, zeroing their attention on a couple unfortunate ticket sellers who happened to be exiting the Union League park at that very moment.

Before any bodily harm could be inflicted on the innocent vendors, the Washington cops' automobile patrol rolled up to the scene and whisked the employees (and the entire Bloomer team) off to safety at the Ninth precinct headquarters, but not before a couple more pop bottles could be hurled in their direction. The police needed their batons to clear a path, and a bicycle patrolman named Benny Williams was plunked in the back with a brick, while half the tall coat worn by Officer Otto Hauschild was torn off.

When the mob gathered at the police station, the Bloomers baseball club was hurried out the back door and driven to the train station, where they caught a shuttle to Baltimore. There was only one arrest: Charles C. Jones, a sixty-eight-year-old teamster who was the alleged ringleader of the Union League ballpark mob. The next day the police promised to launch a full investigation to see if the fans had indeed been defrauded by the game's promoters.

Two days later, a man named F. S. Schmelz, manager of the *real* Chicago Bloomer Girls, traveled all the way from Elmira, New York, to press charges against Kid Carsey. Speaking with a local reporter, Schmelz explained, "My team has been imposed upon, and I will make an earnest effort to have the guilty party punished. My team has a good reputation. I have never scheduled a game and then failed to put in an appearance, even if I knew it would mean a financial loss to me. I believe in playing the game on the level."

By the time of this brouhaha in 1913, the Bloomer Girls were already a well-established novelty act around the country, a brand name worth protecting. Women had been playing baseball almost as long as men, and by the 1890s, the first Bloomer Girls teams began springing up. Eventually, there would be versions of this club in just about every city. There were the New York Bloomer Girls, Boston Bloomer Girls, and the Los Angeles Bloomer Girls. In Philadelphia, there was a professional women's team called the Bobbies, and in Baltimore there was a black bloomers team called the Black Sox Colored Girls. There were literally dozens of female teams crisscrossing the United States and Canada every summer, entertaining fans with a lively playing style.

Florrie O'Rourke was a star for the New York Bloomer Girls, a popular novelty attraction. The team toured the East Coast from 1910 to 1933. *National Baseball Hall of Fame Library, Cooperstown, New York*

It was a commonly accepted practice for each Bloomer Girls team to carry two or three men (called "toppers") on their roster, to help keep ballgames competitive. Future major league stars Rogers Hornsby and Smokey Joe Wood began their professional careers as Bloomer Girls, but the stunt pulled in Washington, where none of the women were actually *women*, seems to have pushed the matter too far.

I think you could make a good argument that before 1925, the Bloomer Girls may have been the most well-known brand in outsider baseball. With so many versions operating across the United States, they received a tremendous amount of newspaper coverage and notoriety. But let's ask the question other chroniclers of the game's history always avoid: were they any good? They billed themselves as world champions, boasted of incredible winning streaks, and promised to "hang tough" with men's semipro teams. But again, was this all just hyperbole?

I conducted a quick study, gathering 100 random box scores from the Bloomers' prime years, roughly 1910 to 1925. The only qualifier was that the games had to feature traveling versions of the Bloomer Girls as opposed to local amateur outfits using the popular name.

In the first 100 games gathered, the professional Bloomers had a 19–78–3 record, good for a .196 winning percentage. Although it's not always easy to determine the sex of their competition, I know of at least four wins and one loss against local female clubs. In a small sample, they certainly seemed to be head and shoulders above the local *women's* teams. But remember, they had two or three *men* in their lineup.

Against male teams, it was a different story. They had a record of 15–77–3 (.163). Against top-notch competition, Negro league teams, and big-city white semipros, they were 0–4. Most of their victories were in the boondocks, against rural teams from places like Wetumpka, Oklahoma, and Ridgely, Maryland. More than half their victories were against teams from towns where the population was less than 10,000.

The Bloomers were a phenomenon, and it's difficult to understand their appeal unless you understand the context. At the time, women weren't expected to exert themselves physically. It was illegal for them to vote, and they were forbidden from wearing shorts in certain parts of the country. Okay, *all* parts of the country. It really wasn't about winning or losing with the Bloomers, it was about playing the game. They truly were at the vanguard of the women's rights movement, playing a game they loved.

◆ 17 ◆

MUSTER ROLL FOR 1914

Bill Veeck was born on February 9, 1914.

Rube Waddell died on April 1, 1914. He was only thirty-seven years old.

As Waddell was struggling through the final stages of his losing battle with tuberculosis, **Rube Foster** was winning on the West Coast with a team now known as the "Chicago American Giants." Playing against mostly Pacific Coast and Northwest League clubs, they went 3–2–1. During the regular season, playing against the top professional black clubs, his team finished 38–13. His best players were **Pete Hill** (the star of the 1905 Philadelphia Giants) and future Hall of Famer **John Henry Lloyd**, who had surpassed Hill as the best all-around African American player in the country.

The best black player in America in the nineteenth century, **Frank Grant**, had retired from baseball and by 1914 was working as a waiter for a catering service in New York City. He died in 1937.

Cap Anson, the so-called architect of baseball's color line, had a long string of failed business ventures, eventually leading to bankruptcy. He had not just built barriers, but burned bridges in the baseball community. After being the game's greatest player/manager during the nineteenth century, he became something of a persona non grata in organized baseball, unable to land a job, let alone acquire an ownership stake in a big-league team he supposedly desired (and felt entitled to). Instead, he organized a semipro outfit in Chicago's City League (called Anson's Colts), even inserting himself into the lineup

By 1914, Cap Anson (left) was performing on the vaudeville circuit, while Rube Foster was building a powerhouse ballclub in Chicago.
National Baseball Hall of Fame Library, Cooperstown, New York

on occasion. Researcher Gary Ashwill has located a box score from August 22, 1908, featuring fifty-six-year-old Cap stationed at first base versus the all-black Leland Giants. Apparently when green (money) was involved, Anson was able to change his position on the issue of black and white players coexisting in the same league. Anson went hitless during the game, and the Leland Giants won 5–0 behind center fielder Pete Hill, who had a hit, then later snagged a line drive, doubling one of Anson's men off first base with his cannon throwing arm. By 1914, Anson's semipro venture had failed financially, and he was performing on the vaudeville circuit, perhaps as a clown.

Charlie "Tokohama" Grant, the man John McGraw had tried to pass off as a Native American back in 1901 during the American League's inaugural season, returned to his hometown of Cincinnati, playing ball with a local team called the Stars. He'd be out of the game completely a couple years later, accepting work as a janitor.

Clark Griffith, who had pitched batting practice to Tokohama back in Hot Springs, Arkansas, was now managing the Washington Senators and on his way to gaining a controlling ownership interest in the team. He had already signed two Cuban players, including Angel Aragon of the Long Branch Cubans, and his club would continue to be one of the most aggressive recruiters of Latin American talent for the next forty years. Later on, he established a lucrative business partnership with the Negro National League's Homestead Grays, who leased his park for many seasons.

Nixey Callahan, former owner/operator of the Logan Squares semipro team, was back in the big leagues, managing Charlie Comiskey's Chicago White Sox. He was finished with the plumbing business.

John McGraw was still managing the New York Giants. His club wouldn't return to Cuba until 1920, this time with a ringer named Babe Ruth in tow, where they would go 8–5–4 in their games against the island stars.

Cyclone Joe Williams, former nemesis of Callahan's Logan Squares, had abandoned Chicago and was now starring for the New York Lincoln Giants, among the strongest black teams on the East Coast. On October 9, 1920, he'd strike out 13 of John McGraw's New York Giants in an exhibition game, en route to 4–1 Lincoln Giants victory. He'd be inducted into baseball's Hall of Fame in 1999.

Forty-six-year-old **Sol White**, former manager of the Philadelphia Giants, had gotten out of baseball completely and was pursuing other opportunities at this time. He'd later make a brief return, as business manager for the Columbus Buckeyes, after Rube Foster formed the first Negro National League in 1920.

Gavvy Cravath, the big slugger who had teamed with Rube Waddell on the old 1911 Minneapolis Millers, was playing right field for the Philadelphia Phillies, where he batted .299, led the National League in home runs with 19, and drove in 100.

Dolf Luque, conqueror of McGraw's touring club in the fall of 1911 and ace of the Long Branch Cubans in '13, would get a cup of coffee with the Boston Braves early in the season before being farmed out to the Jersey City Skeeters in the International League for more seasoning.

Jose Mendez, battling arm problems, was playing shortstop and pitching part-time for the All-Nations, a multiracial club that barnstormed through Iowa, Minnesota, Nebraska, and the Dakotas. The owner of this bunch was a man named **J. L. Wilkinson**, who would later found the famous Kansas City Monarchs.

Eustaquio "Bombín" Pedroso, the dude who no-hit the visiting Detroit Tigers in 1909, was in the states, pitching and playing outfield for the Cuban Stars of Havana, who went 21–16 versus major blackball squads in the Midwest.

Luis Padrón, who batted .310 with 2 triples and a home run versus John McGraw's Giants in 1911, was starring for the Long Branch Cubans, who had transferred to the Class D Atlantic League.

Charlie Comiskey, who had vehemently opposed McGraw's near-signing of Charlie Grant in 1901, was still in charge of the Chicago White Sox. Interestingly, in 1910 he came close to signing Cuban star Luis Padrón. Padrón, who played here in the states with both Cuban teams and white minor league squads, faced a barrage of well-documented racial abuse during his minor league career, as it was strongly suspected at the time that he had "African blood." Thanks to the recent decoding of the genetic code, we now know we are *all* suspected of having a little bit of African blood.

Ban Johnson, the man who turned the Western League into a second major, was still president of the American League but found himself on the side of the establishment this time, battling a new (nonphantom) menace called the "Federal League."

◆ ◆ ◆

On September 5, 1912, Supreme Court justice Delaney affixed his signature to a certificate of incorporation, filed by attorney David L. Fultz of New York's Murphy & Fultz law firm. Thus came into existence an organization called the "Base Ball Players Fraternity." In support of the petition of incorporation were affidavits from seventeen active players, including Ty Cobb, Sam Crawford, and Christy Mathewson. Walter Johnson, the best pitcher in the game, would not only become a member shortly thereafter but also join Cobb as an officer of the new players' union.

Eleven years after the rogue American League toppled baseball's apple cart by opening up improved financial opportunities for players, the new two-league monopoly had righted itself, returned to the status quo, and there was once again a growing discontent among the game's athletes.

The new players' fraternity pursued smaller, winnable issues. For instance, it was common practice at that time for ballplayers to pay for their own uniforms and foot the bill for their own travel expenses after being traded or sent to the minor leagues. Also, after signing their contracts in the off-season, most players never even received duplicate copies for their own records. Such were the primitive business practices back then, and the Players Fraternity got these things changed.

"We got rid of that sort of crap," Ty Cobb recalled more than forty years later, when discussing his involvement with the fraternity.

David Fultz, the attorney in charge of the Players Fraternity, had played for the New York Giants, studied law at Brown, and then built a successful practice after leaving the game. This should sound familiar, since John

Montgomery Ward, founder of the Brotherhood of Professional Ball Players in 1885, had also played for the Giants, studied law at Columbia, and then later built a successful legal practice.

But unlike the Brotherhood, which first threatened to strike, then later founded its own league (the Players League, which lasted only one season), the Fraternity didn't need to take such drastic measures. A bunch of rich guys did it for them.

Led by a man named James A. Gilmore, the Federal League—a minor circuit in 1913—declared itself a third major league before the 1914 campaign. A bunch of successful industrialists and entrepreneurs, with more cash than baseball experience, backed the eight franchises and began opening their wallets, signing as many major league players as they could, often for ridiculously inflated salaries.

During its two years of existence, the feud between the Feds and organized baseball set into motion a crazy bidding war for talent that, looking back, was like the Internet boom for ballplayers. Everybody was getting rich overnight.

The Feds signed a few aging stars, such as Three Finger Brown, Joe Tinker, and Eddie Plank, plus a couple younger guys on their way up, like Edd Roush. But mostly it was marginal talent roped in with large dollar figures. Fringe player Otto Knabe jumped his big-league contract and signed for a $6,500 raise. Philadelphia Phillies pitcher Tom Seaton jumped ship, earning himself a $5,500 pay increase with the Brooklyn Tip-Tops. Scuff ball pitcher Russ Ford, who'd gone 25–39 during his previous two seasons with the New York Yankees, jumped to an outsider club in Buffalo, New York, where his annual pay leaped from $5,500 to $10,000.

Most of the big-name stars, including Fraternity officers Ty Cobb and Walter Johnson, simply used the Federal League as leverage when negotiating with their current employers. Actually, they both signed (or allegedly signed) contracts with Federal League teams before accepting significantly better terms from their current ballclubs.

Ty Cobb went from making $11,333 with the Detroit Tigers in 1913, to $20,000 just two years later. Walter Johnson bent the Senators over a barrel, going from $7,000 to $12,500 in two seasons. Other stars cashed in as well, without leaving the two established major leagues. Boston Red Sox outfielder Tris Speaker nearly doubled the $9,000 he earned in 1913, signing for $17,500 the next year. Same thing with Eddie Collins, who more than *doubled* his salary, jumping from $7,000 to $14,500 during the winter.

Cuban Armando Marsans, who in his previous 154 games with the Cincinnati Reds had batted .297 with 50 stolen bases, left the team midseason to join the St. Louis Terriers of the Federal loop. Former New York Giants Art Wilson and Doc Crandall, who'd played in Cuba during the fall tour back in 1911, bolted from McGraw's club to play in the new league.

Even the scrubs were cashing in: Minor leaguer Jim Bluejacket, offered a very respectable starting salary of $1,800 for his first big-league campaign with the New York Giants, jumped to the Federal League for more money before the season began.

◆ ◆ ◆

Serving as a direct link between the old Players League of 1890 and the upstart Federal League, **John Montgomery Ward** (founder of the old Brotherhood union) became the business manager of the Fed's Brooklyn Tip-Tops in 1914.

Jack Dunn, owner of the Baltimore Orioles of the International League, saw his little baseball juggernaut crushed by the presence of the Federal League's Baltimore Terrapins. Unable to sell enough tickets to stay afloat, Dunn sold his prized recruit, **George Herman "Babe" Ruth** (along with Ernie Shore and Ben Egan) to the Boston Red Sox for $8,000 on July 9, 1914.

In Benton Harbor, Michigan, locals were flocking to a diamond situated on the grounds of a religious commune, where a team of bearded ballplayers were said to play an entertaining brand of baseball as they awaited Armageddon. The next year, 1915, these representatives of the **House of David** hit the road for their first of fifty seasons as barnstorming semiprofessionals.

In September 1914, the Brooklyn Superbas (known today as the Dodgers) beat a new semipro team called the **Brooklyn Bushwicks** 4–1. The Bush-wicks would quickly develop into New York City's most feared semipro powerhouse, often outdrawing the Dodgers on days when their schedules overlapped.

On August 29, 1914, a baby girl named **Jackie Mitchell** was born in Fall River, Massachusetts (hometown of Lizzie Borden). While still in her teens, she became the *second* Fall River lass to make national headlines, as she allegedly struck out Babe Ruth and Lou Gehrig in an exhibition game.

Seven-year-old **Leroy Paige**, later known around the globe as "**Satchel**," was running around the city streets and alleyways of Mobile, Alabama, getting into rock fights with white boys.

Branch Rickey, only thirty-two years old in 1914, was managing the St. Louis Browns in the American League.

Spitballer **Jeff Tesreau** surpassed **Christy Mathewson** as the ace of the New York Giants pitching staff, going 26–10 with a 2.37 ERA. He was second in the league in strikeouts, with 189 on the season.

◆ ◆ ◆

For years, baseball wonks have debated the relative strength of the Federal League, which included a number of major league alumni but few real stars. Everybody is in agreement that it was the worst of the three leagues, but was it even better than the high minors? Using some baseball forensics, we can get some answers. The STARS system shows us how the upstart league, which lasted just two seasons, fit into the larger scheme of organized baseball.

Here are the STARS scores for the three major leagues, from 1914 to 1916. The Fed was competitive but clearly lags behind the two established major leagues. After the Fed folds, notice the jump in quality in both the AL and NL.

17.1

League	STARS Score in 1914	STARS Score in 1915	STARS Score in 1916
American League	326	325	343
National League	318	327	345
Federal League	247	261	---

◆ 18 ◆

TESREAU'S BEARS

As the two major leagues girded themselves against the encroachment of the Federal League, a real war was erupting in Europe. The Federal League, after just two seasons and a number of lawsuits, eventually settled with the baseball establishment and disbanded. As part of the agreement, two ownership groups from the Federal League were permitted to purchase National League franchises, and all qualified players were welcomed back into the fold.

The Base Ball Players Fraternity had made some gains and benefitted significantly from the emergence of the third major league but quickly fell out of favor with its constituents soon after the Federal League disappeared. After reaching a peak of 1,200 members (including both major and minor league players), the union dissolved near the second half of the decade, just as America entered World War I. Regular people had bigger things to worry about, and the players were no different.

In June 1918, Provost Marshall General Crowder issued a "work or fight" order, meaning all men of draft age must either enter the military or work in a war-related industry. Baseball was, of course, considered "nonessential," so the season was shortened, and players scrambled to find their way. One of the newspapers noted "how many ballplayers had suddenly become interested in painting war ships for a living."

Dozens of major leaguers left their teams to "work" for ship-building factories, while more than 150 others joined the military. For most of the ballplayers, factory work meant playing baseball in industrial leagues, where rivalries developed, large crowds filled the stands, and the level of play was on par with the highest minor leagues at the time. When the hostilities overseas ended in 1918, several ballplayers simply never returned to the major leagues.

One of these guys was Big Jeff Tesreau.

◆ ◆ ◆

Born on March 5, 1888, in Ironton, Missouri, Charles Monroe "Jeff" Tesreau was considered a giant during his big-league career. At 6'2" and 225 pounds, the right-hander's size almost stopped his baseball career before it got started. He was so large at seventeen years old that he wasn't permitted to play on the Ironton junior team.

"They said I was too clumsy," Tesreau explained, after making it to the big leagues. "I wanted to play ball, though, and I went out into other fields. I went over to Perryville [Missouri], where I got a job in the mines."

When he wasn't in the hole, Tesreau pitched for the miner's team and did well enough that the independent club of Perrryville signed him to a contract. "I was paid $75 a month," he said, "and that was some money in those days." In 1908, the twenty-year-old won 37 games in the independent Trolley League.

Splitting his time between working in the lead mines and pitching for the Perryville town team, Tesreau caught the attention of a scout named Gordon, who signed the kid to a contract with Austin in the Texas League. Upon arriving in the Lone Star state, the twenty-one-year-old discovered the Austin franchise had been dropped from the league, and he was shipped off, first to Houston, then San Antonio, then Galveston, and finally, Shreveport. During his first year in professional baseball, Tesreau belonged to fully half the teams in the Texas League (as well as the St. Louis Browns, who claimed to have signed him as well), and one team (Austin) that never took the field. After a dizzying rookie year, Shreveport showed mercy, signing the kid to a contract for 1910.

After managing only a 7–11 record his first year in pro ball, Jeff won 15 games and fashioned a stellar 1.91 ERA his sophomore year. The next spring, John McGraw's Giants stopped in Shreveport for a practice game where Jeff caught the attention of the veteran skipper. Mostly, McGraw liked the kid's size and fastball. Mac signed the twenty-three-year-old, who spent the 1911 season pitching for Toronto in the Eastern League. After going 14–9 with a 2.70 ERA, Tesreau won a job with the Giants during the spring of 1912.

He featured a spitter to go along with a Grade A heater. During spring training, Giants coach Wilbert Robinson helped Tesreau add a curveball to his arsenal. Armed with three quality pitches, his first big-league season was spectacular, as the "Ozark Bear Hunter" (a nickname given to him by sportswriter Damon Runyon, even though Tesreau wasn't from the Ozarks and had never hunted bear) went 17–7 to go along with a league-best 1.96 earned-run average. The rookie allowed only 6.6 hits per 9 innings pitched, which was tops in the senior circuit. The Giants, behind the surprising Tesreau, Christy Mathewson, and Rube Marquard, cruised to the World Series but were beaten 4 games to 3 by the Boston Red Sox.

Tesreau won 22 games the next year, then 26 the season after that, and was usually one of the most difficult pitchers to hit in the National League. But in 1917, he had something of a down year, going "only" 13–8, with a team-high 3.08 ERA. He rebounded well enough, though, starting strong in 1918, and by June his earned-run average was back down around his career normal 2.31, but his won-lost record (in an era where managers and media placed

Jeff Tesreau
Pitcher/Outfield

Tesreau's Bears

★

The ace of John McGraw's pitching staff, Jeff Tesreau left the team mid-career to form his own semipro club and coach at the collegiate level. *Courtesy of Scott Simkus*

entirely too much importance on individual wins and losses) was only 4–4. After getting knocked out of the box against the Chicago Cubs in early June, Big Jeff Tesreau walked away from the game. He was only thirty years old, in good health, and his career record stood at 115–72 (.615) with an excellent 2.43 ERA.

John B. Foster, secretary of the New York Giants, said Tesreau told McGraw he was "disgusted with baseball and wanted to get into some other business." In fact, the pitcher joined the Bethlehem (Pennsylvania) club of the Steel League. Because he had already been tabbed Class 4, and was exempt from the draft, Tesreau wasn't joining the industrial league to escape military service. Turns out he wanted to get away from John McGraw.

During the previous spring, McGraw had sent Tesreau down south early to work with pitchers, catchers, and out-of-condition players. When Mac arrived later, he wanted his star pitcher to expose those who had been out partying late at night instead of focusing on baseball. Tesreau refused, believing a player's personal life was his own business, and a feud emerged between these two strong personalities.

In 1919, Tesreau ignored the Giants' orders to return, and instead he pitched for Guy Empey's Treat 'Em Roughs, who called Manhattan home.

The best semipro club in New York City at that time, the Treat 'Em Roughs beat all comers, including the best black and Cuban clubs on the East Coast. Although their roster consisted largely of former and future minor leaguers, major leaguers such as Frankie Frisch, Larry Doyle, Jess Barnes, and Carl Mays made cameo appearances during the season. Marty Kavanagh, who'd played five years in the majors, was a fixture in the lineup all season long.

In 1920, despite several lucrative offers from International League teams, Tesreau accepted a head coaching position with Dartmouth College. He said an offer of "$10,000" couldn't lure him back into Major League Baseball, even if somebody wanted him that badly. Another story said Jeff "found semipro ball lucrative." Because they were drawing more than 7,000 paid customers for Sunday doubleheaders, there's little doubt the Roughs had been paying well.

In addition to running the college program, the Ozark Bear Hunter purchased the rights to the Treat 'Em Roughs, changing their name to Tesreau's Bears for the 1920 season. Like former Chicago White Sox player Nixey Callahan, who left the majors to run the Logan Squares team in Chicago's City League fifteen years earlier, Tesreau was gambling on the public's unquenchable thirst for live baseball. And like the Logan Squares, Tesreau's most lucrative bookings were those against the top African American teams, including the New York Lincoln Giants, Brooklyn Royal Giants, Cuban Stars, Hilldale, and Rube Foster's visiting Chicago American Giants. And as it had been with the Logan Squares, one of their most feared opposing pitchers was none other than Cyclone Joe Williams, now an experienced veteran recognized as the best black pitcher in the country.

How good were Jeff Tesreau's semipro clubs? In 1920, the Bears played tough against Babe Ruth's barnstorming all-star team but lost a doubleheader. A week later, they beat the spitballer's old employers, the New York Giants, 10–9. Interestingly, although he was the ace of the club, Tesreau didn't pitch any of these exhibition games versus big-league outfits, instead giving the stage to youngsters such as Curt "No-Hit" Fullerton and Tom Godfrey, who were trying to break into organized ball. Fullerton later spent several seasons in the major leagues; Godfrey had unsuccessful spring trials with both the Yankees and Red Sox, then later played in the Class D Eastern Shore League.

Perhaps the best indicator of how good this outsider club was is their performance against the best black teams of the era. Going against the likes of the aforementioned Cyclone Joe Williams as well as Cannonball Dick Redding, John Henry Lloyd, Spot Poles, Judy Johnson, Louis Santop, Alejandro Oms, Dick Lundy, Ghost Marcell, Nip Winters, Irvin Brooks, Bingo DeMoss, Cristobal Torriente, Phil Cockrell, and Biz Mackey—just about *every* great African

American and Cuban ballplayer in the country—the Treat 'Em Roughs and Bears more than held their own.

From 1919 to 1921, Tesreau's clubs went 34–39–2 versus the top black and Cuban teams in the world. Tellingly, when Tesreau himself was on the mound, the clubs were 14–6. Without him, they were only 20–33 (.377).

◆ ◆ ◆

By leaving the major leagues in his prime, then pitching dozens of games against the top black teams of the era, Jeff Tesreau is a valuable tool for gauging the quality of the outsider teams in the late teens and early twenties.

For the first time in print, we can share Tesreau's pitching record versus the top black squads (circa 1918 through 1924). Adding in some additional cameo appearances Jeff made with the South Phillies and Brooklyn Bushwicks (two white semipro clubs of nearly the same caliber as the Roughs/Bears), I've thus far located thirty appearances for the spitballer. As expected, he did well, going 18–9 overall with a 3.33 ERA. He struck out 146 batters in 232.1 innings pitched, good for a 5.7 K/9 rate, whereas his major league K/9 rate had been only 4.7 (with a career high of 5.3, accomplished twice). His walks per 9 innings were lower than in the big leagues, but the hits per 9 innings (he allowed 267 against the black clubs) were *much* higher than his work in the majors. Some of this might be attributable to their home park, the Dyckman Oval, which had an awkwardly short center-field fence, favoring the hitters.

Let's go ahead and line up Jeff's work versus the top black teams against that of the two top black pitchers of the era, Joe Williams and Dick Redding. To establish some control over the dataset, we'll only use Williams's and Redding's work from the same period as Tesreau's, 1918 to 1924. These guys were all very similar in age; Williams was the oldest, having been born in 1886, while Tesreau was born in 1888 and Redding in 1890. Again, this is their individual body of work against the black teams; everybody against *basically the same level of competition*:

18.1

Pitcher	W	L	ERA	G	GS	CG	IP	H	BB	K
Dick Redding	46	37	3.13	99	76	66	721.1	732	194	405
Joe Williams	32	25	2.42	64	53	46	469.0	468	90	322
Jeff Tesreau	18	9	3.33	30	27	25	232.1	267	44	146

Tesreau could still pitch, and had he been a black man, he would have been an outstanding star in the Negro leagues. But Williams, although slightly older, was clearly better. He had the same control as Tesreau but was tougher to hit and struck out more men per 9 innings.

As for their outings, head to head, *against* Jeff Tesreau's Bears, this is how Cyclone Joe and Cannonball Dick fared:

18.2

Pitcher	W	L	ERA	G	GS	CG	IP	H	BB	K
Dick Redding	2	1	3.60	4	3	2	20.0	16	4	9
Joe Williams	2	1	1.65	4	4	3	32.2	16	9	31

◆ ◆ ◆

When news broke that Christy Mathewson, legendary Giants pitcher, was suffering from tuberculosis, Tesreau had a reconciliation of sorts with McGraw, appearing once again on the Polo Grounds pitching mound. In 1921, Jeff suited up for the Giants "old-timers," who played McGraw's current edition in a five-inning exhibition game, raising funds for their ailing ex-teammate. Roger Bresnahan was there, as was Art Devlin, Fred Tenney, and Fred Merkle. Hooks Wiltse started for the old-timers and pitched three effective innings before being replaced by Big Jeff Tesreau. Still in fantastic shape, and only thirty-three years old, Tesreau walked one but didn't allow any hits or runs in his two innings of work against the Giants.

NEGRO NATIONAL LEAGUE

Rube Foster's Negro National League was *not* the first all-black professional baseball organization. Let's dispel that widely accepted kernel of misinformation right here, at the beginning.

Black teams had tried to become members of the white National Association, dating back to the 1860s and 1870s, but they were denied entry. In 1887, the eight-team League of Colored Baseball Clubs was formed, with professional squads representing New York, Boston, Philadelphia, Baltimore, Washington DC, Pittsburgh, Louisville, and Cincinnati. With poor planning and little in the way of financial backing, the league folded after only two weeks. The Boston team was literally stranded in Louisville with no money to return home.

Infielder Sol White was a member of the Pittsburgh franchise in the old League of Colored Baseball Clubs. He'd later become Rube Foster's manager on the Philadelphia Giants super team of the early twentieth century, then briefly serve as business manager for an outfit in Rube Foster's new Negro National League (NNL) in the 1920s.

In 1907, Rube Foster left Sol White's team for Chicago, where destiny awaited him. Undeterred, White entered his Philly Giants in the freshly minted National Association of Colored Professional Clubs of the United States and Cuba that same season. The league name was a mouthful, but they played a short season, finishing enough games to crown an actual champion. There would be no encore campaign in 1908. This league (and yes, it was a *real* professional baseball league) has been largely forgotten today.

Way back in 1886, one year before the League of Colored Baseball Clubs did its Hindenburg impersonation, there was talk of starting a ten-team Southern Colored Base Ballist league. This organization doesn't appear to have ever gotten off the ground, but in 1920—the same year Foster and his cronies formed the NNL—a new Negro Southern League was founded with eight teams scattered throughout Florida, Georgia, Tennessee, Louisiana, and Alabama. Their very first season, nearly every one of their eight franchises successfully completed a schedule of 70 or 80 games. The league would last more than twenty years and become the de facto blackball Triple-A, launching the careers of young stars such as Satchel Paige and Turkey Stearnes, who later moved up to the great northern black leagues.

When Rube Foster met with the other team owners at Kansas City's "colored" YMCA in February 1920 to draw up blueprints for the NNL, they enjoyed a number of advantages over their predecessors. These could probably be separated into three parts:

- A customer base growing at an explosive rate

- A maturing, sophisticated media network

- Baseball *experience*

At the beginning of the twentieth century, trickles of black people began fleeing the oppressive South and moving to northern cities, where factory jobs were readily available. By 1920, the black populations of most northern urban centers had more than doubled. Detroit, which had only six thousand black residents in 1910, would see this figure rise to one hundred twenty thousand by 1929. From 1916 to 1918 alone, nearly half a million African Americans traveled north, taking advantage of a labor shortage created by World War I. Over the decades, *millions* of black people moved north in what came to be known as the Great Migration. This was to become Rube Foster's customer base, and it was growing daily.

Newspapers were the king of all media at this time, mostly because they were the *only* media. Radio was still in the developmental stage, and television was a madman's science fiction experiment. Black newspapers, catering to their community and focusing mostly on the issue of social equality, dated back to the mid-1800s. But it wasn't until the emergence of the *Chicago Defender* that there was a black media outlet with national influence.

Founded in 1905 by Robert S. Abbott, the paper was a small-time affair, more or less published out of an apartment for several years. It wasn't until 1910 that Abbott hired his first full-time employee. Within a couple years, his paper went from an initial print run of three hundred copies to a circulation of more than one hundred thousand. At about the same time the Negro National

League was being founded, it is estimated that the *Defender* was being read by more than five hundred thousand people each week.

Based in Chicago, Foster's team was just a long fly ball away from the *Defender*'s headquarters. Abbott and Foster were friends, two of the city's elite black entrepreneurs, involved in the same social circles. The *Chicago Defender* had been the leading voice during the Great Migration, urging blacks to bolt the South for fresh opportunities north of the Mason-Dixon Line, and it also became the biggest advocate of the new Negro National League, providing ample coverage of league activities and urging readers to support the enterprise.

But just as important as the growing black population in the North and the Negro National League's relationship with the most powerful black media outlet in the country was simply the experience level of the leading figures in the league. I'm talking here about Chicago's Rube Foster, Kansas City Monarchs owner J. L. Wilkinson, and Indianapolis ABCs leader C. I. Taylor. In fact, their experience as baseball entrepreneurs might actually have been more important than the first two points listed earlier.

Back in 2008, author Malcolm Gladwell wrote about the importance of experience in his bestseller, *Outliers: The Story of Success*. In his book, Gladwell argued there is a direct correlation between logging ten thousand hours of intensive development and practice and those who eventually achieve a high degree of success in their chosen fields. Ten thousand hours translates roughly to ten years of development.

Rube Foster, after taking over the Leland Giants in 1910, had been running a team for ten years before he helped found the Negro National League, battling for survival, learning how to handle players, and building his Rolodex of team owners, stadium operators, and promoters. He was ready in 1920. He'd logged his ten thousand hours.

Same with ABC's owner C. I. Taylor, who'd started managing back in 1904 in Birmingham, Alabama. By 1910, he was running the West Baden Sprudels in Indiana, then took over the Indianapolis ABCs in 1914. He'd gone through the same ups and downs as Foster had.

Likewise with Wilkinson, a white businessman from Iowa who founded a traveling girls' team in 1909. In 1912, he created the All-Nations team—whose roster included whites, blacks, Native Americans, Cubans, and Asians—and cut his teeth trying to earn profits barnstorming through whistle-stop towns in Nebraska, Minnesota, Iowa, and the Dakotas.

Not only had these men paid their dues, they'd already established rivalries with one another. Several years before the Chicago American Giants and Indianapolis ABCs became charter members of the new Negro National

League, they were already fierce competitors/business partners who'd played against one another in front of ten thousand paying customers.

The Negro National League wasn't perfect by any stretch of the imagination, but it *does* make perfect sense why it succeeded to the extent that it did at that precise moment. The convergence of a growing customer base, the relationship with the nation's top black media outlet, and the battle-tested experience of several key figures meant the timing was ideal. Rube Foster's brainchild set into motion a series of leagues that existed (sometimes hanging on by a string but persevering nevertheless) for nearly forty uninterrupted years, launching the careers of more than forty Hall of Famers.

◆ ◆ ◆

Before the Negro National League was founded in 1920, the all-black (and Cuban) outsider clubs had put together an impressive resume:

- ◆ They had defeated white major league clubs, dating back to the 1800s.

- ◆ Operating in a neutral environment (Cuba), the African American clubs had performed on par with visiting major league teams.

- ◆ From 1901 to 1919, blackball clubs had gone 127–75 (.629) against white minor league teams, the majority of the games being against teams of the highest classification.

When talking about on-field talent, the conventional wisdom among historians is the Negro leagues hovered somewhere between Triple-A and major league caliber. Even in the contemporary newspaper accounts, sportswriters felt the same way. In interviews after their careers, the players themselves offered a mixed assessment. Some, such as Hall of Famer Buck Leonard, believed the league was about Triple-A ability. Former Chicago American Giants pitcher "Sug" Cornelius thought it was *better* than the white big leagues. And Art "Superman" Pennington, during our encounter in the baseball bunker, said it was simply "a third major league, man."

On one point, almost everybody agrees: the Achilles' heel of the black leagues was pitching depth. It wasn't that the black teams didn't have good pitchers in the 8 and 9 spots in the bullpen; it's that they *didn't have* eight or nine pitchers. They could only afford to carry fifteen or sixteen players, total, so the emergency starts and mop-up relief appearances were often handled by position players.

For the first time, we actually have statistical evidence to verify the pitching issues. As we mentioned earlier in the book, the black teams weren't the only ones playing exhibition games versus semipro, college, and minor league clubs. Back before 1950, the white big-league clubs did quite a bit of this as well, on off-days or on Sundays in cities where baseball was banned on the Sabbath. Looking at the runs scored and runs allowed versus identical levels of competition, we're offered a glimpse into the relative abilities of the white *and* black big-league clubs. These figures are cobbled together from 5,742 games played from 1901 to 1950.

19.1

Major League vs. Various Levels	RF	RA
High minors	6.12	4.33
Semipro	6.86	3.02
College	9.82	2.57

19.2

Negro League vs. Various Levels	RF	RA
High minors	4.31	3.37
Semipro	6.18	3.77
College	8.18	3.64

Obviously, based on the run differential, both the major leaguers and the Negro league teams dominated these levels of competition. There's no debating they were at the top of the talent pyramid. But how they did it is instructive. Against the lower levels, the white major leaguers both *scored more* and *allowed fewer* runs than the blackball teams.

Against the high minors (Triple-A in today's classification system) the major leaguers scored nearly two runs more per game than the black clubs did. But they also allowed about one more full run per 9 innings in these games. The black pitchers/defense were better against Triple-A, according to table 19.2. Is this the kind of evidence that contradicts the conventional wisdom?

Probably not. I suspect these were different run-scoring environments, with contextual issues such as ballpark factors contributing to the disparity. But just as importantly, there was also a different priority level associated with these exhibitions. For the black clubs, playing a white minor league team was a big deal, an important part of their schedule. It was common to use one of their aces in these games, as they wanted to prove themselves. With the white big leaguers, it was a different story. Often it was the low men on the totem pole, the rookies, and replacement-level arms at the end of the bullpen bench pitching in these exhibition games.

◆ 20 ◆

CONTINENTAL DIVIDE

THE GRAY-HAIRED GENTLEMAN stood behind a small table, gun in one hand, Bible in the other. In front of him lay the white, hooded robe favored by the Ku Klux Klan. It was December 1924, and the aspiring spiritual leader posed for newspaper photographers to announce he was severing his ties with local Klavern 14 of New Jersey, saying the racist organization was "an iniquitous fake."

A few months later, this same man announced his intentions to run for governor of New Jersey under a new third party promoting an anti-Klan platform. It had been quite a whirlwind for the sixty-year-old gubernatorial candidate. Just eighteen months earlier, he and his new bride (number six, for those keeping score at home) had shown up at his brother's doorstep in Cleveland, penniless and hungry. The couple's honeymoon had consisted of crisscrossing the country, preaching on street corners, telling anybody who'd listen that they were going to hell, while at the same time shaking them down for financial donations.

It was a tough sell.

Prior to becoming a reverend in the unauthorized branch of the "Church Army" (the Evangelical Church of England's version of our Salvation Army), he'd studied law, performed in a traveling comedy troupe, served in the military, been a practicing hypnotist, and had spent a year in jail for dabbling in unlicensed medicine.

Using a technical term borrowed from today's psychological community, this gentleman was what we would now call "bat-shit crazy."

His name was George H. Lawson, and in 1921 (three years *before* becoming a Klan member, then an anti-Klan gubernatorial candidate) he had tried to found the first fully integrated major league in baseball history.

Rev. Lawson
Commissioner

Continental Baseball League
★

George Lawson spent some time in jail, became a street preacher, ran for governor, and tried to found an integrated major league. Later on, he fell off a ladder and died. *Courtesy of Scott Simkus*

Lawson, it turns out, had a baseball background. He'd been involved with several minor league teams and leagues as an owner, administrator, and promoter. He'd even organized a baseball tour of England, taking a group of amateurs overseas to play a series of exhibition games. The tour became notable in the British press not so much for the baseball but for the exploits of Lawson himself, who apparently abandoned the games to chase his then-wife around the country with a gun, as she was allegedly involved in an illicit affair with another man.

George Lawson's younger brother, Alfred, had pitched briefly in the major leagues and spent another ten years or so in the minors. Al had befriended a young John McGraw back in 1890, and together they organized and participated in one of the first baseball tours of Cuba. In another one of those bizarre instances of baseball serendipity, Al Lawson had briefly been teammates with African American second baseman Frank Grant back during the days when a handful of blacks were permitted to play in the minor leagues.

As for George's Continental League in 1921, it wasn't his first attempt at creating an integrated major league. Back in 1910, he'd tried bootstrapping something called the United States League, which was to include eight franchises in places such as Boston, Brooklyn, Newark, and Baltimore. He initially wanted to include several all-black clubs, then later amended his plan to include "three black players" on each otherwise all-white team. A month before the season began, Lawson resigned from his leadership post (he was probably forced out), and the reconstituted league debuted, operating out of smaller New England towns instead of the big cities initially promised, and *without* any black players.

But the whole thing seemed so much more plausible in 1921, as Lawson tried to prop up the Continental Baseball League (CBL). After the Black Sox scandal in 1919, when eight Chicago White Sox players conspired to throw the World Series and were shortly thereafter banned from organized baseball, there was a growing discontent among the game's fans. Some folks were upset with the "crooked" players who'd tampered with the game's integrity by conspiring with gamblers. Others were upset with baseball's establishment because they believed some players involved in the affair (most notably Shoeless Joe Jackson) had been treated unfairly during the adjudication process. And there was the usual flare-up of discontent among the players themselves, as ownership groups sought to tamp down salaries after the collapse of both the Federal League and the Base Ball Players Fraternity.

Again, Lawson sought to form an eight-team league, with four all-black teams and four white clubs. At the top of his recruitment list were stars Shoeless Joe Jackson, Eddie Cicotte, and the six other White Sox who had been blacklisted by organized baseball for their part in the fixing scheme. Lawson's plan also included signing eight full-time umpires, with four blacks included in the mix. He sent a letter to Rube Foster, owner of the Chicago American Giants, whose team had just been crowned champions of the new Negro National League, inviting him into the fray.

I'm paraphrasing here, but Foster, who had better business instincts than most, said, "No thanks, and by the way, don't put *any* teams in our Negro National League cities." Rube didn't want anybody messing with what he knew was a pretty good thing.

Although he wasn't able to lure any of the major black teams, or any of the banned Chicago White Sox players, the league got off the ground, albeit barely, with several CBL franchises playing exhibition games in April and May. The league's flagship franchise, the Boston Pilgrims, were clobbered in a doubleheader by Heinie Zimmerman's Bronx Giants. Zimmerman, like the guys from the White Sox, had recently gotten kicked out of organized ball for bribing teammates in an attempt to fix games. But by the end of May, Lawson's league simply disappeared from the radar.

Poof! Gone.

The Continental Baseball League had followed Lawson's classic business strategy. First off, start with a wildly ambitious plan. Second, convince a bunch of gullible, information-starved newspaper reporters across the country to write about it. And finally, initiate a complete nuclear meltdown of said plan by simply pressing the START button.

What if he hadn't been such an idiot?

What if Lawson had possessed the interpersonal charm to persuade men such as Rube Foster and J. L. Wilkinson into the fold? Foster and Wilkinson knew how to run profitable baseball teams under some of the most burdensome business conditions imaginable. What if Lawson had access to financiers with deep pockets, as James A. Gilmore had, when he turned the Federal League into a third major back in 1914? And what if the Continental Baseball League teams had employed the top bird dogs and scouts from around the country, gathering up the best talent available?

How good could the Continental League have been if Lawson had actually pulled it off? The notion gives us a unique opportunity to see how much *major league* talent was hidden, or exiled, on the fringe in 1921. Let's do George Lawson's work for him and retroactively build this alternative association. One caveat: unlike all of the other upstart major leagues (the American Association, Union League, Players League, American League, and Federal League), the Continental will *not* be allowed to poach talent from the two established major leagues. Starters and key bench figures on National and American League clubs are strictly off limits, as this fictional eight-team league (four white, four black) is cobbled together.

The rosters will be constructed using talent from four areas: the outcasts, the fugitives, the refugees, and the freaks. *And please keep in mind: this league never happened!* This is simply what could have been, had the constellations been aligned differently.

From Rube Foster's Negro National League, we can lure their four best teams: Rube's Chicago American Giants, Wilkinson's Kansas City Monarchs, the St. Louis Giants, and the Indianapolis ABCs. These are the outcasts. Each team is strengthened by the acquisition of talent from the other four black clubs, plus the independent African American and Cuban teams playing on the East Coast. There will be no fewer than twelve future Hall of Famers on these four clubs, including Oscar Charleston, Pete Hill, Cyclone Joe Williams, Bullet Rogan, Andy Cooper, John Henry Lloyd, Judy Johnson, Louis Santop, Ben Taylor, Biz Mackey, Cristobal Torriente, and Jose Mendez.

More than a dozen fugitives will be signed from white semipro teams. Three men formerly associated with Tesreau's Bears will be part of the mix: Tesreau (of course), pitcher Curt Fullerton, and catcher Paddy Smith. Thirty-year-old Joe Harris, who batted .375 in a part-time role for the Cleveland Indians in 1919 before leaving organized baseball to play in the outlaw leagues, would start at first base for one team. In the real world, Harris rejoined the majors in 1922 and eventually started for the Pittsburgh Pirates in the 1927 World Series. Also part of this class is twenty-five-year-old pitcher Milt Gaston, who was dominating the semipro ranks with a club called the Paterson Silk Sox but would later pitch for eleven seasons in the major leagues.

The Black Sox would spearhead the refugees, players kicked out of organized ball for nefarious activities but given a new lease on life in the Continental League. Shoeless Joe Jackson, Eddie Cicotte, and their teammates would be joined by other ne'er-do-wells Joe Gedeon, Hal Chase, Benny Kauff, and Cozy Dolan.

Roughly one-third of the new Continental League would consist of the freakishly talented prospects (and veterans) from the white minor leagues. Dazzy Vance was thirty years old, buried in the Southern Association, and by all rights should have been in the major leagues. He gets signed by the Continental. Lefty Grove is dazzling the competition (25–10, 2.56 ERA) in the International League. Veteran Chief Bender went 13–7 with a 1.93 ERA for New Haven in the Eastern League and was still major league caliber. Pie Traynor, Kiki Cuyler, and Goose Goslin, all starring in the minors, might have been attracted by the promise of big dollars in a new loop.

Also coming over from the minor league ranks would be Ike Boone, Buzz Arlett, Reb Russell, and Lefty O'Doul, all record setters from the lower levels. O'Doul, of course, would bat .349 during his major league career and would later be inducted into the Japanese Baseball Hall of Fame for his pioneering efforts in spreading the professional game overseas.

Other curiosities residing on the benches of the Continental League clubs are Olympic gold medalist/outfielder Jim Thorpe, who batted .358 for Toldeo in the American Association in 1921; Maurice Archdeacon, record holder for fastest time ever recorded in circling the bases (he batted .325 and stole 53 bases in the International League in '21); and Chinese/Hawaiian third baseman Buck Lai, whom we'll discuss in more detail later on.

Just in terms of diversity and athleticism, the Continental would certainly look much more like what we see today on TV when we flip on the MLB Network than the other two loops. The average age of the two hundred players in this fictional league would have been 27.9, which is just about in line with the other two major leagues.

There are nineteen future Hall of Famers in the Continental League, versus fifteen in the American League and fourteen in the National. Using the STARS system, we can see *precisely* how these three leagues would have compared to one another, in terms of paper talent. I'll spare you the details for now, but a specially engineered version of STARS was created for the Negro league players to account for what might have been, had they been allowed into an integrated major league environment. Worth noting: I use a conservative projection, where only 9 percent of the top black Americans and Cubans are granted opportunities in a color-blind big league.

20.1

1921 Professional Leagues	STARS Score
American League	353
National League	344
Continental League	330

The two established leagues get a slight edge (mostly in pitching depth), but it would have been very difficult to notice any difference in the quality of play between the three major leagues. This isn't like the Federal League where there was a noticeable drop. So here we have a hypothetical example, in 1921, of an *entire league* of major league talent hiding on the outside. Nearly two-thirds of the Continental League's players, by hook or by crook, were *not* part of the establishment yet were actively playing baseball at the time. The other third were in the minors, with some of them (such as Lefty Grove) stuck in a perpetual state of arrested development as they played in leagues that elected to retain their talent, instead of selling it, by circumventing the minor league draft system in existence at the time.

The rosters of the **Fantasy Continental League** teams used in this study are the following:

Chicago Black Sox: Chick Gandil, Joe Gedeon, Swede Risberg, Buck Weaver, Happy Felsch, Ike Boone, Joe Jackson, Grover Hartley, Jim Poole, Manuel Cueto, Ernie Padgett, Fred McMullin, Ben Paschal, Jim Thorpe, Frank Reiger, Eddie Cicotte, Lefty Williams, Milton Gaston, Jack Bentley, Sheriff Blake, Jeff Tesreau, Jack Warhop, Larry Benton, Lefty O'Doul, and Eddie Gerner.

Philadelphia Continentals: Hal Chase, Max Bishop, Joe Boley, Heinie Zimmerman, George Harper, Reb Russell, Benny Kauff, Jimmie Wilson, Dick Hoblitzell, George Grantham, Luke Boone, Cozy Dolan, Maurice Archdeacon, Howard Lohr, Frank Crossin, Dazzy Vance, Lefty Grove, Jack Ogden, Tommy Thomas, Dave Danforth, Larry Cheney, Bill James (no, not that one), Frank Woodward, Hugh Bedient, and Chief Bender.

Pittsburgh Continentals: Joe Harris, Buck Herzog, Ray Brubaker, Pie Traynor, Bob Fothergill, Kiki Cuyler, Goose Goslin, Benny Bengough, Gavvy Cravath, Chuck Dressen, Tom McMillan, Sammy Hale, Fred Merkle, Bunny Brief, Paddy Smith, Harry Krause, Ray Kremer, Jean Dubuc, Vic Aldridge, Oscar Tuero, Johnny Couch, Carmen Hill, Bert Gallia, Pug Cavet, and Jimmy Clinton.

NEW YORK METROPOLITANS: Joe Hauser, Sparky Adams, Ray French, Fritz Maisel, Earl Webb, Hack Miller, Jigger Statz, Pinky Hargrave, Sam Crawford, Jack Barry, Jake Pitler, Buck Lai, Duffy Lewis, Jim Viox, Mickey Lalonge, King Bader, Buzz Arlett, Jesse Petty, Doc Crandall, Earl Whitehill, Freddie Fitzsimmons, Ernie Koob, Oyster Joe Martina, Curt Fullerton, and Nick Cullop.

CHICAGO AMERICAN GIANTS: Edgar Wesley, Bingo DeMoss, Bobby Williams, Dave Malarcher, Jimmie Lyons, Cristobal Torriente, Jelly Gardner, George Brown, Leroy Grant, Bob Fagan, Bill Riggins, Johnson Hill, Valentin Dreke, Pete Hill, Jim Brown, Dave Brown, Tom Williams, Tom Johnson, Jack Marshall, Otis Starks, Bill Holland, Dick Whitworth, Phil Cockrell, Cyclone Joe Williams, and Ed Rile.

KANSAS CITY MONARCHS: George Carr, Irvin Brooks, Dobie Moore, Ghost Marcell, Hurley McNair, John Donaldson, Bullet Rogan, Frank Duncan, Lemuel Hawkins, Bunny Downs, John Beckwith, Sam Mongin, Doc Dudley, Otto Briggs, Bruce Petway, Rube Curry, Sam Crawford, Cliff Bell, Andy Cooper, Jose Leblanc, Connie Rector, Slim Branham, Ping Gardner, Oscar Levis, and Zach Foreman.

INDIANAPOLIS ABCs: Ben Taylor, Frank Warfield, Dick Lundy, Ramon Herrera, Chaney White, Harry Kenyon, Crush Holloway, Biz Mackey, Bill Pettus, Connie Day, Morten Clark, Bartolo Portuondo, Alejandro Oms, Rev Cannady, Russell Powell, Jim Jeffries, Jose Mendez, Dicta Johnson, Bob McClure, Roy Roberts, George Britt, John Taylor, Jesse Hubbard, String Bean Williams, and Nip Winters.

ST. LOUIS GIANTS: Robert Hudspeth, Clint Thomas, John Henry Lloyd, Judy Johnson, Bernardo Baro, Oscar Charleston, Charlie Blackwell, Louis Santop, Tullie McAdoo, Eddie Holtz, Joe Hewitt, Candy Jim Taylor, Spot Poles, George Shively, Dan Kennard, Bill Drake, Dizzy Dismukes, Jimmy Oldham, Bill Gatewood, Bill Force, Luther Farrell, Dick Redding, Red Ryan, Isidro Fabre, and Luis Padrón.

One hundred of these players were performing in the Negro National League or with independent professional black clubs on the East Coast. More than thirty of the white men were playing semiprofessional baseball or had been blacklisted by organized baseball. The remaining seventy players were part of the established minor league system. Together, they would have formed a league virtually indistinguishable from the two established major leagues.

◆ 21 ◆

FEAR OF A BLACK PLANET

SIX YEARS AFTER HIS FAILED ATTEMPT at propping up a third major league (and just two years after his failed—largely unknown, I suspect—run for governor of New Jersey), George Lawson was working as a lowly house painter when he fell from a ladder, suffered a cerebral hemorrhage, then died shortly thereafter. He was sixty-three years old.

There was never an integrated Continental Baseball League. Even if there wasn't a lunatic at the helm, it doesn't take a master's degree in American history or sociology to understand such an enterprise would have had very little chance of survival, given the state of race relations in our country at that point. Putting this fictional league together on paper is one thing, but there were still thousands of little events, both big and small, related and unrelated, that needed to occur before Jackie Robinson could successfully don a Brooklyn Dodgers uniform.

Yet two teams from this surrealist baseball universe did, in fact, meet for a championship series in the fall of 1921. The St. Louis Cardinals (87–66, third place in the National League) squared off against the all-black St. Louis Giants (42–32, third place in the Negro National League), for the supremacy of Mound City.

The Cardinals were without the services of Rogers Hornsby, who had bolted for California, where he'd play in a winter league with Ty Cobb and George Sisler. The Giants had their full roster, but not the super-sized bunch proposed in our previous chapter. With all of the games hosted at Sportsman's Park, the Cardinals won a tightly contested series at three games to one. The Giants' lone victory was notable, though: a 6–2 decision over future Hall of Famer Pop Haines. Oscar Charleston starred at the plate with two home runs during the four-game set.

The *Sporting News*, writing specifically about the Cardinals-Giants series on the front page of their October 13, 1921, issue, called the games "bad stuff" and wondered, "Who's to blame for letting the Cardinals play the negroes?" The anonymous reporter figured if team manager Branch Rickey had been in St. Louis (he was in New York, watching the World Series), he might have prevented his club from "joining the black and tan league."

Hmm.

◆ ◆ ◆

A year earlier, Babe Ruth and Carl Mays toured the eastern seaboard with a team of mostly minor league all-stars, playing several games with the top black teams of the era. They lost their first game to Cannonball Dick Redding and the Bacharach Giants 9–4, though Ruth smoked one over the Shibe Park fence for a home run.

A week later, Babe's stars split a two-game series with Hilldale, an emerging black powerhouse from Philadelphia, featuring future Hall of Famer Louis Santop. Babe's club played a total of sixteen games in three weeks, mostly against white semipro teams. According to figures published in *Variety* magazine (December 31, 1920), the Yankee star was paid $22,000 for his efforts. His teammate Carl Mays had signed for three weeks, at $3,200, whether he pitched or not. Jeff Tesreau, Lefty O'Doul, Wally Schang, and Yankees catcher Fred Hoffman all suited up for Ruth's outfit at various times during the tour.

Although charging the exorbitant price of a dollar fifty per admission, the Bronx Giants (run by former major leaguer Heinie Zimmerman) sold 16,200 tickets for their game with Ruth's all-star team. In the suburbs, games with Ruth's bunch attracted a minimum of 2,500 fans. The games with the black teams probably approached 10,000 in attendance. The tour was profitable.

There is some debate about how much Ruth really made during the barnstorming tour. In a January 1921 interview with the *Sporting News*, Ruth claimed he made "$10,000 touring around the east after the regular season" then another $11,000 in Cuba for eleven games played with John McGraw's team. One historian believes Ruth may have earned nearly $40,000 for his twenty-seven postseason exhibition games.

Either way, it was a huge chunk of change. Ruth's salary with the New York Yankees in 1920 was "only" $20,000. Including spring training, this pencils out to roughly $115 per game, for 175 games scheduled. Using the more conservative figures from the *Sporting News*, Ruth was earning an astonishing $778 per game during the postseason barnstorming tour.

People at the top took notice. Judge Kennesaw Mountain Landis, installed as commissioner of baseball in the wake of the horrific World Series gambling scandal in 1919, aggressively sought to curtail the barnstorming efforts of the players. A huge feud erupted between Ruth and Landis in 1921, involving the slugger's postseason baseball business ventures. This was mostly about money, as organized baseball's cartel sought to wrap its iron fist around any (and every) money-making venture involving its teams and star players.

Officially, the league detailed its objections (again in the *Sporting News*), which I'll paraphrase here in three bullet points:

- The players are too tired to perform at their very best after a long six-month season.

- Losing games to inferior competition due to fatigue or indifference casts Major League Baseball in a poor light.

- The players increase their risk of injury when performing on subpar baseball diamonds.

◆ ◆ ◆

The handwringing over barnstorming games with outsider teams predated Commissioner Landis's reign.

Back in the fall of 1909, Rube Foster's Leland Giants lost an incredibly close three-game series against the powerful Chicago Cubs. Joe Tinker and Frank Chance opted not to play, while the Leland Giants were still one year away from acquiring John Henry Lloyd, Frank Wickware, and Bruce Petway—three players who would help elevate the club to near major league caliber in 1910, but it was a fiercely contested series nevertheless. Mordecai "Three Finger" Brown won the opener, 4–1. Rube Foster had a 5–2 lead going into the ninth inning of Game 2, before things unraveled and the Cubs rallied for a controversial, umpire-aided, 6–5 win. In Game 3, future Hall of Famer Brown won for the second time over the Lelands, 1–0.

The *Sporting Life* noticed things hadn't been easy for the Cubs, as written in a November 1909 editorial:

Suppose the Cubs had lost their three games to the Leland Giants, and, by the way, none of the big leaguers' victories was easy, does any one think there would not be a large number of persons who would have been convinced firmly that the Lelands would be right up there fighting for the National League pennant, if they were asked into that organization? It is all right to make money [barnstorming], but let us make it without losing our dignity.

White semipro teams such as the Tesreau Bears, Paterson (New Jersey) Silk Sox, and Brooklyn Bushwicks won their share of games against barnstorming major league outfits, but there was only *one* outsider group who beat the big leaguers more often than they lost: the Negro league clubs.

Through fines and intimidation, Czar Landis and Major League Baseball curtailed, but didn't fully eliminate, these postseason barnstorming junkets. The biggest reformation successfully imposed was to eliminate the practice of entire teams, using their actual team names, playing in unsanctioned exhibition games. After the early 1920s, you no longer saw the St. Louis Cardinals (or New York Giants, or whomever) playing the all-black St. Louis Giants in exhibition games. It was always an ad-hoc all-star team of some sort; i.e., the Earle Mack Stars, the American League All-Stars, the Bustin' Babes, or whatever. The objective was to protect the brand equity, although they certainly wouldn't have used that term back then.

Perhaps the most popular barnstorming outfits in the late 1920s were those featuring Babe Ruth and Lou Gehrig of the New York Yankees. *National Baseball Hall of Fame Library, Cooperstown, New York*

I might be wrong, but I get the impression that although ownership had all the power, the real equity at this point was in the fandom's affinity for their favorite players. People loved their local team but weren't yet "rooting for laundry" as comedian Jerry Seinfeld later quipped when describing the modern affection for pro sports teams, where the players are highly paid mercenaries and rosters change from one season to the next.

Real teams were sometimes called different names by different papers in the same city. And often they were strongly associated with their skipper. The Philadelphia Athletics were the Mackmen, after Connie. The Cleveland Indians were actually known as the "Naps" for a while, after manager Napolean Lajoie. The Brooklyn Dodgers were the Robins at one point, in honor of skipper Wilbert Robinson.

Team names were fluid in the past; logos and merchandising weren't used in any sort of sophisticated manner. Landis had an instinct for the future good of the game. It involved restoring the integrity of on-field competition by cracking down on the bad elements and taking steps that made the teams and leagues more valuable than individual players.

The September 24, 1932, issue of the *Chicago Defender* had a different take on the issue:

Has Judge Landis Blocked Games with Race?

For the first time in many years there will be no games between teams composed of Race players and all-star clubs recruited from the major leagues, and fandom is wondering why. That is, there will be no games played in cities where major league clubs are located, according to information just received. The Kansas City Monarchs will play a team harboring the Waner brothers of Pittsburgh, but Kansas City is far removed from the major circuits. Besides, the Monarchs will get just one series as compared with the two or three it asked.

A Big Change

The decision of the majors to pass up playing before Race fandom is quite a shift in things from what has occurred in the past. At one time the St. Louis Stars played the Browns or Cardinals post-season games after the close of each season. The American Giants played all-star nines, and Detroit and Cleveland did likewise.

There is quite a coincidence in the arrival of the order and appearance of the Chicago Cubs at the top of the heap. Many are of the opinion that the Cubs, a lily-white organization, would be at the root of such a move if the thing came up for consideration at either of the league or interleague meetings.

Robert A. Cole, owner of the American Giants, made every attempt to get one of the all-star teams for his park, but failed to land the attraction. The Chicago White Sox management is known to have advised its players against such games, even though several of the players are to participate in barnstorming.

Fonseca, manager of the Sox, is taking no chances, perhaps, on having his club, which was able to beat the Boston Red Sox out of the cellar rights, to hurt their chances to repeat the accomplishment next season.

Nobody can be certain of the motivations, but beginning in the 1930s, there was a near complete elimination of barnstorming games pitting intact major league clubs versus Negro league outfits. Most of the white-versus-black series after this point featured ad-hoc white clubs, sometimes mixing major and minor leaguers, and even semipros, in the same lineup, which provided a convenient alibi for any setbacks on the diamond.

◆ 22 ◆

STRANGER THAN FIKKKTION

O N AUGUST 20, 1927, two thousand cash-paying patrons filtered into Washington's Griffith Stadium, home of the Senators, to watch a benefit baseball game between two amateur clubs. Manager Hessler's Junior Order squared off against the Knights of the Ku Klux Klan.

The Junior Order had revenge on their minds. The previous season they'd been smoked, 8–4, by the elder hoods. Not that this was anything to be ashamed of: the Ku Klux Klan had a formidable team in 1926, winning more than 75 percent of their games in and around the DC area. Their contests were covered extensively in the *Washington Post*, right there next to Walter Johnson and the Senators, as well as the Negro league's Baltimore Black Sox. This was the world at that time.

The Klan's biggest victory of 1926 had to be their 4–0 whitewash of the Hebrew Stars on Labor Day. The Jews had a good team—in the middle of their lineup was little Abe Povich, only 5'3" tall, but considered one of the best amateur athletes in the capital. Abe's brother was Shirley Povich, who later became a legendary sportswriter in Washington, and his nephew was Maury, who'd make a gazillion dollars a generation thereafter, exploiting uneducated people's personal problems on a controversial television program. Surely you remember the "Who's your baby daddy?" stuff.

Against the Klan, Abe Povich went 1-for-2, coaxing a base on balls.

In their 1927 rematch, the Junior Order beat the older Klansmen 5–3. No mention of what the fund-raising efforts were intended for.

◆ ◆ ◆

Abe Povich (left) and Sonny Kremb (right). *Courtesy of Scott Simkus*

In Philadelphia, one of the best semipro clubs was the South Philadelphia Hebrew Association, known more commonly as the SPHAS. Owned and operated by Eddie Gottlieb, this (mostly) Jewish club dominated the city's white semipro baseball scene and was a formidable opponent of the best visiting black clubs from the Negro leagues.

Lefty Vann, a former minor leaguer who played for Gottlieb in the early 1930s, claimed to have earned $600 a month while manning first base with the SPHAS, which was "the most money I ever made in my life."

Gottlieb was a master sports promoter, involved in professional basketball for more than fifty years as owner of the Philadelphia Warriors during Wilt Chamberlain's reign, then later as a league official for the NBA. In 1971, he was inducted into the Naismith Memorial Basketball Hall of Fame.

Never one to sit still, Eddie owned and operated the Negro National League's Philadelphia Stars franchise, from 1936 until 1952, after Jackie Robinson had reintegrated organized baseball. None other than future Hall of Famer Oscar Charleston was managing this bunch when they finally ran out of gas in the early 1950s.

◆ ◆ ◆

Not to be outdone, Philadelphia's Catholics got involved in high-level semipro baseball as well. The Nativity Catholic Club of the early 1920s was a talented, morally upstanding bunch. In six games, they went 2–4 against Hilldale, the Bacharach Giants, and the Brooklyn Royal Giants, three of the most outstanding professional black clubs in the East. I haven't yet tracked down their games against the SPHAS, which I trust was a rivalry of biblical proportions.

◆ ◆ ◆

In September 1925, Rats Henderson and the Bacharach Giants beat the Bloomer Girls, 11–8, in what was described as a "comedy" game. As mentioned in chapter 16, Rogers Hornsby started his professional baseball career as a diamond drag queen, playing for the Bloomers.

◆ ◆ ◆

In addition to being a Bloomer, and then a Cardinal (and later a Giant, a Cub, a Brave, and a Brown), Hall of Famer Rogers "the Rajah" Hornsby was also a longtime, card-carrying member of the Ku Klux Klan. No, not the baseball team. The actual political organization. Hornsby was a difficult personality with more than enough venom to spread around, but as far as we know, he wasn't a hood-wearing, cross-burning lunatic. As explained by Hornsby biographer Charles Alexander, like other prominent southerners (Rogers was from Texas), Hornsby was likely "conscripted into the Klan as it made a push to become a legitimate social organization" in the 1920s. Having the Rajah on the roster, as a semiactive participant, lent an air of prestige to whatever klavern he belonged to.

Near the end of his playing career, Hornsby participated in a number of exhibition games with Negro league teams, and by the 1950s and '60s he was coaching black and Latino players without any known incidents. In the late 1950s, as a coach with the Chicago Cubs, Hornsby worked closely with all-star shortstop Ernie Banks, a Negro league alum, who Rajah said was "a fine ballplayer."

◆ ◆ ◆

Early in his life, Oscar Charleston, an African American, was said to have ripped the hood off a Klan member during an intense standoff somewhere in rural Indiana. Whether or not this is true, or just one of those apocryphal stories, isn't really clear at this point. But Charleston *was* a tough hombre—serious, dignified, and disciplined after having spent a couple years in the military.

Back in 1915, during a postseason exhibition game against a number of white Federal League players, then-teenager Charleston beat the crap out of a couple unruly guys and got thrown into jail.

Later in his life, Charleston had to suffer the indignity of traveling in a rattletrap bus, crisscrossing the Midwest as manager of the Indianapolis Clowns. This was in 1954, when dozens of black men were finding jobs in organized baseball as players or part-time scouts. Just six years later, Gene Baker (a former Kansas City Monarchs and Chicago Cubs infielder) became the first black manager in the history of organized baseball when he took over the Batavia (New York) team in the New York–Pennsylvania League; yet here was Oscar, running a novelty outfit with a woman at second base (all glove, no stick), a drunken midget named Spec Bebop goofing around in between innings, and a dude named King Tut, who wore a glove the size of a chaise longue (literally), making fans laugh with his baseball-inspired minstrel routine.

The golden age of the Negro leagues had long since passed, and sometimes the Clowns found themselves performing in front of just a couple dozen entertainment-starved hayseeds. The third wheel of their entertainment package, along with Bebop and Tut, was a cigarette-smoking white guy in clown makeup named Ed Hamman, who did some juggling stuff and performed a couple on-field routines with an actual duck.

Cable TV had not been invented yet, folks.

◆ ◆ ◆

Ed Hamman was a former minor leaguer who later played, managed, and eventually became a team owner in outsider baseball.

Courtesy of Scott Simkus

Ed Hamman was actually a pretty good baseball player who had appeared briefly in the lower minor leagues before joining the barnstorming House of David ballclub in the late 1920s. By 1932, he was playing shortstop for an outfit called the Nebraska Indians, touring the country with a bunch of talented Native American athletes from the Haskell Indian Nations University in Kansas.

Hamman's teammates appeared in the box scores under the names of Little Bear, Canoe, Rock, Running Deer, Big Fire, and Lone Star. One of Hamman's other teammates that season was a lanky, older fellow named Jimmy Claxton.

◆ ◆ ◆

John McGraw had unsuccessfully attempted to pass Charlie Grant off as an American Indian back in 1901, in order to sneak the African American into the upstart American League. McGraw's efforts were blocked by Charlie Comiskey, among others, but just fifteen years later, a man named Hastings (a Bay Area baseball impresario of Native American descent) pulled one over on the Pacific Coast League's Oakland Oaks.

Hastings convinced the Oaks management that Jimmy Claxton, the left-handed pitcher who would later barnstorm with clown/shortstop Ed Hamman, was a full-blooded Native American, when in fact he was of mixed race. Claxton's father was black, his mother white.

And this is how, on May 28, 1916 (thirty-some odd years before Jackie Robinson), a black man pitched two ballgames in one of the nation's most talent-laden minor leagues. His actual work on the hill was less than stellar, as he appeared "nervous" according to newspaper accounts. In just 2.1 innings pitched, Jimmy allowed 4 hits, walked 4, and closed out his minor league career with a 7.72 ERA.

Jimmy Claxton made a brief appearance in white professional baseball. *Courtesy of Scott Simkus*

Manager Rowdy Elliott, who was just twenty-four years old and a kid himself, released the twenty-three-year-old Claxton a couple days later without explanation. In an interview conducted decades later, Claxton said a "friend" had tipped Elliott off to Claxton's true ethnic heritage and that was the end of his little adventure.

Claxton went on to have a long career as a vagabond moundsman, pitching for various semipro clubs across the country. In 1932, at the age of thirty-nine, he finally made his debut in the black majors with the independent Cuban House of David (CHOD). His most prominent teammate there was Luis Tiant Sr., a Cuban pitcher whose son would carve out his own legend with the Boston Red Sox during the 1960s and '70s.

The CHOD's principal owner was a man named Syd Pollock, who'd later run the Indianapolis Clowns for a couple decades, before selling the club to . . . Ed Hamman.

◆ ◆ ◆

In the years predating commercial air travel, the Pacific Coast League might as well have been located on a different continent. Because of its pleasant climate,

Lim Popo
Firstbase

Zulu Cannibal Giants

★

Negro league legend Buck O'Neil got his start with one of the oddest, most controversial teams from outsider baseball, the barnstorming Zulu Cannibal Giants, who played in faux-African face paint and grass skirts. The Cannibal Giants were a predecessor of sorts to the Clown brand, which was deemed less offensive to the African American community. *Courtesy of Scott Simkus*

and the fact it was three thousand miles away from civilization (read: New York), odd things happened on the coast.

You had black guys like Jimmy Claxton finding themselves in uniform, teams regularly playing 200-game schedules, and star players such as Buzz Arlett (who hit 432 home runs in his minor league career) choosing to stay out west instead of pursuing the greener fruits of Major League Baseball.

This is probably how Barney Joy, a dark-skinned Hawaiian (of Malaysian descent), put together an excellent season with the San Francisco Seals in 1907. Joy was the best baseball player on the Hawaiian Islands during the first decade of the twentieth century, and based on the personal recommendation of a friend, he was offered a contract with the Seals.

A large, 200-pound lefty, Joy had what was described as a hard sinker, as well as a wicked change-up the pitcher himself had dubbed the "Kanaka Korker." If we had to pick a modern comp, fellow Hawaiian native Sid Fernandez is an almost perfect fit, both in size and substance. During Joy's first exhibition game with the Seals, he struck out the first five batters who stepped inside the box. During the regular season, he made 40 starts, going 17–21 with a respectable 2.45 ERA in 334.1 innings pitched. His WHIP (walks and hits allowed per 9 innings pitched) was tenth best in the league, attracting attention from no fewer than eight major league franchises.

The Boston Braves of the National League eventually won the recruitment battle, but the crafty Hawaiian never made it into the majors. Shortly after it was announced that he'd be joining the Braves in 1908, a bizarre smear campaign fanned across the nation's papers, bringing into question the pitcher's race. He's "as dark as an Ethiopian" said one paper; another flat out claimed he was a "negro."

The Braves backed out of the deal shortly thereafter, and Barney Joy did *not* become the first Pacific Islander in the major leagues. In fact, Joy returned to Hawaii the next year, pitching for local teams the rest of his career.

◆ ◆ ◆

In 1916, the same year Jimmy Claxton was enjoying his brief fling in the Pacific Coast League, a ballclub known as the Chinese Travelers zigzagged its way around the country, playing colleges, minor league squads, and professional black teams.

During the first half of the season, they went 51–30, and among the others, had played tough against Oscar Charleston and the Indianapolis ABCs. They weren't really Chinese but rather had come to the mainland from Hawaii. A number of their star players, including William Tin Lai (better known as Buck) and Vernon Ayau, were Hawaiians who had played with and against Barney Joy back on the islands.

Barney Joy
Pitcher

HAC

Honolulu Athletic Club

★

Hawaiian Barney Joy's major league ambitions were thwarted when he was deemed "too dark" for organized baseball. *Courtesy of Scott Simkus*

During the fall of 1915, this same Chinese Travelers club visited Cuba, where their arrival was greeted with lackluster enthusiasm by the local press. It was assumed the locals (who included both major and minor leaguers on their rosters) would demolish these Asian visitors. After a couple of losses, the Hawaiians rebounded, beating future major league star Dolf Luque, as well as Bombin Pedroso, the guy who had no-hit the Detroit Tigers in 1909. The Hawaiian guys shocked their hosts, nearly splitting the series.

Almost half of the Chinese/Hawaiian roster would eventually play minor league baseball here in the states, but by far their best athlete was third baseman Buck Lai. As a high schooler on the islands, he was a basketball star and had set several track and field records, both in the sprints and the long jump, which he won with a leap of 22'6". The Olympic record for the broad jump at that time was just 24'11'.

As a ballplayer, Buck Lai was an outstanding defensive third baseman and base runner. After his last tour with the Hawaiian team, he stayed in New York, pursuing a career in professional baseball. He hooked up with Bridgeport in the Eastern League (EL), where he batted .293 during his first season. He'd play three more seasons in the EL, before jumping into the semiprofessional scene, where he played with and against the likes of Jeff Tesreau and Hall of Famer John Franklin "Home Run" Baker.

In 1928, although he was already approaching his mid-thirties and well past his prime, our old pal John McGraw invited Lai to the New York Giants spring training. McGraw and Rogers Hornsby had butted heads, and the Rajah had been shipped off to the Boston Braves after the 1927 season, which opened up an infield spot McGraw hoped Lai might fill.

♦ 23 ♦

HOT CORNER IN THE JAZZ AGE

THE CAREER RECORDS OF THREE STAR third basemen from the 1920s are listed in table 23.1. One is already in the Hall of Fame, one was a candidate back in 2006 (but didn't get elected), and one is a man you just learned about in the previous chapter:

Player	G	AB	R	H	2B	3B	HR	SB	AVG	SLG
Player A	248	1044	158	310	30	4	4	38	.297	.345
Player B	804	3041	494	897	139	50	27	66	.295	.400
Player C	531	2019	334	588	66	22	10	51	.291	.361

The stats are against Negro league competition, played almost exclusively in the East. These three men not only faced the same competition; they played head to head dozens of times.

Player B is Judy Johnson, the Hall of Fame corner man for the old Hilldale and Pittsburgh Crawfords teams. Player C is Oliver "Ghost" Marcell, selected by John Henry Lloyd as the greatest third baseman in blackball history. And Player A is the man featured in the illustration at right.

You may have noticed he wasn't black. And since we're getting technical, he wasn't really *white* either. This is William Tin "Buck" Lai, and although he was raised in Hawaii, his parents were originally from mainland China.

Buck Lai spent nearly twenty years playing in outsider baseball. *Courtesy of Scott Simkus*

To make the numbers a little easier to follow, let's prorate their career figures over the course of a traditional 154-game season:

23.2

Player	G	AB	R	H	2B	3B	HR	SB	AVG	SLG
Buck Lai	154	648	98	192	19	2	2	24	.297	.345
Judy Johnson	154	583	95	172	26	10	5	13	.295	.400
Ghost Marcell	154	586	97	171	19	6	3	15	.291	.361

To be clear, Buck Lai didn't really play in the Negro leagues, he played *against* them. As one of the top semiprofessional ballplayers in New York City, Lai squared up against every great black pitcher, from Cyclone Joe Williams and Cannonball Dick Redding to Satchel Paige and Leroy Matlock, during his twenty-year career in outsider baseball.

Although we haven't adjusted for ballpark and a variety of other things, Buck Lai clearly belongs in the conversation with Johnson and Marcell. Not saying he's as good as Judy or Ghost, I'm merely suggesting his numbers are so close to theirs, and his statistical sample so large—over 1,000 at-bats—that we need to take notice. To ignore his performance against the black teams, to ignore his statistical similarity to a Hall of Famer and a Hall of Fame candidate, would be analytical bankruptcy.

Why is this such a pressing issue? Because we sort of know how good Buck Lai was: he played several years of minor league baseball in the white Eastern League, starting at third base for manager (and future Hall of Famer) Ed Walsh. And we can tell from his record that he was *not* a Hall of Fame–caliber player. Does this mean a mistake has been made in the evaluation of blackball stars Judy Johnson and Oliver Marcell? Possibly.

On the one hand, it's possible that Buck Lai might have been a much better player than his brief track record in organized baseball suggests. In an e-mail interview, historian John Holway (who interviewed nearly 100 Negro leaguers back in the 1970s) said several of the black players mentioned Buck Lai by name when remembering the top players they'd crossed paths with. The black players respected Lai.

The Eastern League was Class A ball, the equivalent of Double-A baseball today, and Buck Lai, who spent parts of four seasons there, was a league-average hitter. Career .260 mark in a place where everybody hit about .260. It wasn't that he was terrible; he batted .293 his first year (1918), then followed that up with .260 and .265. In 1921, he injured his hand, missed considerable time, and could manage only .229 in 275 at-bats. Buck left organized baseball after the season and split his time with the Brooklyn Bushwicks and South Phillies from Philadelphia, two of the premier semipro teams on the East Coast.

Buck continued to improve as a ballplayer and by the mid-1920s was the second- or third-best player on the Bushwicks, a Double-A-caliber semipro team who featured several former and future major leaguers on their roster. He was one of the top two or three hitters on the team, and in January 1928, John McGraw and the New York Giants invited Buck to spring training. Although he was almost exclusively a third baseman (I have him at third in 247 of his 248 games against black teams), McGraw said Lai was getting a shot to fill the second base vacancy left by the departure of Rogers Hornsby.

No pressure, dude. Hornsby had just batted .361 with 26 home runs and 125 RBI. Buck Lai had just turned thirty-three years old by the time he arrived at Giants camp and didn't have a snowball's chance. Well, actually, he wasn't really given much of a shot, as he didn't appear in any of the early games. It seems the Lai tryout may have been a publicity stunt, and judging by newspaper reports, Buck wasn't too thrilled about it. He wanted a legitimate shot at making a major league roster but wasn't given an opportunity.

Almost immediately, McGraw tried selling Buck to Little Rock, but Lai refused. He had a wife back in New Jersey and was finishing up some additional college work. Buck begrudgingly accepted a position with Jersey City in the International League but quit after four games and returned to the Bushwicks.

In a 1931 *Brooklyn Eagle* story, some additional light was shed on Lai's ill-fated trial with the Giants. It's implied if Lai could have made the big-league team, he would have stayed in organized baseball. Anything less would not cut it. He had just passed his bar exam and was making out well in law. He wasn't going to walk away from that profession unless it meant something really big.

In the story, Lai said he got his baseball fix with the Bushwicks, who played at home four days per week. No travel, good side money, and some of the best competition in the world.

◆ 24 ◆

THE (ALMOST) REAL ROY HOBBS

IN MARCH 1928, OTTO MILLER, a Brooklyn Robins scout, caught a train to Philadelphia where he was scheduled to have dinner with a thirty-year-old semipro outfielder named Eddie Gerner. In his briefcase, Miller, who'd caught nearly 1,000 games for Brooklyn before retiring in 1922, had a blank contract and a certified check.

Brooklyn had a miserable season in 1927, going 65–88 and finishing sixth in the National League. General manager Dave Driscoll wanted Miller to get this guy's signature on a contract before the end of spring training. They'd had some luck with late bloomers in the past, having plucked thirty-one-year-old future Hall of Famer Dazzy Vance out of the minor leagues a few years earlier.

At dinner, Eddie Gerner brought along friend Howard Lohr. The thirty-six-year-old Lohr was something of a mentor to the younger Eddie and was friends with Robins GM Driscoll, having played for him ten years earlier. Lohr had a couple cups of coffee in the major leagues, and he and Gerner had gotten to know one another while competing in the East Coast's high-stakes semipro baseball circuits. They'd played against one another and had been teammates on occasion. They were both born in Philadelphia; both lived there, worked there, raised families, and would eventually die in the city of brotherly love.

Miller had to catch a train back to Brooklyn, so he didn't waste too much time before revealing his cards. The Robins had been watching Gerner's progress the previous couple summers, he explained. They not only liked what they saw, they believed Gerner had what it took to step right in and have an immediate impact.

And yes, the scout confessed, he knew about Gerner's checkered past, and they'd do whatever needed to be done to clean the slate.

◆ ◆ ◆

Turns out, Gerner had already played in the National League eight years earlier, as a member of the world champion Cincinnati Reds. Eddie, who threw and batted left-handed, had been something of a child prodigy, signing his first professional contract in 1915, at age seventeen, with Albany of the New York State League. Although the youngest pitcher on the staff by a good five years, he led the Senators in appearances with 51 but finished with a disappointing 4–22 ledger.

The next season he returned to Albany, where he finished second on the team in wins, with 15, and appearances, with 39. The only pitcher better than him on the club was twenty-eight-year-old major league veteran Dixie Walker, who went 25–18 in the Class B association. Although Gerner should have still been in high school, people were now referring to him as a sure bet to make the major leagues. It's notable that Gerner also chipped in at the plate, batting .286 in 123 at-bats. It was a low-offense environment, and Gerner's mark was actually the second highest average on the team for anybody with more than 100 at-bats.

In 1917, Eddie moved up to Montreal in the prestigious International League. He was only nineteen years old on a team where the average age was just under thirty, but he led the starters in wins (20), innings pitched (337), and fewest walks per 9 innings (3.0) and was second in ERA (2.94). Gerner and the team's other teenage phenom, seventeen-year-old Waite Hoyt (7–17, 2.51 ERA), were thought to be on the fast track to big-league stardom.

And then America got itself knee-deep in a World War. Gerner left organized baseball in 1918, pitching for a war-related factory team.

Eddie Gerner
Outfield

Brooklyn Bushwicks
★

After a brief major league career, former pitcher Eddie Gerner became one of the top hitters in New York City's independent baseball ranks. *Courtesy of Scott Simkus*

In 1919, with everything settled overseas, Gerner found himself in a Cincinnati Reds uniform. At twenty-one years old, Eddie was a big leaguer, having apparently benefitted from his development in the shipping league. The pennant-winning Reds had a good team, and Gerner wasn't used much after his debut on May 14, appearing in only five games total. It was likely he was used for batting practice and exhibition games during the season, while "learning" by watching Reds aces Hod Eller, Dutch Ruether, and Slim Sallee. For the year, Eddie finished 1–0 with a 3.18 ERA and was voted a full World Series share by his teammates.

As had been the case since he began playing competitive baseball, Gerner had been the youngest player on the 1919 Reds, the closest teammate being a full three years older than Eddie. After a year of experience working with the veterans, manager Pat Moran expected big things from his young lefty in 1920, as Cincy got set to defend its title.

◆ ◆ ◆

Everything seemed to be going great as Gerner skyrocketed up the professional ladder, but then something very peculiar occurred during spring training in 1920: Eddie couldn't throw strikes. Here was his opportunity to earn a larger role with the club, and he could no longer throw a baseball over the damn plate. In 17 innings of work, he walked *16* batters and hit 3 others with pitched balls. By the beginning of April, his spring training earned-run average stood at 4.24, and the team decided to shut him down, give him a rest.

They weren't going to farm him out—this wasn't a death sentence with the big club—but we're not exactly sure what was going on. Gerner may have had a sore arm, or he may have had one of those Rick Ankiel deals, where he lost his nerve on the mound. But as Gerner struggled, the Reds stood behind him.

Gerner came north with the big-league team and rode the pines for a couple weeks. Then one day, near the middle of May, he didn't show up at the ballpark. He disappeared. It came out in the papers a few days later that he'd jumped his contract, signing with the outlaw Oil City, Pennsylvania, team. A couple of wealthy industrialists from Oil City and Franklin, Pennsylvania, had decided to start an independent, two-team league, throwing out wads of cash to lure a couple dozen former, and future, major leaguers.

Within a couple weeks, Gerner was not only pitching for Oil City but pitching well. Naturally, the Reds were pissed off. They had Commissioner Judge Landis put the kid on the black list. Eddie would need to return to Cincinnati to reinstate his good name, but that would never happen.

What *did* happen during the seasons of 1920 and '21 was rather interesting, as Gerner reinvented himself as a ballplayer.

◆ ◆ ◆

At the restaurant in Philly, Otto Miller, the old Brooklyn scout, handed Eddie Gerner a certified check and told him the Robins would "clear things up with the league" when he signed. In fact, Gerner's name had already been taken off the black list in 1925, but he chose to be put on the voluntarily retired list and continue playing semipro ball, rather than report to the Reds.

The check had Gerner's name on it, and the amount was $5,000. Miller excused himself from the table to give Lohr and Gerner a chance to talk things over.

Just a couple days earlier, Gerner had surely read about his teammate Buck Lai's tryout with the New York Giants. Lai and Gerner both played for the Brooklyn Bushwicks and were, in fact, the two best players on the best independent team in New York City. Lai's trial with John McGraw's team didn't end well, with Buck opting to come home to play for the Bushwicks instead of playing minor league baseball.

But Gerner's situation was different; he was being offered cash money to sign, not a half-baked tryout. It wasn't the biggest signing bonus ever, but five grand was more than most working stiffs made in a year.

Otto Miller returned from the men's room and sat down in the booth, pulling out an ink pen and the contract. Gerner thanked Miller for coming all the way to Philadelphia to meet with him, thanked him for the kind words he had shared about his baseball ability and potential as an outfielder. And then Eddie did something that shocked not only Otto Miller but his good friend Howard Lohr as well: he pushed the check back toward the Brooklyn scout and told him he'd have to think about it. He had a job, he explained, and he couldn't just walk away. Maybe, he suggested, if the terms were favorable, he could join the Robins when they came north to start the regular season. Maybe.

Miller put the check back in his briefcase, picked up his hat, and headed back to the train station, shaking his head the entire way. Eddie Gerner ultimately chose to remain with the Bushwicks and would never get another offer from a major league club. It would later be revealed that Gerner wasn't interested in quitting his day job. Between his income as a shipping clerk for a pharmaceutical company and the money earned as a highly prized semipro ballplayer in both New York and his hometown of Philadelphia, he was happy with his lot in life.

◆ ◆ ◆

After jumping his Reds contract and joining Oil City, Eddie discovered he could throw strikes once again. Oil City carried fifteen or sixteen men on their roster, and Eddie was used pretty much as he had been during his four years in professional baseball: he started every three or four days and pitched relief in between.

Near the end of his first season outside of organized baseball, Oil City lost three position players; two defected to a rival club for the promise of more cash, one man got injured. Gerner, for the first time since he was a school boy in Philadelphia, was pressed into playing a regular position. Manning right or center field, Gerner batted near the bottom of the order but surprised people with the stick. Slowly, the hits started coming. There were singles and doubles and then a home run.

By the end of the season, the guy who had spent the last five years of his life focusing on pitching was now hitting on par with teammates Manuel Cueto (the Cuban who *also* jumped the Reds after the 1919 season, after getting screwed out of his World Series share); Steve Yerkes, who had played several years of Major League Baseball; and Joe Harris, who'd batted .375 in limited time with the Cleveland Indians in 1919 before skipping out on organized ball. Harris, of course, would later re-emerge with the Pittsburgh Pirates, starting at first for their 1927 World Series team.

◆ ◆ ◆

The next season, 1921, Eddie Gerner signed with the Fleisher Yarns in his hometown of Philadelphia. They played a more challenging schedule than Oil City, booking a couple dozen dates with Hilldale, the Cuban Stars, and several of the other top-notch black outfits. Plus, they played in front of crowds that often exceeded 6,000 or 7,000 people.

Gerner continued to pitch, winning a reported 24 games by late July, but he also played outfield full time when he wasn't on the mound. Instead of batting near the bottom of the order, he moved up toward the middle. The Yarners played in a hitter-friendly park, and Gerner took advantage. In 55 games thus far uncovered, he went 75-for-185 (.405) with 14 home runs and 36 runs scored. The former big-league pitcher was now making a name for himself as a power hitter, regularly cracking balls off the wall and over it. A year or two later, the top semipro teams in New York came calling. Gerner first joined the Bay Parkways (where Hank Greenberg would later get his start in semipro ball), then jumped to Max Rosner's elite Bushwicks in Brooklyn.

When Gerner batted .405 in 1921, he struggled against the tougher black teams, managing only .256 with 1 homer in 12 games. This would change in New York. With the Bushwicks, Gerner continued to improve and was known to get into hitting duels with opposing black stars Oscar Charleston, John Henry Lloyd, and John Beckwith, often matching them hit for hit and power for power. Gerner was now the best white baseball player in New York who didn't wear a Yankees, Giants, or Robins jersey.

By the mid-1920s, what did Otto Miller and the Brooklyn Robins see when they watched Eddie Gerner? He was the best hitter on the Bushies, topping .400 with relative ease, but we can isolate his stats versus the black teams to get a more specific gauge of his true talent. Keep in mind, the Bushwicks' games were played in Dexter Park, which was a pitching haven.

Gerner's career numbers are jaw-dropping. If he was a black player, we might be throwing his name in the same bucket with all the other unknown all-time greats. As it stands, Gerner is somebody just now being rediscovered. Was he the "almost real" Roy Hobbs, the top white semipro talent in the 1920s? Could he have starred in the major leagues?

Here's how Eddie fared against the greatest black teams in the world. I'll let you decide:

24.1

Year	Team	G	AB	R	H	2B	3B	HR	SB	AVG	SLG
1918	I.C.B.U	1	4	0	0	0	0	0	0	.000	.000
1921	Fleisher Yarn/ Harrowgate	12	39	5	10	0	0	1	0	.256	.359
1922	Germantown	1	4	0	1	0	0	0	0	.250	.250
1925	Bay Ridge	2	8	1	2	1	0	0	0	.250	.375
1926	Bay Ridge	3	12	1	4	2	0	0	0	.333	.500
1927	Bushwicks	25	99	15	34	4	1	3	2	.343	.495
1928	Bushwicks	24	94	19	38	12	1	1	1	.404	.585
1929	Bushwicks	29	112	23	44	8	3	2	0	.393	.571
1930	Bushwicks	17	69	15	29	8	2	1	0	.420	.638
1931	Trenton	1	5	2	2	1	0	0	0	.400	.600
	Career vs. Negro Leagues	115	446	81	164	36	7	8	3	.368	.534

◆ 25 ◆

JIMMY CLINTON

Aᴀ𝐅ᴛᴇʀ ᴛʜʀᴇᴇ ᴄᴏɴsᴇᴄᴜᴛɪᴠᴇ ʟᴀsᴛ-ᴘʟᴀᴄᴇ ꜰɪɴɪsʜᴇs in the International League, during which the club averaged 97 losses, the Skeeters did the residents of Jersey City, New Jersey, a huge favor and closed up shop after the 1915 season. Nobody could take the pain any longer. The Skeeters had finished dead last or second to last seven out of eight years. The last time they'd finished *above* .500 was back in 1907, when they clawed and scratched their way to a meager 67–66 mark, good enough for fifth place in the eight-team Eastern League.

In their place emerged an independent professional baseball team known simply as the Jersey City Club. Apparently there wasn't enough money in owner Dave Driscoll's budget to come up with a cleverer moniker. But in lieu of a flashy nickname, Driscoll's bunch *did* offer something folks in Jersey City hadn't witnessed in quite some time: winning baseball. The team carried a small roster—roughly twelve men—but most had cups of coffee in the major leagues, and they quickly established themselves as a powerhouse in the New York/New Jersey semipro baseball scene.

The real star of this bunch was one of the few men who had *not* played Major League Baseball, a pitcher by the name of Jimmy Clinton. For two seasons, Driscoll's group rode the coattails of Clinton's pitching arm, beating numerous big-league and top-flight black baseball clubs during the summer. In September 1916, Jimmy shut out the Cincinnati Reds on 2 hits. In his next start, he lost to the St. Louis Cardinals 5–0 but struck out 8 men in the process, including Rogers Hornsby twice. At the end of the year, he held the Washington Senators to 3 runs, recording his second victory over a big-league team. At about this same time, he also added a victory over the talented Cuban Stars, striking out 7 in the process.

But it was the next year, 1917, that Jimmy Clinton and the Jersey Club had their breakout summer. The team's right-handed star led the club to wins over the New York Giants, Boston Braves, Pittsburgh Pirates, and Cincinnati Reds. He also notched another victory over the Cuban Stars. There were three losses to white major league clubs as well (the Yankees, Giants, and Senators), but this was more due to poor defensive support (13 errors in three games) than poor pitching on the part of Clinton, who went the distance in every contest.

News of the club began appearing regularly in New York City's major papers. Because of their track record, the fans of Jersey City supported the

While pitching for outsider teams, Jimmy Clinton had a winning record versus major league teams. *Courtesy of Scott Simkus*

club well during their weekend games, and owner Dave Driscoll started to think bigger. There was talk of bringing the team to Ohio, where they would compete in a national semipro championship tournament. He also mentioned a potential postseason trip to Puerto Rico, where they would make some money by spreading the game on the islands. Finally, Driscoll settled on the unthinkable—he wanted to secure financing to reenter the International League in 1918—arguably the top minor loop in the country. They'd finished the 1917 campaign with a 34–4–1 mark and were ready to test their mettle with the big boys.

◆ ◆ ◆

With the help of industrialist Harry Doherty (who ran the Doherty Silk Sox factory and ballclub), plus the financing of Jersey City businessman Joseph Moran, Driscoll was able to put together a ballclub and refurbish the home field in time to join the International League. In the starting lineup on Opening Day were three position players from the previous year's independent juggernaut: Howard Lohr, Joe Harter, and Jimmy Irving. On the mound was none other than Jimmy Clinton.

Clinton limited visiting Rochester to 7 hits, striking out 4, as Jersey City won the lid-lifter, 9–2. Center fielder Joe Harter singled and scored a run. Left fielder Howard Lohr, who had been the cleanup hitter and star of the independent J. C. Club, went 2-for-4 with a stolen base.

But the next day, things became weird. Lohr, who'd had brief trials with both the Reds and Indians, bolted the Skeeters, who had readopted the old team name, and rejoined the semipro ranks. Later on, he'd provide consultation to friend and fellow semipro legend Eddie Gerner, who turned down a generous offer from the Brooklyn Dodgers in 1928. Joe Harter, who batted .300 in the opening series, left the club two days later, following Lohr back into the outsider baseball ranks.

Jimmy Clinton stuck around for one more start, shutting out Toronto (the eventual IL champions), 4–0, on 2 hits. Jimmy struck out 5 men, walked 4, and made three clean plays on defense. After the game, with a perfect 2–0 record, a 1.00 ERA, and only 9 hits allowed in 18 innings pitched, Clinton *also* quit the team.

Fans would soon discover that Clinton, Lohr, and Harter had joined the Doherty Silk Sox, who were one of the kings of independent professional baseball during that era.

I'm reading between the lines here, but based on some preseason promises that were not kept, it appears the tenuous relationship between Doherty and Driscoll had collapsed before the first pitch of the Jersey City Skeeters' season was ever thrown. In fact, just days before Opening Day, a heinous act of vandalism destroyed much of the Jersey City Skeeters' newly refurbished ballpark.

According to the local papers, "Vandals . . . tore down picket fences, wrecked the grand stand stairs, smashed every pane of glass on the property and laid waste practically to every fixture on the grounds."

I'm not suggesting Doherty had anything whatsoever to do with this, nor does it sound like the handiwork of teenage boys looking to have some random, albeit troublesome fun. It appears vicious and premeditated.

The papers continued, listing additional damages caused at the ballyard:

At the entrance to the park the box office was wrecked. The stairs leading to the upper seats in the grand stand were hacked in different places, apparently with an ax and broken window glass and bottles were scattered about the floor of the lower parts of the main structure. A telephone booth that originally stood in the rear of the grand stand was torn from its place and hurled down the stairs. It lay, smashed to bits, at the foot of the stairs. This booth had been installed by the Telephone Company at a cost of $150. Scores of iron seats of the grand stand were wrested from their fastenings and many of the partitions separating the private boxes were torn asunder.

In the upper part of the grand stand, where Driscoll maintained a private office, the wreckers held high carnival. The doors of the office were ripped off, evidently with a crowbar, and the interior woodwork smashed in every conceivable manner. Papers that Driscoll had stored away there were torn into shreds and the skylights were broken.

A $250 mowing machine was found in the bleachers and in a condition beyond repair. Benches were ripped from the bleachers, and the fence in back knocked down. The players' benches were wrecked and the wire screening in front of the grand stand torn down. The dressing rooms at the end of the field are a complete wreck. The shower baths were destroyed and the lead pipes carted off. The lead pipe, however, was the only thing carried away, so far as Driscoll could see yesterday.

When asked if he had any suspicions of who might be behind the damage, Driscoll said, "How do you expect me to know when the police don't know?" What was most disturbing to Driscoll was how the police failed to hear any of the vandalism occurring, as they patrolled the neighborhood on foot the previous evening. It was befuddling. Although he was interviewed several times about the damage, not once did Driscoll suggest he believed kids were behind any of this.

Before the season, the Doherty Silk Sox were committed to transferring their three best players to Jersey City's new International League franchise. Otto Rettig, Franky Bruggy, and Bibbs Raymond were supposed to augment Driscoll's team. Instead, within one week of the season opener, the exact opposite occurred, with the Doherty outfit cannibalizing the Skeeters' roster, grabbing stars Lohr, Harter, and Jimmy Clinton.

Now, honestly, there isn't anything connecting the dots between the ballpark destruction and the Doherty team. But since we're merely having some fun here, trafficking in random speculation about things that occurred ninety-five years ago, I'll offer one theory before moving on.

During the winter of 1917–18, as Driscoll was hatching his plan to reenter the International League, there were numerous heated discussions at Jersey City City Council meetings about what to do with old West Side Ball Park, which was falling into a state of disrepair and happened to sit on a large parcel of valuable real estate. A city commissioner by the name of Moore had broached the subject of having the municipality purchase the land and develop it into a residential area, where "7,000 people could live, in six and eight family dwellings."

Moore brought along an army of architects, bankers, and builders to one of the meetings. The Real Estate Board of Hudson County was represented by a committee of nine men. The chamber of commerce was represented at the meeting as well, as were the building and loan guys, who had an entire corner of the room to themselves.

Although Moore said he was merely "suggesting" this idea to his fellow Jersey City commissioners (as if he had just come up with it in the shower that morning), he had all the numbers already worked out for the project, to the tune of $3 million in potential contracts for developing the neighborhood.

"I am opposed," said Commissioner Gannon, "to a municipality going into the land business. I would rather see the Government lend $1 for every dollar our banks and private investors would lend, and thus form a participating mortgage plan." About half the commissioners shared Gannon's position.

At the same meeting, Rev. William Martin of St. Matthew's Episcopal Church "took a fling" at the suggestion of building new homes on the baseball park site. He was in favor of government but pointed out that a few blocks south of the ballyard there were seventy-five vacant lots, with the streets graded and fire lines and sewers already installed.

The final speaker of the day was Myra Meade, an architect (and perhaps the only woman in the room). As she began her presentation, all hell broke loose as the first commissioner (Moore, the guy who hatched the big idea of turning the ballpark into a residential neighborhood) went out of order, explaining—loudly, I presume—how the guys "could sell their own land" if they wished and form a municipal construction company and issue stock. If he sensed his opportunity to grab some quick kickback cash slipping away, he was right.

The idea was voted down a short time after.

A month or two later, Joseph F. Moran purchased the property for $75,000 and kept the ballpark there, intact. It was a large parcel, and some of it was earmarked for building a new warehouse, which was more in keeping with the industrial nature of the area. Moran, it was later revealed, was now a partner with Driscoll in the new ballclub. This is probably why the alliance with Doherty fell apart, as it was no longer necessary.

It seems that political graft might have been behind the destruction of the ballyard just days prior to the Skeeters' opening game. Might have been, the same way bears might shit in the woods.

As for the team itself, Dave Driscoll lost his number-one starter, leadoff man, and cleanup hitter after just one week of baseball. It was a mad scramble after that, and the club never seemed to right itself, finishing with an abysmal 30–94 record, good for last place. Jersey City was right back where they started in minor league ball—the cellar. The next year, 1919, they went 56–93, seventh place in the International League.

In 1920, Driscoll put his brother-in-law, Patrick Donnelly, in charge of the Skeeters and accepted the general manager's position with the Brooklyn Dodgers. Apparently the Dodgers had been impressed with Driscoll's 86–187 (.315) ledger the previous two years. He stayed on as GM in Brooklyn until 1932.

◆ ◆ ◆

The vandalism and politics surrounding the real estate may have been outside Driscoll's control, but he certainly could have saved himself some grief over the player personnel issues in 1918 if he'd paid closer attention to the tea leaves.

Like dozens of others at the time (including Eddie Gerner), Harter, Lohr, and Clinton were baseball mercenaries. All three had outstanding full-time jobs, and although they may have had the ability to play Class A ball or in the majors, they used baseball as a means to supplement their regular income.

According to a *Variety* magazine article from December 31, 1920, Jimmy Clinton was believed to be the highest paid semipro player on the East Coast. According to the piece, Clinton was paid $75 per game to perform for the Paterson Silk Sox in 1920. He was also an outstanding basketball player in the early days of the game, earning $25 per contest during the winter. All told, in combination with his wages as a successful insurance salesman in New York City, Clinton was said to earn upward of $15,000 per year, with zero overnight travel.

Babe Ruth and Ty Cobb were earning roughly twenty grand at this time, but lesser lights, not so much. Pitcher Walt Kinney of the Philadelphia Athletics made about $4,000 (which is like $43,000 today), Lee Magee of the Cubs made $4,500, and Swede Risberg (who was about to be banned from baseball for his role in the Black Sox scandal) made only $3,250.

Fifteen thousand dollars was an impressive income. Walter Johnson made only $16,000 pitching for the Senators. Even if the *Variety* article is a gross exaggeration and Clinton only made, say, a third of the reported $15,000 figure, he was doing what he loved, when (and where) he wanted to.

In addition to playing ball in the New York City area, Joe Harter worked as a tax collector for the city of Irvington, New Jersey. Howard Lohr was an accountant for the Philadelphia Railroad. These men were educated, white-collar workers who had options other ballplayers didn't.

They were afforded the opportunity of having their cake and eating it, too.

◆ ◆ ◆

Jimmy Clinton is completely forgotten today but was a legend in New York City before 1950, the same way superstar playground basketball players became legends a couple generations later.

With the playground basketball legends of the 1960s and '70s, the narrative always centered around "how good" somebody might have been in college or the NBA if they hadn't gotten into drugs, been shot, dropped out of school, or somehow otherwise screwed up their opportunities. The stories about the days when Player X outplayed Dr. J or Pistol Pete Maravich in a YMCA gymnasium were the currency that funded their reputations.

The same stuff was true with Jimmy Clinton. Sportswriters at the time wondered what he might have accomplished in the big leagues had he had the inclination to give it a try. If he didn't have that lucrative insurance job with a good bank in New York, they wrote, who knows what he might have done? The stories of him defeating the great black teams and the New York Yankees and Pittsburgh Pirates became the currency that funded *his* reputation.

In a very specific way, Jimmy Clinton's resume is very similar to that of talented black pitchers of the same era, such as Cyclone Joe Williams, Cannonball Dick Redding, and John Donaldson. We only know of their potential through anecdotal evidence and a slowly emerging (albeit fragmentary) statistical record. And in Clinton's case, he actually pitched against Williams and Redding and beat them.

In the late 1940s, Max Rosner, longtime owner of the Brooklyn Bushwicks (the best semipro team in New York City history), named Jimmy Clinton to his all-time greatest team. Joe Press, who was involved as a player and manager in the New York baseball scene for forty years, named Clinton to *his* all-time team.

A group of experts was gathered during World War II to select the all-time greatest semipros. They limited the discussion to what a player did on local semipro ball fields, regardless of how far he advanced in organized ball later on. Again, Jimmy Clinton was crowned the king of the hill, ahead of Jimmy Ring, who pitched twelve years in the major leagues, and a number of others.

Finally, in 1959, Jimmy Clinton was elected to the semipro Hall of Fame. During a reception held at a banquet hall on Long Island, Clinton, near seventy years old at the time, received a plaque and said a few words.

Jimmy Clinton not only pitched against Cyclone Joe Williams, he beat him several times. And because Clinton also pitched against the likes of Babe Ruth, Rogers Hornsby, and dozens of other major leaguers, understanding how good he was might help calibrate our understanding of the Negro league pitchers.

◆ ◆ ◆

Using a collection of newspaper stories spanning four decades, I'll paint a word picture describing Clinton's pitching repertoire. When he was younger, he was said to possess one of the finest curveballs in his league. Later on, when he was in his athletic prime, he was known primarily for his wicked spitball. The pitch had a sharp, downward break, and Clinton frequently faked wetting the ball, so half the time his opposition didn't know what was coming. He mixed in a nasty knuckleball and was sometimes called "Crossfire" because he'd change his arm slots and come at the batter from different angles. His control, even of the wet ones and knucklers, was said to be impeccable. He was a handful on the pitching mound.

According to a 1950s newspaper article, three men who had similar stuff (meaning high-quality spitters) were Cyclone Joe Williams, Cannonball Dick Redding, and Phil Cockrell of Hilldale.

I went near cockeyed studying census records for two hours, trying to uncover when Clinton was born. My best guess (although I am not positive) is around 1889. Working backward, we can reconstruct key moments of Clinton's baseball career.

In 1959, he was elected to the semipro Hall of Fame.

In 1929, he wrapped up his pitching career at the age of about forty years old. Based on box scores, over the previous five or six seasons, he'd become increasingly *less* effective on the mound, rarely finishing his starts and sometimes getting roughed up early in ballgames.

In 1925 he had probably the last great season of his career as he hurled for the champion College Point club and beat a group of all-stars featuring Babe Ruth batting in the 3 hole.

The year 1921 marked Clinton's only full season as a member of the Brooklyn Bushwicks. He was 1–1 against Negro league teams that season.

In 1919, he pitched for Guy Empey's Treat 'Em Roughs. He went 11–6 during the summer, including a string of seven consecutive victories. For comparison's sake, former and current major leaguers Jeff Tesreau, Jesse Barnes, Pol Perritt, Carl Mays, and Rube Benton went a combined 11–8 pitching for Guy Empey's team, which faced mostly major black teams throughout the summer. Clinton was the ace among these guys.

As previously mentioned in the article, Jimmy Clinton was 2–0 with a 1.00 ERA for the Jersey City Skeeters in 1918. He quit the club after one week, joining the semipro Doherty Silk Sox.

In 1917, pitching for the independent (nontraveling) Jersey City Club, Clinton was 4–3 versus intact major league teams.

In 1916, his first year with Dave Driscoll's Jersey City team, Clinton was 2–1 versus big leaguers and 1–1 against blackball teams.

In 1914, Jimmy Clinton was 15–1 for the Poughkeepsie Honey Bugs, champions of the Class D Atlantic League. This means, in his final 18 minor league decisions, the right-handed spitballer was 17–1 (!). Sportswriters from other towns in the loop complained because Clinton only joined the team when it was his turn to pitch and spent the rest of the week at his day job with a New York bank. He was twenty-five years old and already using baseball to his advantage, not the other way around.

From 1908 to 1913, Clinton pitched for a number of semipro clubs, developing his wet one and knuckleball. He continually declined offers from minor and major league teams because . . .

In 1907 he'd had a rough experience playing for Providence in the Eastern League. He was only eighteen or nineteen years old, playing with a veteran crew led by manager (and future Hall of Famer) Hugh Duffy. Clinton was easily the youngest kid on the team, where the average age was about twenty-five. Although he impressed with his curveball, described by opponents as "one of the best in the loop," he finished with a 3–6 mark, allowing 107 hits in 102 innings pitched. An article the following season said Duffy and Clinton didn't see eye to eye and that the kid didn't get steady work from the old-timer. Duffy went so far as to put the speedy Clinton into the outfield. Clinton asked for, and was eventually given, his release. He hooked on with Allentown in the Atlantic League, where he supposedly won all his games but two.

In 1905, Clinton pitched for the Elizabeth YMCA and was said to be offered a contract by the New York Yankees. He allegedly made his professional debut with Paterson in the Hudson River League, although this isn't yet confirmed.

In 1902, there was a story about three newspaper boys who were arrested in Manhattan for pelting persons going to and from the trains, theatergoers, and others with dirty snowballs. The boys were apparently congregating near 42nd Street by Grand Central Station. A petition had been signed by several hundred businesspeople, imploring the police to deal with these rascals.

The police hid around the area and observed the boys. They watched them pelt men and women. Drivers of cabs and coaches suffered especially.

According to the story, "Women stopped to shake the water from their faces and soiled snow from their hair and clothing, while men did the same, often turning to shake their fists at the newsboys."

Three boys were arrested and spent the evening at the Children's Society rooms for the night. The ringleader was a thirteen-year-old lad who called himself "Jimmy Clinton."

Not sure if this is our guy. If so, I can't imagine it felt too good getting plugged in the face by one of his original wet ones.

◆ ◆ ◆

In the minor league games we can thus far confirm, Jimmy Clinton was 20–7 during his awkward professional career.

In exhibition games against major league clubs, Clinton was 6–5 with a 2.72 ERA. In 109 innings pitched, he allowed only 87 hits, walked 29, and struck out 56 batters. Because most of these games were played during the waning days of the dead-ball era, Clinton's 4.6 K/9 rate is high, comparable to the top strikeout men of the era. Big leaguers managed only a .225 batting average (87-for-387) versus his vast arsenal of junk.

Against Negro league teams, Jimmy was 9–5 with a 2.84 ERA. In 130 innings pitched, Negro leaguers batted .236 (114-for-483), walked 38 times, and struck out on 90 occasions. His 6.2 K/9 rate would be among the leaders in the blackball circuit.

Add all this stuff together, and Jimmy Clinton was 35–17 against meaningful competition. In half of these games, he was backed by semipro teammates whose defense may have cost him a couple additional victories. I don't think it's a stretch to suggest Clinton might have been a major league star if he'd chosen that path.

◆ 26 ◆

BIG BANG THEORY

Josh Gibson's Plaque in Cooperstown:
Considered greatest slugger in Negro baseball leagues, power-hitting catcher who hit almost 800 home runs in league and independent baseball games during his 17-year career.

Babe Ruth's Plaque in Cooperstown:
Greatest drawing card in history of baseball. Holder of many home run and other batting records. Gathered 714 home runs in addition to fifteen in World Series.

Did Negro league legend Josh Gibson really hit "almost 800" home runs during his professional career? *National Baseball Hall of Fame Library, Cooperstown, New York*

JOSH GIBSON WAS ELECTED to the Hall in 1972. No doubt he was the greatest slugger in blackball history (tops among the outsiders), but the estimate of "800 home runs" was simply a guess, based mostly, I suppose, on the profile included in Robert Peterson's watershed book, *Only the Ball Was White*, published back in 1970.

Contemporary stories regularly lauded Josh Gibson and his astonishing single-season home run totals. He was said to have clubbed 69 round-trippers one season, 75 during another. One year, according to people Peterson spoke with, Josh pounded out 89 long ones.

During his first full season with the Homestead Grays, twenty-year-old Gibson was said to have blasted more than 70 home runs with this legendary team. It's one of those stories that has been passed down for decades, becoming an important part of his legend.

The problem is, back in 2009, author Phil S. Dixon tracked down nearly *every* box score from the Homestead Grays' 1931 season and discovered it simply wasn't true. Gibson had hit "only" 40 home runs. We have credible single-season figures for a couple other summer seasons as well: Gibson hit 34 home runs in 1932, during a 135-game slate with the Pittsburgh Crawfords; and in 1941, he notched 33 (in only 94 games played) with the Veracruz Blues of the Mexican League.

◆ ◆ ◆

Babe Ruth was part of the Hall's inaugural class back in 1936. He was the most famous player in the world at that time and is still the game's most recognizable name. You can make a compelling argument, given his time and place (regardless of whether or not his league was integrated), that Ruth was the greatest player ever. I certainly believe he was.

Unlike Gibson, every home run in Ruth's official career was meticulously tracked. He did, indeed, hit 714 home runs during his career, plus another 15 during World Series play. That gives him 729. But wait, he also hit one home run in an All-Star Game and another during his brief minor league career. This gives him 731.

Josh Gibson was said to have hit nearly 800 bombs against "league and independent" competition. We have 731 home runs for Babe Ruth against mostly "league" competition. But what about the "independent" games? Like the Homestead Grays, the Yankees played a number of exhibition games (both preseason and midseason) during Ruth's career. All major league teams scheduled exhibition games on off-days at that time. Those home runs *aren't* included in Ruth's 731.

Plus, we know from Ruth's frequent barnstorming wars with Commissioner Landis that he played lots of postseason exhibition games against independent clubs. How many home runs did he hit in those games?

Luckily, we live in the golden age of baseball research, where obsessive sorts spend hours and hours poring through old papers, counting stuff up.

Back in 2007, author Bill Jenkinson published a detailed accounting of just about every single home run hit by Babe Ruth during his career, including league stuff and barnstorming games with the outsiders. This includes winter ball in Cuba, exhibition games in California, games against the black clubs—the whole enchilada.

Let's go ahead and list these figures, year by year, showing Ruth's *complete* home run record:

26.1

YEAR	HR
1914	2
1915	5
1916	4
1917	2
1918	18
1919	54
1920	76
1921	76
1922	55
1923	64
1924	75
1925	32
1926	65
1927	88
1928	81
1929	60
1930	63
1931	69
1932	47
1933	39
1934	46
1935	10
TOTAL	**1,031**

The mind-boggling figures look like something from the PED era. Ruth's single-season high was 88 during the famous 1927 campaign when the Yankees marched to a World Series sweep over the Pittsburgh Pirates. After the season, Ruth and Gehrig embarked on a cross-country tour, scrounging up a couple extra dollars. Ruth added another 19 taters to his season total during these games. For his career, Ruth hit no fewer than 1,031 home runs against "league and independent" competition. More than 70 percent of those were collected against major league teams. It's impressive.

It's difficult to work on this chapter without sounding as if I'm trying to denigrate Josh Gibson. I'm not. As of this writing, Gibson has the second highest career batting average in Negro league history (.361). He's number one in home runs per at-bats, and because he took his share of walks, he's almost certainly number one in OPS (on base plus slugging). Toss in the fact he played his entire career in some of the most difficult home-field hitting environments in professional baseball at the time (Forbes Field, Greenlee Field, and Griffith Stadium were his club's home grounds), he almost assuredly sits on top of the black-ball list in OPS+. When discussing the greatest right-handed batters of all time, it would seem foolish to not include Gibson's name in the same conversation with men such as Rogers Hornsby, Jimmie Foxx, and Frank Thomas.

And rest assured this chapter isn't intended to prop up the legacy of Babe Ruth. Lord knows he doesn't need my help. Entire forests of trees have been felled to print books focusing on George Herman Ruth's life and career. If there was *never* another book written about Babe, it wouldn't tarnish his legend one bit, and it might help save the environment.

It's not exactly fair comparing just anybody's career to that of Babe Ruth's, but because Gibson has become so inextricably linked with him (he was known as the "Black Babe Ruth" and the "Brown Bambino" throughout his career), we had to start there.

Undoubtedly, Josh Gibson is the most legendary of sluggers from the world of outsider baseball. When Ted Williams came into the American League in the late 1930s, he remembers veteran players pointing out the incredible distances where the black catcher had hit home runs in the various big-league parks. Gibson was somebody the white players knew, and discussed openly, at the time. When pressed for which black players they believed could make the grade in major league ball, Gibson and Satchel Paige were invariably the first names to come up.

But how many home runs did Josh Gibson actually hit? A large percentage of the box scores and game stories from the catcher's career are still missing, but we have enough information to make an educated guess.

We'll use three methods: the E-Z Form, the E-Z-Plus Form, and the Long Form. Should be interesting to see the different projections and how close we get to Cooperstown's claim of "almost 800."

Easiest of these is obviously the E-Z Form. Josh Gibson played seventeen seasons in black professional baseball, and we have credible season totals for three of these years. He hit about 40 home runs in 1931, his first full season in black professional baseball. He is credited with 34 in 1932, in a shorter season with the Pittsburgh Crawfords. And he knocked out 33 in 1941 while playing in Mexico. He averaged 35.6 home runs per year, according to these figures. Multiply this figure times seventeen seasons and we get 606 home runs.

The are a multitude of problems with this method. Number one, Gibson didn't play seventeen *full* seasons. He joined the Homestead Grays on July 25, 1930, then was in and out of the lineup after his young wife passed away while giving birth to their first child that same year. Because of his late signing, and the personal stuff, he should be credited with only a half season. In 1937, he bolted the Grays to play a short season in the Dominican Republic, with Satchel Paige, again missing a lot of potential action during the summer. In 1940 we have a big hot mess, as Gibson allegedly spent the spring in Puerto Rico, then jumped over to Mexico, where he appeared in only 22 games. We're really not clear at this point exactly how much baseball Gibson played that summer, but it appears to be something less than a full season.

Also, we're missing his winter league home runs from Cuba and Puerto Rico, where he mashed 33 in five different off-seasons. It's easy enough to throw those in, then adjust his total summer "seasons" down to sixteen to account for his abbreviated stints. The revised E-Z Form total is 603 career home runs. Not much of a difference from the E-Z Form.

◆ ◆ ◆

In the second method, the E-Z-Plus Form, we'll calculate Gibson's career totals based on games played, instead of seasons. As of this writing, I believe I have about 46 percent of Josh Gibson's career collected. This includes everything—Negro league contests, semipro, Latin America, exhibition games versus major and minor leaguers, and All-Star contests.

I have box scores (or documented accountings thereof) for roughly 996 of the 2,148 games I suspect Josh Gibson played during his career. Gibson is credited with 245 home runs during these games. Using some basic mathematics, we can project the Brown Bambino with having belted 532 home runs during his illustrious career, versus all levels of competition.

There are a multitude of problems with this method, as well. Most importantly, the 996 box scores distort the competition level and most likely skew the home run totals. For instance, only 177 box scores (18 percent) have been collected against white semipros. This is an issue because roughly half of his career was played against this type of competition. We'll need to adjust for this information gap to get a more credible career projection for Gibson.

And this takes us to the Long Form.

◆ ◆ ◆

Not any one season during Josh Gibson's career was the same, but they all followed similar patterns. It was common for his teams to travel south during March for their spring tour. Among other places, Gibson trained in Hot Springs, Arkansas (where John McGraw ran Chief Tokohama through his famous tryout in 1901), New Orleans, Texas, Florida, and Alabama.

After limbering up for a week or so, the team immediately jumped into exhibition games, earning gate receipts versus Negro Southern League (NSL) teams, black colleges, black semipro teams, and other major league Negro teams training in the same area. Because this was the Jim Crow South, where black and white folks weren't allowed to urinate in the same facilities, let alone play ball against one another, Gibson didn't face any white competition during these Deep South junkets.

In addition to their regular lineup, the black teams used two or three additional players during these games (mostly pitchers), but the contests were otherwise hotly contested. For the Negro Southern League clubs (considered inferior to the higher-paying, more famous northern teams), defeating a major blackball club was a big deal.

Although the games didn't count in the league standings, the won-lost figures from these spring tours *were* usually included in a club's overall season total. It was part of their identity. The Gibson home run totals for 1931 and '32, for instance, include games played during the spring. Josh missed one entire spring tour (1932), due to appendicitis. In the Long Form, we'll account for this missing tour, then project his totals based on an average of about 20 spring training games per season, using his actual recorded figures against NSL teams, black colleges, and the other major league blackball clubs.

During their return home, Josh Gibson's teams often played white minor league clubs in 10 or 12 late-spring, preseason tune-ups. Most of these games were against Class D outfits from the Middle Atlantic League, whose franchises were all within driving distance of Pittsburgh. I have box scores for 15 of these games, which accounts for perhaps a third of all the minor league exhibitions Gibson appeared in. In these 15 games, Josh Gibson was 27-for-63 (.429) with six doubles, four triples, and only one home run. In the Long Form, we'll prorate the catcher's numbers based on how many minor league box scores I believe are missing.

The regular season included a slate of roughly 50 to 75 scheduled games against Negro National League (NNL) opponents. The NNL of the 1930s and '40s was based in the East, and newspaper coverage wasn't as thorough as it had been in the 1920s. We know, for instance, that roughly 40 percent of Gibson's box scores are missing and may have never been printed anywhere. But we *do* have the boxes for the other 60 percent, and using these we can calculate his home run figures per game and at-bat, and we can figure out how often Josh Gibson rested during the NNL season.

It's important to understand how often he rested so you don't overestimate how many home runs he may have hit in those missing ballgames. Turns out, Gibson was extremely durable. Although he was primarily a catcher, he appeared in nearly 90 percent of his team's league games. Over the course of a 154-game season, he would have played in 135 to 137 games, which is a lot for a catcher. Using all this information, I figure Gibson hit close to 200 home runs in official league games, during what were extremely short seasons compared to the white major leagues.

During the summer, there were also interleague games scheduled with major black teams from the West, such as the Kansas City Monarchs and Chicago American Giants. Most historians lump these in with his career totals, and we'll go ahead and do the same, accounting for the missing box scores.

As previously mentioned, a *huge* part of Gibson's regular season was played against white semipro teams. I figure this was almost 50 percent of his career, meaning he likely appeared in more than 1,000 of these contests in small towns and big cities across the country. Why so many games against the semipros? Money. The black versus white games were an irresistible event and were typically more lucrative than the official Negro league bookings. I've collected 177 of these games involving Josh's teams, of which Gibson appeared in 153. If you're curious, his numbers looked like this:

26.2

Josh Gibson vs.	AVG	SLG	G	AB	R	H	2B	3B	HR
Semipro teams	.423	.798	153	624	179	264	61	19	45

Semipro was the heart of outsider baseball, and I suppose it is widely misunderstood by fans today because it's a category that simply no longer exists. There are no longer teams of grown men making part-time money playing baseball at night and on weekends, in front of paying audiences of one thousand, or five thousand, or ten thousand people. But back then, there were.

There were always a handful of patsies on the summer docket, but by and large, the semipro competition was not chopped liver. The evidence suggests the best of these clubs were actually *better* than lower-level minor league teams, and by a wide margin. Gibson and crew had a much more difficult time playing against the semipro Brooklyn Bushwicks, for instance, than they did against the Middle Atlantic League teams, who were part of organized baseball. Of the pitchers I can positively identify, at least 20 percent of the men Gibson faced in those 153 semipro games had major league or minor league pitching experience.

No, Gibson's .423 batting average isn't against major league or even Triple-A-level competition, but it isn't meaningless, either. We'll use the known semipro figures to flesh out this missing part of Josh's career. I have him with roughly 300 homers against semipro teams during his seventeen seasons.

The final step in the Long Form is to add in the all-star games (0 home runs in 12 games but a .459 batting average versus the best black pitchers in the world), postseason contests, and barnstorming tours with major league and minor league clubs (he batted over .400 against both). Adding *all* of this material together—accounting for missed games, illness, Latin American junkets, lost box scores, official league contests, spring tours, playoff games, barnstorming tours, square dancing events, bobbing for apples, quilting bees, and everything else under the sun—I figure Josh Gibson appeared in roughly 2,148 games from 1930 through 1946. During this span, I estimate he clubbed no fewer than 639 home runs. I happen to think this is a pretty good guess.

It seems the Cooperstown plaques have overestimated Josh Gibson's career home run totals by 20 to 30 percent, and they've *underestimated* Babe Ruth's by roughly the same percentage.

But hey, that's baseball, right?

◆ 27 ◆

ARMAGEDDON ALL-STARS

D URING THE 1930S, news reports drifted northward every March about the mysterious band of baseball gypsies who dared challenge the toughest of major league teams. Sponsored by a religious sect in Michigan, with a roster comprised of ballplayers from the sect, this group of vagabond diamond drifters held their own against Bill Terry, Mel Ott, and the New York Giants; battled valiantly versus Babe Ruth, Lou Gehrig, and the mighty Bronx Bombers; and easily disposed of the lowly St. Louis Browns, 1–0.

According to newspaper stories, members of this ballclub, called the House of David, had to abide by certain rules. They were nonsmoking, chaste vegetarians who refused to shave or cut their hair. In deference to their religious beliefs (and despite their obvious on-field baseball wizardry), they refused to pursue professional careers in the secular world of organized baseball. The House of David played the major leaguers in the spring, then semi-pro and minor league teams in the summer, sometimes logging more than 200 games and 20,000 travel miles annually, because they loved Jesus and they loved baseball, though not necessarily in that order.

Although a mere historical baseball footnote today, the House of David was the most famous independent professional team in the 1920s and '30s and the source of a couple genuine mysteries: Were they *really* good enough to compete with major leaguers? And how did they become so popular?

To understand the House of David baseball team, one needs to start at the beginning, with the man who founded the religious commune. And to understand this man, one needs to make peace with a series of scandalous events that propelled the sect to national prominence in the 1920s.

The House of David's sketchy past has been almost completely forgotten now, but the details surrounding the group's rise to fame may ring uncomfortably familiar today.

Before World War I, all systems were go at America's fastest-growing doomsday commune, the Israelite House of David, based in the quaint fruit-marketing community of Benton Harbor, Michigan, nestled along the southeastern shores of Lake Michigan. Founded in 1902 by a Kentucky-born broom maker and former traveling salesman by the name of Benjamin Purnell (along with his wife, Mary Purnell), the sect grew to include more than one thousand two hundred followers at its peak, most of whom lived and worked on the colony's one hundred and thirty-acre property. The centerpiece was Purnell's mansion, called Shiloh, which remains to this day. The male population's most distinguishing features were their lengthy hairstyles and Rumpelstiltskin beards.

King Benjamin Purnell, a gregarious 240-pound vegetarian, claimed to be the seventh messenger of Christ and believed it was his responsibility to gather the twelve lost tribes of Israel in anticipation of the millennium. Gathering the tribes evidently entailed building a business empire worth over $10 million at its peak, approximately $115 million today. The House of David had its fingers (or better yet, its *beards*) in a number of operations, including a greenhouse, a dairy, a print shop, therapeutic springs, several farms, a bakery, a vegetarian restaurant, several Oldsmobile dealerships, and multiple hotels. They operated the Eden Springs Amusement Park, which was a major tourist attraction in southwestern Michigan, and sponsored several House of David musical acts, including a band billed as "The Long-Haired Demons of Jazz," which played the vaudeville circuit and regularly appeared on radio programs.

They even marketed House of David bottled water in nearby Chicago. This was a clever little business concept whereby the colony sold Lake Michigan water to a large city of people who lived along the shores of . . . Lake Michigan.

One story, which may or may not be apocryphal, says that when a Benton Harbor street car company refused to hire two colony members because of their unfashionable hairstyles and facial hair, Purnell stormed over on his white horse and purchased the entire operation, installing bewhiskered minions in leadership positions. True or not, the story speaks to the locals' collective memory of Purnell as a personally aggressive, powerful figure not to be trifled with.

Around 1913, under the direction of King Ben, the colony built a full-size baseball field on its property. At first it was used as a recreational outlet for colony members, then later rented out for ballgames between top-notch, noncolony semipro teams in the area. Eventually, the House of David fielded its own ballclub, which challenged local teams the first few years, perfecting its game before venturing off the compound and on the road to serve as another promotional (and profit-generating) vehicle for the colony.

By the early 1920s, the House had developed several talented ballplayers and instituted a popular pepper ball routine, a baseball precursor to the Harlem Globetrotters' Sweet Georgia Brown basketball act decades later. During the fifth inning of each game, several House players formed a semicircle in the middle of the diamond and whipped up a jaw-dropping baseball juggling routine. The House of Beards was not the first to blend sport with a trademark on-field entertainment act, but they were among the most successful.

As far as local amateur teams went, the House was fairly competitive; and with the value-added appeal of the exceptional pepper ball schtick and those mesmerizing beards, they gained notoriety. Venturing farther away from the familiarity of southwestern Michigan to the larger towns and cities of the Midwest, the House encountered tougher competition. Losing teams (beards and juggling baseball acts notwithstanding) didn't draw too well on the road, and the House of David had no interest in propping up unsuccessful businesses.

Like the Bloomer Girls—the supposedly all-female team that often used cross-dressing men in its lineups—the House had no choice but to recruit

At the height of its popularity, the House of David team attracted large crowds. This photograph shows a game versus blackball's Chicago Giants, played at the HOD compound in Benton Harbor, Michigan. *National Baseball Hall of Fame Library, Cooperstown, New York*

ringers, ballplayers from outside the colony—talented infidels, if you will, embedded at key positions like pitcher and shortstop. By the mid-1920s, the majority of their starting lineup featured noncolony members, paid to grow beards (or wear false ones), play ball, and put on a good show.

According to court records, as of 1928 the team had generated "over $125,000" in profit during team manager Francis Thorpe's fourteen years at the helm—equivalent to about $1.5 million today. Not bad for a still pretty obscure traveling baseball team, and a substantial fraction of the House of David's overall earnings.

Just as the House of David team was poised to establish a genuine national presence, something occurred that threatened to stop it dead in its tracks. Not just the baseball team, mind you, but the greenhouse, dairy, therapeutic springs, farms, bakery, restaurant, car dealerships, bottled water plant, Eden Springs Amusement Park—all were put in serious jeopardy.

Turns out King Benjamin Purnell got caught with his pants down.

Literally.

As early as 1910, before the baseball team existed, rumors and accusations circulated about unsavory activities on the House of David compound. Lurid stories popped up in newspapers, not just in Michigan but all over the country, about Purnell's alleged sexual proclivities. One of the requirements of membership in the House of David was a vow of celibacy; yet every two or three years Michigan law enforcement showed up, sniffing around the compound, following up on various leads, few of which panned out.

King Benjamin always shrugged off these accusations, maintaining that he was simply "a man of God." After sixteen years, prosecutors were at long last able to substantiate their charges that this man of God used his power to indulge a predatory appetite for teenage girls. Purnell was arrested on November 17, 1926, after forty-two months on the run, a big chunk of which, it was suspected, he had spent hiding at secret locations in Canada. Suffering from ill health, he had returned to Benton Harbor frail and gray—and was promptly turned in by Bessie Woodworth (a former ward of Purnell) and her husband, Emerald, who accompanied twenty Michigan policemen as they broke into the House of David compound. There had been a $4,000 bounty offered for information leading to the capture of Purnell.

The next day, Purnell posted $50,000 bail and returned to the compound; it wouldn't be until the following spring that his case would actually go to trial.

From the time the trial began in mid-May to the issuance of the judge's decree six months later, the legal fortunes of the House of David and the Purnells received almost daily coverage in newspapers across the country. This was Enron meets David Koresh. This was Jonestown, Heaven's Gate, and baseball—*combined*—and people just couldn't get enough of it. The trial finally achieved what all the bearded baseball teams and bottled water and dairy farms couldn't: it put the House of David colony on the national map for good.

The testimony was considered shocking at the time. The central allegation was that King Ben had for many years demanded sexual access to the young women of the colony, excusing the practice as a "purification ritual." When the police began asking questions, the women were quickly married off in group ceremonies to teenage boys from the colony in order to shield them from interrogation by the authorities. Oftentimes the kids didn't even know one another before the matrimonial ceremony.

According to witness Elizabeth Smith Wheeler, who had been both a resident of Shiloh while Ben was there and a participant in one of the group wedding ceremonies, Purnell lived in a two-room apartment on the second floor of the mansion and kept as many as thirty or forty girls quartered in the building at any given time.

Elizabeth Wheeler moved to the colony with her family at the age of thirteen. They were originally from Birmingham, Alabama, and had learned that King Ben and Mary believed themselves to be "the second coming of man" and that Benjamin was the "younger brother of Jesus Christ" and could do no wrong. It was further claimed that it was King Ben's duty to lift the veil of sin, that he could "cleanse the blood of others." If you belonged to his cult, there'd be a special place in heaven waiting for you.

Elizabeth Wheeler's family was one of hundreds who decided to pack up their junk, move to Michigan, and give their entire life savings to the man with the long beard. Wheeler was eventually separated from her family and moved inside Purnell's Shiloh. After she turned sixteen, King Ben began "visiting" her room late at night. According to courtroom testimony, he "visited" Wheeler on a regular basis over a period of nearly two years, and she was warned never to confide these circumstances to anybody (especially to her family or Mary Purnell), her silence secured by the knowledge that "terrible things would occur" to those she loved most if she betrayed her vow of silence.

What kinds of terrible things? There were reports of nearly two dozen people who had disappeared while living on the compound in Benton Harbor. One eyewitness claimed to have seen Purnell push a loaded revolver in the face of his own brother-in-law during an altercation inside the compound's mansion. William E. Smith, father of one of the young women involved in the scandal, admitted under oath that he was "practically asked once to commit murder." And police discovered at least one dead body (a young girl) in a shallow grave on the premises.

Judgment day came in November 1927. Newspaper accounts of the trial leading up to this day read back like some theatre of the absurd. It had the Scopes monkey trial atmosphere, with the proceedings often interrupted by laughter from the gallery, as the case, its entertaining characters, and bizarre testimony attracted large crowds. A gaggle of unfashionably bearded men in suits bounced around spewing scripture, or nonsense that was supposed to sound like scripture. There was Benjamin Purnell himself, mortally ill with tuberculosis, being wheeled in and out of the courtroom all summer. He was long, gaunt, all sunken eyes and scraggly gray beard: weak and dying but defiant to the very end.

The presiding judge, the honorable Louis H. Fead, didn't find the proceedings humorous in the least bit and showed little mercy at the end of the road. Despite the best efforts of the defense team, headed by one H. T. Dewhirst (the House of David's chief lawyer; more on him in a moment), Purnell was found guilty of fraud. In December 1927, Judge Fead signed a decree ending the temporal rule and authority of Benjamin and Mary Purnell over the House of David and its business affairs, including the baseball team. The King was forbidden from associating at any time (and in any way) with any woman or girl from the House of David who was less than twenty-five years old. And Benjamin and Mary were both given thirty days to evacuate the compound for good.

The state had also sued to dissolve the House of David itself, but Fead put this on hold while a local bank conducted a complete audit of the operation. There were three key objectives: uncover all of the revenue streams and figure out exactly how much money this place was generating; resolve the multitude of class action lawsuits pending against the House of David; and refund monies to family members of the colony who had donated their life savings to join the cult but who now wished to leave the institution.

After the meat had been stripped off the bones, the bank and state of Michigan would return whatever was left of the House of David to the remaining members.

Seems pretty simple, but it wasn't. Exactly two weeks after Judge Fead's decree, King Benjamin F. Purnell, self-proclaimed brother of Jesus Christ, dropped dead. It was eerily reminiscent of William Jennings Bryan's death just five days after his humiliation at the Scopes trial two years earlier. Believers put Purnell in a box and waited patiently for three days. Although he claimed that he'd live forever, he never came back. Sometimes it's hard to live up to the pressure of your big brother's legacy.

The death of King Ben, coupled with the legal appeal process, changed the complexion of what had been a two-decade-long odyssey to bring down the House of David. With the sexual predator out of the way, the state lost a little bit of its zeal, and this is where H. T. Dewhirst comes in.

Dewhirst was a longtime member of the House of David colony and confidant of King Ben. He had been a circuit court judge in his native California before packing up and joining the House of David, where he quickly gained a seat on the board of directors and became Purnell's right-hand man. He served the House of David as the cult's corporate attorney, handling incorporations, contracts, and acquisitions and protecting the House against legal actions and minimizing its liabilities.

When Ben was finally captured and brought to trial, Judge Dewhirst seemed the natural choice to represent him in the courtroom proceedings. Dewhirst understood everything happening inside the walls of the Benton Harbor compound and, given his long personal relationship with Ben, presumably had the man's best interests at heart. And anyway, who wouldn't want to represent the brother of Jesus Christ in a trial?

(A quick aside: serving on the House of David board alongside Judge Dewhirst and King Benjamin was the previously mentioned Francis Thorpe. Not only had Thorpe helped found the original House of David baseball team and managed it for years, he was present at many of the group wedding ceremonies, standing by with a pocket watch to assure the proceedings began precisely at the stroke of midnight.)

As it happens, H. T. Dewhirst had two sons (Bob and Tom) who were both pretty good baseball players. They were both in their late teens when the trial took place and had been honing their baseball skills with the House of David youth teams for a number of summers. The younger brother, Tom, wound up as the player-manager of the House's Central States traveling team in the 1930s and became known as the "Bearded Babe Ruth."

The House eventually won an appeal against the state's dissolution suit, whereupon open warfare broke out between Dewhirst and Mary Purnell. It was a gruesome mismatch, turning friends into foes. In the end, Dewhirst shrewdly grabbed control of about 90 percent of the cult's businesses, property, and cash, leaving the widow Purnell with only a decimated remnant.

From what had reportedly been a $10 million empire, Mary eventually settled for the paltry sum of $60,000 cash, a small farm, and a couple of small businesses, including an unfinished hotel in downtown Benton Harbor. Dewhirst got the amusement park, bowling alley, cabins, mansion, hotels, logging operation, boats, farms, bottled water business, therapeutic springs, baseball field, ballclubs, the Long-Haired Demons of Jazz and other bands, along with the publishing company, bakery, vegetarian restaurant, and undisclosed cash assets. This was a worse deal than Lou Brock for Ernie Broglio.

As for King Benjamin himself, he never left the original facility, as specified in Judge Fead's decree. To this very day, his mummified body lies in state at Shiloh, "until the day when he shall arise from the dead and lead his followers into the promised land."

Don't hold your breath.

Mary Purnell licked her wounds and shuffled across the street to set up her own religious operation, the City of David. Several of the original baseball players, including Francis Thorpe, Doc Talley, John Tucker, and Andy Anderson—the guys who perfected the pepper ball routine—went with Mary and founded a new traveling ballclub. Not to be outdone, Dewhirst put his boys in charge of the original House of David club and franchised out another couple of versions to two promoters named Ray Doan and Louis Murphy. This is why, throughout the 1930s, there were often four or five legitimate House of David baseball teams traveling around the country, in addition to numerous imitators. The promoter Syd Pollock, who would later run the black Indianapolis Clowns, had his Cuban Stars team grow beards in 1932 and play their spring training games as the Cuban House of David—but they had to shave the beards off in May for the beginning of the East-West League (Negro league) season.

Ray Doan turned out to be something of an outsider equivalent to Bill Veeck. He took the notoriety of the House of David name and ran with it. He built up a network of quality opponents and developed a sophisticated marketing machine that helped attract large crowds on a consistent basis. He hired some big names, most notably 300-game winner Pete Alexander, who became a House of David player-manager in the early 1930s, along with fellow Hall of Famer Chief Bender and female stars Babe Didrikson and Jackie Mitchell. He paired his team with the Kansas City Monarchs (one of the most famous black professional teams of the period) for long barnstorming tours in the West. And when the beards were not enough, Doan was the man who put baseball players—even the mighty, dignified Monarchs—on the backs of donkeys and made them play one or two innings while riding atop the beasts.

Not to be outdone, Louis Murphy arranged for his version of the House of David franchise to become an adjunct member of organized baseball, honoring the reserve clause and scheduling dozens of spring training exhibition games against major league (and minor league) teams during the 1930s. Murphy, who had originally started out as a promoter and booking agent for the

House, was eventually sued by Dewhirst in 1935 when it was alleged he was operating the East Coast ballclub without the written permission and consent of the Benton Harbor commune.

The very next year, the other promoter Ray Doan was sued by Dewhirst for failure to pay royalties earned from his touring band of Davidian ballplayers. Doan then countersued the religious commune for $50,000 in damages, claiming the Benton Harbor headquarters had damaged the value of the brand "by putting five House of David teams and two colored versions on the road."

Business gets ugly sometimes.

Before the relationship between the franchise holders and the colony leadership became strained, the 1930s House of David teams' main selling point was their claim to have defeated "75% of their opponents, plus several Big League teams to boot." In truth, this was the most important selling point. You could have your big beard and juggling balls, but if you couldn't furnish a team capable of putting a consistent beat-down on the local sandlotters, you weren't going to have a profitable independent baseball team for long. There were literally dozens of teams who attempted to hit the road but were later forced to stagger home midstream, penniless and hungry, when they failed to live up to their own hype. For what it's worth, 75 percent seems to have been the magic number for successful barnstorming teams. All the biggest baseball gate attractions (white, black, male or female) claimed to have won more than 75 percent of their scheduled games. After examining the box scores, it turns out some of these teams (the really good ones, such as the Negro League's Homestead Grays) really did hover around, or above, this benchmark of success.

So what about the House of David? Were they really that good? We've tracked down the won/lost records reported in the press for four of their seasons, showing an interesting progression:

27.1

House of David	W	L	T	PCT.
1917	17	13	0	.567
1928	110	56	6	.663
1935	146	50	0	.745
1936	160	52	0	.755

In 1917, the team was just getting started with a thirty-game schedule, most of their competition coming from nearby Chicago and southwestern Michigan. By 1928, they were a well-known national commodity, traveling around the country. By the mid-1930s, they had reached their apex, appearing in spring training exhibitions versus big-league clubs in March, then winning prestigious semiprofessional tournaments during the summer. When you mash these numbers together, you come up with a winning percentage of .717 over the course of 600-plus games. Not bad, really—and pretty close to the 75 percent they regularly touted.

But now a word about published won/lost records, as opposed to records researchers build up game by game: many teams fudged their totals for marketing purposes. No doubt a traveling team who wins 75 to 80 percent of their contests is a much sexier gate attraction than a group boasting, say, a .560 or .610 winning percentage. Even the famous Negro league teams, who had no real need to tinker with their impressive track record, were known to beef up their victory totals a bit in PR pieces during the late 1930s, when they were the top independent baseball attractions in the East. So in baseball research we tend to grant more credibility to won/lost records compiled from individual game reports and box scores.

We've uncovered almost 20 percent of the David's box scores from 1928, 1935, and 1936, 106 games over three seasons in which they have a reported aggregate winning percentage of .725. The years from 1928 to 1936 represent the very height of the Bearded Ones' excellence and popularity. It was during this span that they took the $6,400 purse at the 1934 *Denver Post* Tournament, hiring Satchel Paige to win the semifinal against Chet Brewer and the Kansas City Monarchs, 2–1. And yes, they defeated three major league teams in exhibition games, including both St. Louis clubs and the Philadelphia Athletics— but something strange jumps out when we do the math. The team's record for these 106 games with box scores adds up to an underwhelming 54–52, or .509. I can't confirm this with certainty at this point, but it appears the House of David may have been falsifying their "official" won-lost records in their contemporary press releases.

So let's widen our scope a bit. I'll spare you the method behind the madness, but I guesstimate that the official House of David teams played around 6,500 games from 1920 to 1950. Our goal was to locate 10 percent of their games, or 650, over this period, to see if we could learn something from this sample. The games needed to meet three criteria. First, they had to feature legitimate Benton Harbor House of David teams, either from the original colony, Mary's City of David, or Louis Murphy's outfit. Second, we needed to be able to classify the competition (i.e., categorize their opponents as either semipro, minor league, major league, Negro league, or college). And third, the boxes and line scores needed to be from games played from 1920 to 1950.

◆ ◆ ◆

In terms of quality, when one examines the pedigree of the ballplayers and their achievements on the diamond, it's really difficult to differentiate between the various factions. On balance, they all possessed a similar ability and talent level.

In attempting to gather 10 percent of the box scores, we actually managed to overshoot our goal, coming up with 766 games. Here's the quick and dirty:

27.2

House of David	W	L	T	PCT.
1920–1950	323	431	12	.428

So in those 766 games, the House of David's winning percentage plummets to .428, which is bad. There's a sabermetric term for this: *oops*. Instead of closing the gap from our three-season sample, we're actually creeping further away from the alleged 75 percent winning percentage.

Let's categorize this stuff by competition level:

27.3

House of David vs. Various Levels	W	L	T	PCT.
Major League	3	33	0	.083
Negro League	10	40	2	.200
Minor League (White)	16	40	0	.286
Minor League (Black)	22	29	2	.431
Semipro	270	286	8	.486
College	2	3	0	.400

A couple of quick takeaways from the chart. First of all, yes, they defeated a few major league teams. Three times. They also *lost* to the big leaguers. In fact, they lost more than 80 percent of the time. Now, we haven't uncovered *all* their games against the big boys, but in the three dozen we have to work with thus far, they went 3–33. That's a pretty rough 36-game stretch, man.

Not only did they lose, they often lost badly. The Phillies slugged them 17–2, the St. Louis Browns beat them 13–1, the Senators smoked 'em 18–8, and the Brooklyn Dodgers squeaked out a 19–3 victory in 1932. The major league players may or may not have appreciated the spectacle of these bizarre spring training exhibitions, but they clearly showed very little mercy once the first pitch was thrown.

Oh, and the other thing one notices in table 27.3 is that the House of David didn't have a winning record versus *any* level of competition. Makes you scratch your head a bit.

Listed in table 27.4 are the run-scoring statistics for the Beardos, organized by competition level:

27.4

House of David	RF	RA	RPG
Major League	2.86	8.25	11.11
Negro League	3.77	6.75	10.52
Minor League (White)	4.30	6.52	10.82
Minor League (Black)	5.19	5.47	10.66
Semipro	5.17	5.02	10.19
College	7.00	6.20	13.20

Clearly, the House of David teams weren't as good as advertised. Some might even consider them as big a fraud as King Ben had been.

What is perhaps just as interesting (and valuable) is that we've detected some meaningful patterns in what before seemed to be an unstructured mess of information. There are no conclusive answers here, and many qualifiers should be slapped on this study (sample size, variable teams and quality over thirty years, and so on), but consider that we have managed to compare major league teams, Negro league teams, and minor league teams by virtue of their record against a common opponent. Like in the Rosetta Stone chapter, these records can be recovered, and they can tell us things, or begin telling us things, about the hidden secrets of baseball history.

♦ 28 ♦

THE OTHER JACKIE

On April 2, 1931, a teenage girl named Jackie Mitchell made national headlines by striking out Babe Ruth and Lou Gehrig in a spring training exhibition game. The Chattanooga Lookouts of the Class A Southern Association had signed the seventeen-year-old five days earlier, and more than four thousand people witnessed her remarkable debut against the New York Yankees.

A couple days later, Judge Landis voided her contract, in what some folks have called an egregious example of misogyny. There are those who believe Jackie Mitchell was a legitimate pitching prospect whose career was snubbed out in the same discriminatory manner as that of the hundreds of African American men who were denied an opportunity to play Major League Baseball because of the color of their skin.

These people are nuts.

Mitchell's story has inspired a number of books, many built around the theme of gender equality and redemption. Like a lot of old-time baseball tales, hers is a series of random puzzle pieces, all shaped exactly alike. One can be lazy—or worse, have an agenda—and haphazardly graft together several of these pieces, creating a grossly distorted, fun-house mirror portrait of the facts.

I believe this is sort of what has happened with Mitchell's story. It has metastasized over the decades. Let's review the popular version of the story, in bullet point form:

♦ When she was a young girl, her family lived next door to Dazzy Vance, who was pitching for the Memphis Chicks at the time. Young Jackie learned how to pitch from Dazzy.

◆ She struck out "9 sandlotters" in an exhibition game when she was fifteen or sixteen years old, catching the attention of her male competitors.

◆ Joe Engel, general manager of the Chattanooga Lookouts of the Southern Association, heard about this young phenom, signing her in 1931.

◆ In her professional debut, against the visiting New York Yankees, Mitchell came out of the bullpen and baffled Babe Ruth and Lou Gehrig with her curveball, striking out both men.

◆ Judge Landis voided her contract soon after the incredible debut, forcing her to play professionally on the barnstorming circuit with a variety of teams.

◆ Mitchell retired from baseball after the 1937 season, because she was "frustrated with the demeaning conditions" associated with playing

Jackie Mitchell (left) meets Babe Ruth (center) and Lou Gehrig (right), just prior to striking them out.
National Baseball Hall of Fame Library, Cooperstown, New York

ball on the fringe. On more than one occasion, she was required "to pitch while riding a donkey."

◆ In later years, she came to be viewed as a heroine in the decades-long struggle for women's rights. It has even been suggested Jackie Mitchell was like the Jackie Robinson of women's athletics.

Now we'll go through the annotated version of Mitchell's career, with my commentary after each bullet point:

◆ As a young girl, her family lived next door to Dazzy Vance, who was pitching for the Memphis Chicks at the time. Young Jackie learned how to pitch from Dazzy.

There is probably some truth to this. Vance last pitched for Memphis in 1920, and Jackie would have been young, maybe six or seven years old, but I'm sure she could have learned how to grip a curveball from the guy. Why not? You have to learn it from somebody, right? And the connection to Dazzy became a huge part of her promotional resume, used extensively throughout her barnstorming career, as part of the newspaper promotional pieces. The two were photographed with one another on several occasions.

◆ She struck out "9 sandlotters" in an exhibition game when she was fifteen or sixteen years old, catching the attention of her male competitors.

I don't know anything about this specific game (I can't find the puzzle pieces), but I'll take it at face value. I'm sure it's true. As a term, *sandlotter* usually referred to teenagers back then, whereas *semipro* usually referred to adults. So, at fifteen or sixteen, we're talking about the equivalent of our modern youth league's Babe Ruth, Pony, or Colt ball. And having coached some of this stuff over the years, I estimate the league average at this level of baseball is more than one strikeout per inning. That is, the *average* of all the pitchers' games combined equals more than one K per IP. Go any younger, and the typical game would have *two* strikeouts per inning. Striking out guys is simply how a large percentage of the outs are recorded at the teenage level. Even in American Legion ball, where the players are maybe sixteen to eighteen years old, the typical pitcher punches out one per inning. I believe Jackie had some genuine ability, and it wouldn't surprise me one bit if she was a "league average" strikeout ace at the American Legion level.

♦ Joe Engel, general manager of the Chattanooga Lookouts of the Southern Association, heard about this young phenom and signed her to a professional contract during the spring of 1931.

In a 1940 *Time* magazine article, they called Joe Engel the "Barnum of Baseball," as in Barnum & Bailey's Circus. Engel was one of those great old-time baseball lifers but is largely forgotten by today's fans. He pitched with the Washington Senators during the Walter Johnson era, then he became a terrific scout for the team after his playing career was finished. Later on, he'd move to Tennessee, working as the general manager of the Chattanooga Lookouts in the Southern Association. At Chattanooga, he gained a national reputation, based on a series of outlandish promotions designed to drum up attendance. On one Opening Day, he had the team enter the playing field riding atop elephants. One time he traded a shortstop for a turkey. He raffled off houses and automobiles, and one time . . . he had a girl pitch in a real live game versus Babe Ruth and the New York Yankees.

♦ In her professional debut, against the visiting New York Yankees, Miss Mitchell came out of the bullpen and baffled Babe Ruth and Lou Gehrig with her curveball, striking out both men.

In the days leading up to her appearance versus the Yankees, the story went across the national newspaper wires. Jackie Mitchell, left-handed teenager, would start against the New York Yankees. In fact, some stories promised she'd get to pitch against Babe Ruth. This had all been predetermined.

Well, she didn't start the game. Instead, Engel made his manager shrewdly wait until two men had batted in the first inning before summoning Mitchell in from the bullpen to face the Babe. This was a keenly orchestrated ruse: 5'8" teenager Mitchell came in and whiffed Ruth. The Babe, who was no stranger to oddball promotions or theatrics, feigned his indignation, threw his bat, and to the delight of the crowd, got into a little argument with the umpire before returning to the bench.

The next batter was Lou Gehrig. Gehrig was a gentleman, of course, but about as boring as a piece of white toast, so he dutifully took three strikes, then returned to the dugout without much fanfare. Lou was followed by Tony Lazzeri, who bunted the first pitch foul, before taking four straight balls for a walk. Mitchell was immediately lifted for a new pitcher and never appeared in another game for the Lookouts.

A week or so later, the United Press ran a story where several anonymous players took Mitchell's skills to task, saying she didn't have the stuff to pitch professional baseball. When asked directly about the incident, Babe Ruth went on the record with this:

> Don't you say anything to hurt this little girl! She's all right. I got perhaps 50 fan letters asking me if I was "going to let her strike me out." Four boy scouts personally asked me the same question at Chattanooga.

> Reprinted from the *Sun* (Wilmington, Delaware). Article by Foster Eaton (United Press). When asked specifically about his angry outburst with the umpire after striking out, Ruth just smiled and walked away from the reporter.

◆ Judge Landis voided her contract soon after the incredible debut, forcing her to play professionally on the barnstorming circuit, with a variety of teams.

The intimation by some historians regarding the Landis ban has been, "They needed to keep her out, or she was going to rock the gender apple cart, embarrassing some of the game's biggest male stars," and that the contract negation was some sort of sexist discrimination. I think Landis may have even said something to the effect that women "weren't physically equipped to play professional baseball" on a daily basis. I know several players echoed those specific sentiments anonymously in articles published at the time.

My own personal take is Landis voided the contract to stop Joe Engel, not Jackie Mitchell. Don't get me wrong—Landis may have been a sexist pig, but I don't know that he was atypical, considering the era. But what I *do* believe, given the time and place, is that Landis was actually trying to *take the chivalrous route*. By saying he was concerned about her physical well-being, instead of lambasting Engel for the cheap stunt (or worse, proclaiming Mitchell a total farce), he gave everybody an opportunity to save face. Indirectly, he helped preserve

Mitchell's opportunity to make a few dollars on the barnstorming circuit, thanks to the ambiguity regarding her true talent level.

Why was he out to stop Engel? Integrity of the game. It's one thing to draw fans with pregame promotions and giveaways; it's another to orchestrate in-game stunts.

◆ Mitchell retired from baseball after the 1937 season because she was "frustrated with the demeaning conditions" associated with playing ball on the fringe. On more than one occasion, she was required "to pitch while riding a donkey."

I would suggest the demand for Mitchell dried up. Quickly. Fact is, she didn't put on a good show, and more often than not, based on contemporary newspaper reports, fans seemed disappointed in her performance or relieved when she was mercifully taken out of the game. And as harsh as this may sound, I believe I'm actually being kind here.

This is actually one area where I've collected some of those puzzle pieces and have been able to fit them into their proper spots. The only way to figure out how good Jackie really was is to look at how she fared versus other competition. If she could strike out Ruth and Gehrig in her "professional debut," then surely she must have ripped through lesser lineups with relative ease.

And it so happens that she didn't. In fact, it's really difficult to find any good outings at all, and when you do, they always have one or two of those "wink wink" sentences embedded in the story, mentioning "how courteous" the men were to not run out their ground balls, and so on.

Probably one-third of the stories simply avoid mentioning the particulars of her outing at all, instead recognizing her appearance and parroting the exciting material from her press release. I guess if you don't have anything nice to say, you don't say anything at all.

And then there were the reporters who didn't give two shits about hurt feelings or Mitchell's box office, they simply reported the facts as they occurred. If Jackie pitched two innings, and the teams mutually agreed to "not count the runs" scored off Mitchell, then that's what they reported. The honest game stories could be rather gruesome, and I've included two excellent examples here. Both of them are game accounts featuring Jackie pitching versus semipro men's teams.

July 9, 1931—Florence (AL) Times
Chattanooga Junior Lookouts vs. Southern Rails of Sheffield
Miss Mitchell was treated most rudely in the one inning that she tossed the ball up to the plate, the Rails counting three runs on four hits, two of them being screeching triples off the bat of Charlie White and Bill Crittenden. [She also walked one and struck out none.]

July 18, 1933—Unknown newspaper
House of David vs. Westchester (PA) Grays
Jackie has a slow dropping curve which can be seen from the bleachers. Apparently she could not manage it last night, even after an unusually long warm-up. And so it was with vocal relief that Walsh, speedball hurler, replaced her in the second and the game began.

What's most puzzling is, even in her "good" outings, you can't find her striking out *anybody*. Here, this young lady fanned the mighty Babe and Lou, but she can't punch out the lowly semipro guys. She pitched for the House of David for a while, but even they let her go as she wasn't adding value (let alone victories) to their product. In later years, she came to be viewed as a heroine in the decades-long struggle for women's rights. Again, it has even been suggested Jackie Mitchell was like the Jackie Robinson of women's athletics.

Heroine? Sure, why not? She's an interesting figure from the fringe in an era where women athletes weren't treated very well.

There were many talented female ballplayers before 1950. If we made a list of the very best, I'm not sure Jackie Mitchell would rank in the top 100, based strictly on her actual skill level. Clearly, she wasn't in the same stratosphere as female pioneer ballplayers such as Toni Stone and Connie Morgan, who performed admirably in the Negro leagues, or Alta Weiss, who pitched semi-professionally for fifteen years, earning enough money to put herself through medical school.

But that's just my two cents.

◆ 29 ◆

1934

Two recurring themes in this book are that Major League Baseball was neither always monolithic, nor its talent static. During the first fifty years of its existence, baseball was a much smaller business than it is today, and its existence hinged on its ability to weather both external and internal challenges.

During these volatile decades, some of the best teams and players in the world were not part of the official major leagues. Talent fluctuated from one year to the next; guys jumped to the Players League, or the Federal League, or the semipro ranks. Or they held out for more money, or they quit the game altogether and went back to work as butchers, or insurance salesmen, or farmers. Other men were banned from the game for bad behavior, while still others were in the high minor leagues, earning decent salaries, which may have mitigated their desire to move up.

The same things were true in the Negro leagues, but to an even more extreme degree. It was *never* a monolith, and its distribution of talent from one year to the next (or one week to the next) can only be described as the very definition of chaos. There was almost no central authority, teams regularly violated the most basic tenets of running successful small businesses, and like the white big leagues, blackball's existence hinged on its ability to weather both external and internal challenges. Several times, from 1920 to the mid-1930s, the Negro leagues proved unable to weather these storms, folded, and were quickly reconstituted by new regimes, in new formats, with new money, and new problems. Players who jumped contracts, or had been banned for bad behavior, were quickly reinstated. These kinds of things confused their fan base and angered the black sportswriters who wanted to support a strong black major league but found it difficult from one summer to the next to understand what the hell was happening. Simple things, such as publishing league standings where the wins and losses balanced, proved to be elusive throughout almost the entire history of black baseball.

This madness certainly helped fuel organized baseball's decidedly low opinion of the professional black leagues. Branch Rickey, who broke the color barrier in Brooklyn, thought the Negro National League was nothing more than a "racket" run by criminals (which was partly true). Hall of Famer Hank Greenberg (the first true star of Jewish ancestry), when he was general manager of the Cleveland Indians, went to see an all-black, East-West, all-star game as a guest of Abe Saperstein (the Harlem Globetrotters guy) and later admitted he couldn't envision any of the players as having major league potential because he thought "they were all just a bunch of clowns, so I looked at the game with prejudiced eyes." And Bob Feller (who didn't think too highly of any ballplayer not named Bob Feller) predicted Jackie Robinson would fail miserably with the Dodgers because he was "too strong in the shoulders" or some other racist malarkey.

So beginning in the 1970s, led by a small army of well-intentioned baseball historians and the Negro league veterans themselves, a wildly enthusiastic campaign was launched to restore black baseball's dignity. Books were published, several all-time greats were inducted into Cooperstown, and the *Sporting News* (which back in the day rarely had kind words for outsider baseball—or blacks) printed maudlin pieces about the poor fellas who were denied opportunities in the white major leagues.

And from this campaign emerged a treasure trove of wonderful new baseball stories, some true, some half true: folklore from the great black baseball leagues. Stories about Josh Gibson hitting 89 home runs and Cool Papa Bell stealing 175 bases in one season.

So, were the Negro leagues a racket, filled with clowns and muscle-bound athletes who were "too strong in the shoulders" to be good at baseball? Or was it a secret gold mine featuring some of the most unbelievably talented ballplayers of all time? As the fog clears, it becomes increasingly apparent the Negro leagues were actually something in the middle. Some great teams and players, performing in leagues with some teams and players who weren't really all that good. In terms of talent, the Negro leagues were, more often than not, horribly unbalanced.

And yet the question still persists: exactly how good were the *best* of the Negro league teams?

As credible Negro league statistics emerge, reconstructed by groups of talented researchers, analysts have the information needed to move us closer to the truth.

It doesn't mean the work has been easy.

◆ ◆ ◆

In my humble opinion, one of the biggest miscalculations made by some Negro league historians is to take the racial mix of Major League Baseball in the late 1970s, when nearly 33 percent of the game's most important players were black, and project that exact figure backward, as if this percentage should always be static. If one-third of the best ballplayers were black in 1979, the theory goes, then the same should have been true in 1959, and 1939, and 1895. And this, of course, is entirely wrong.

This approach ignores the fact that every baseball-playing community (white, Asian, Latin American, black) goes through a process of evolution. The best players in Japan in the 1930s would have had a difficult time in the lowest minor leagues (as we'll illustrate in an upcoming chapter), but by the 1960s, there was a handful of men who could have started in the majors. But even today, although there have been a number of wonderful stars (Ichiro Suzuki, Hideki Matsui, Yu Darvish, Hideo Nomo), one team of Japan's very best players would probably be only fair-to-middling here during the course of a full major league campaign.

Same process existed for the African American players and teams, albeit during an earlier time. From 1885 to 1899, the top black teams in the country (the Cuban Giants, Cuban X-Giants, Page Fence Giants, Columbia Giants, and Big Gorhams) were 59–101–1 (.369) against white major and minor league teams. From 1900 to 1915, the top black (and Cuban) teams in the world improved, going 146–111–11 (.568) versus white major and minor league teams.

Ah, let's just go ahead and place these figures in a table, which is easier to understand:

29.1

Negro/Latin Teams vs. MLB/Minors	G	W	L	T	PCT.
1885–99	162	59	101	1	.369
1900–15	268	146	111	11	.568
1916–30	169	109	57	3	.657
1931–45	143	88	53	2	.624

An unmistakable pattern of improvement emerges, then a slight dip backward in the 1930s and 1940s.

◆ ◆ ◆

One of the things I did *before* I began sorting won-lost data (I didn't want to bias my assessment), was to go through every Negro league team's roster, year by year, earmarking guys I legitimately believed could have had major league careers, had the game been integrated. This doesn't mean I necessarily thought they would have been stars, or even starters; I just wanted to isolate the quality athletes. I started with the Hall of Famers and the guys who were HOF candidates (or Hall of Famers in Cuba). Then I worked my way through the all-stars and perennial league leaders and added the dudes who had short, spectacular careers (Chino Smith, who batted near .400 during six seasons at the top of blackball but passed away at age thirty-one due to cancer, is an exemplar here) or long, steady careers, dumping all these names into a spreadsheet.

Everybody else (which is to say, *most* of the Negro Leaguers) were designated as "minor leaguers," meaning they had value, just not as much as the other guys.

Once this was done, I could go year by year, calculating how many Negro leaguers *might have been in the majors*, had the two, eight-team white major leagues been fully integrated. That table looks like this:

29.2

Year	Potential Major Leaguers	Percentage in an Integrated MLB
1910	23	8.5%
1915	31	11.4%
1920	53	19.5%
1925	72	26.5%
1930	70	25.6%
1935	70	25.6%
1940	61	22.4%
1945	63	23.1%
1950	43	15.8%

What is immediately noticeable, especially when examining the data in conjunction with the teams' won-lost record against white teams in table 29.1, is the rapid ascent in talent, then slight dip backward from the late 1930s through the early 1950s. I don't exactly know why. One guess is that the instability of blackball franchises during the Great Depression, coupled with World War II, had a negative impact on young talent filtering its way into the major black leagues (and if you're familiar with the large number of players who fled to Mexico in the early 1940s, including guys like Roy Campanella and Larry Doby, it's *not* that: I've included those men in the spreadsheet).

By the 1940s, you had an unusually large number of aging veterans such as Cool Papa Bell, Jud Wilson, Willie Wells, Biz Mackey, and Mule Suttles still holding down important starting jobs in the circuit, even as some of these guys were approaching their mid-forties and were well past their primes.

Far below the 33 percent advocated by some baseball historians, the actual number of potential black/Latin major leaguers before integration hovered from 19 to 26 percent. By the time Jackie Robinson became an All-Star with the Brooklyn Dodgers, I would argue (due to World War II, mostly, and perhaps a slight *overestimate* of how much big-league quality existed from 1925 to '35) that the black talent pool the majors drew from was as thin as it had been in thirty years. By 1950, I estimate the league would have been only 16 percent minority had everybody (e.g., Willard Brown, Bus Clarkson, Ray Dandridge) been given a fair shot.

I looked at the performance of black minor leaguers in 1950 to come up with this figure. Some of these men had horrible experiences in the white minors: managers who didn't want to play them, teammates who shunned them, hotels who wouldn't allow them entrance, spectators who caused them all sorts of grief. Because I'm basing their potential on their *actual performance*, it's possible the numbers plummet because of the immeasurable pressures of being part of the first wave of integration. Some guys, like Willie Mays, Ernie Banks, and Larry Doby, excelled, while others, such as Willard Brown and Dan Bankhead, wilted. Or, to be perfectly honest, perhaps the reason some of the guys didn't make it has nothing to do with pressure at all—they simply weren't good enough. It's a realistic explanation.

◆ ◆ ◆

By 1962, I'd argue that baseball was statistically colorblind. I'm referring to the athletes here, not management and coaching opportunities. If you could play the game, you'd get an opportunity to prove yourself. And if you were really, *really* good—regardless of skin color—you'd probably get *several* opportunities at proving yourself. By the early 1960s, Major League Baseball had become a true meritocracy.

With this in mind, it's notable that only 20 percent of the major league game's key contributors in 1962 (key contributors being defined as *one of the top seventeen most frequently used players on each big-league roster)* were African American or dark-skinned Latino. In 1965, this figure bumps up to 22.9 percent. In 1970, it's roughly 25 percent, and by 1975, 27.7 percent of the game's key contributors (meaning those who started or played key roles on the bench) are people of color. Then, by 1980, when the popularity of baseball in the black community reaches its apex (it would decline, systematically, in the ensuing decades, setting off a bizarre, irrational panic later on), 30.8 percent of the key players are either African American or Afro-Hispanic.

Were the game's gatekeepers becoming more and more racially tolerant, giving additional opportunities to minority ballplayers as each decade passed? No, not really. What was happening was the talent base was growing in a very consistent, measurable way. Nobody would have recognized this at the time, but this is precisely what was occurring.

The game had been racially tolerant since at least 1962. One only need look at the top minor league rosters (and leader boards) at that time to see there was no longer any blatant, systematic discrimination preventing African Americans and dark-skinned Latinos from excelling in baseball. If you could play the game, man, you'd get a shot at proving yourself. And when there *were* instances where black athletes didn't rise above Double-A or Triple-A (or whatever) in the early 1960s, it isn't in any way disproportionate to the number of talented white dudes who never got a taste of the big time. Making it to the top in pro ball is a tough racket, regardless of one's color.

◆ ◆ ◆

The funny thing is, I've spent years working through all of these things, collecting material and trading e-mails with various experts and baseball analysts, not because I want to make a profound statement about black and white athletes, or human nature, or any of the tired, socioeconomic stuff preferred by some of today's academically inclined sports historians. I've devoted a significant part of my life to this work because I simply *want to know how good the goddamn Pittsburgh Crawfords were*!

Numerous outsider and blackball teams pique my interest, of course, but I'm using the Crawfords as an example here because of their vaunted reputation. One would be hard-pressed to find a modern compilation of the greatest Negro league teams in history and *not* see the mid-1930s Pittsburgh Crawfords listed at, or near, the top. And for good reason: their star-studded roster included Hall of Famers Satchel Paige, Josh Gibson, and Cool Papa Bell in their primes, as well as aging HOFers Oscar Charleston and Judy Johnson, among others.

They were considered awesome in their time but, like all blackball teams, they are also still something of an enigma. They didn't win the league championship every year during their reign (1932–37). They had some key players come and go (to North Dakota and the Dominican Republic, jumping the team midseason to make more dollars playing for semipro or Latin American teams), and they lost a number of games to lower-level, white minor league teams.

There was one particularly disastrous spring tour in 1932, for example, when the Crawfords lost seven of eleven games versus white Western League teams. In terms of producing future major leaguers, the Western League was clearly the *worst* of the four Class A minor leagues at that time (Class A being the equivalent of today's Double-A), meaning the Crawfords had a tough time holding their own against intact teams from the eighth-best white league in organized baseball.

A closer examination of the box scores provides some answers. Yes, the Crawfords had Satchel Paige, Oscar Charleston, and Double Duty Radcliffe out there (and those men performed well), but they were also missing more than half of their starting lineup. Judy Johnson didn't make the tour. Rap Dixon and Hall of Famer Jud Wilson weren't there. And Josh Gibson, who'd had an operation for a burst appendix, was recuperating back home in Pittsburgh. It was Satch and Oscar and Duty—and a bunch of replacement-level guys, essentially black minor leaguers—getting their lunch handed to them out in Omaha, Nebraska.

On the other hand, when the Crawfords were at full strength, they administered some serious punishment against Dizzy Dean in the fall of 1934, beating Diz a couple times when he was just about the best pitcher in the world. And then during that winter, a handful of Crawfords—including Bell, Paige, and shortstop Chet Williams—traveled to Los Angeles with some other blackball luminaries, completely obliterating several Pacific Coast League (Triple-A) all-star teams, winning 34 of 39 decisions.

These are the components—their star-studded roster construction, the games versus minor and major leaguers, the other anecdotal stuff—around which the Pittsburgh Crawfords' reputation has been formed. But there are always caveats and question marks. When they didn't do well, they were missing key players. When they *did* beat Dizzy Dean, he wasn't backed by his Cardinal teammates but rather by a mix of major and minor leaguers—or semipros. And when Satchel, Cool Papa, and Chet dominated the PCL teams in the winter of 1933–34, their club had been augmented with superstars like Mule Suttles, Willie Wells, and others.

And all of these things bring us back to the regular season. The Crawfords always performed well in the Negro National League, winning roughly 64 percent of their games from 1933 to 1936. Today, that would be like averaging 103 wins per season, which is rather impressive stuff. But the 800-pound gorilla in the room is the question regarding the relative quality of the league in which they participated.

We know there were some other great clubs during the 1930s, most notably the Chicago American Giants, but from top to bottom, what are we talking about here in terms of talent? Could the Pittsburgh Crawfords win even 50 percent of their games if they had been inserted into the American or National League? Forget the World Series teams, could Satchel Paige and the Pittsburgh Crawfords beat Paul Waner and the fifth-place Pittsburgh Pirates in a short series?

This is why understanding how black baseball talent evolved from 1885 to 1915 (and from 1962 to 1980) is critical to understanding the overall quality of black baseball back in the 1930s.

◆ ◆ ◆

MODIFIED STARS SYSTEM

By taking the list of black players I believe would have been major leaguers had the game been integrated in the 1920s and '30s, we can create a modified STARS system based on careers that might have existed, had the circumstances been similar to the 1960s or '70s. This is the reason for going through the trouble of estimating what percentage of Major League Baseball might have been black, had the game been colorblind in the 1920s, '30s, and '40s. We can rebuild careers, assign points, and design a modified STARS system compatible with the regular STARS system.

Under this program, Satchel Paige—who in real life entered the big leagues at forty-one years old, pitching from 1948 to 1953—instead gets credit for a career projected to have occurred from 1928 to 1953, had the game been colorblind. Catcher Roy Campanella, who didn't get a major league opportunity until he was twenty-six, comes up a few years earlier under the modified STARS system. And men such as Buck Leonard and Cool Papa Bell, who *never* played in the major leagues, are given full credit for careers spanning fifteen and twenty-two years, respectively. Players' career paths basically follow those forged during their actual Negro league careers, with some adjustments along the way. If they played twelve seasons at the top of blackball's talent pyramid, they're usually given credit for twelve seasons in the white majors, as well. Notable exceptions include the career of Hall of Famer Jud Wilson, who continued playing in the black leagues until he was nearly fifty years old. It's highly unlikely this would have occurred in the white majors: I've chopped a large chunk from the end of his career to approximate a more realistic career path. And the same has been done for many others.

Everything else about the modified STARS system for Negro leaguers functions exactly the same as it does for white professional ballplayers. Athletes are given credit for the years they were projected to have played in the major leagues. Their scores are adjusted according to their age. And they're given appropriate credit if they have been elected to the Hall of Fame.

During testing, the same results crop up. Specifically, the blackball teams with higher STARS scores are always near the top of the standings, while the lower-graded teams finish near the bottom. The one glaring difference is the disparity between the haves and the have-nots in blackball, confirming what a number of analysts have always known: there was a huge disparity in the talent level from team to team, muddying the overall league quality.

This doesn't mean that Satchel Paige and Oscar Charleston weren't great players or deserving of their Hall of Fame status (because they were—and they are). It just means they were performing in leagues that weren't necessarily major league quality. This is nothing to be ashamed of.

But if we care about the game's history and the legacy of teams such as the Pittsburgh Crawfords, we should want the truth. And if we're going to continue suggesting the Pittsburgh Crawfords rank right up there with the incredible 1927 New York Yankees and 1906 Chicago Cubs, it might be nice to have something beyond anecdotal evidence. Engineering a properly weighted STARS system for the Negro leagues (based on statistical and demographic data instead of folklore) could be a huge step in pushing forward our understanding of the game's past.

◆ ◆ ◆

Before jumping into how the Pittsburgh Crawfords grade out compared to other Negro league teams (and white major league clubs) in the 1930s, let's quickly review where the Negro National League stood during its inaugural season of 1920 in order to understand the progression.

According to my system, the white major leagues would have been roughly 19.5 percent black in 1920 had the game been a true meritocracy. This doesn't mean all of these players were part of Rube Foster's Negro National League, because they weren't. Many of the country's best black players, such as Cyclone Joe Williams, were playing with independent clubs in the East, clubs that were *not* part of Rube Foster's league. Using the major league STARS calculations from chapter 20— which discussed the Continental Divide—we can see how the Negro National League would have fit into the larger scheme:

29.3

Professional Baseball Leagues	STARS Score
American League (1921)	353
National League (1921)	344
Negro National League (1920)	223

The earliest Negro National Leagues were very good but not major league timber. Thanks in large part to the quality of their top four teams (Chicago American Giants, Detroit Stars, Kansas City Monarchs, and Indianapolis ABCs), the Negro National League was arguably the best minor league in the country in the early 1920s. If it had included the best players from the independent Eastern League clubs, it could have been something much better, probably superior to the old Federal League of five years earlier.

By my estimation, the top four teams would have been favorites in any of the high minor leagues (the PCL, International League, and American Association), as well as the old Federal League, but they would have likely finished dead last had they been in the major leagues. The bottom four teams in the Negro National League are what really drag down the circuit. The Cuban Stars, St. Louis Giants, Dayton Marcos, and the Chicago Giants (not to be confused with the *American* Giants) would have struggled to compete in the high minors, let alone the big leagues. The last-place Chicago Giants, who finished 5–31 (.139), were no better than a Class D outfit.

Now, how far did things progress over the next fifteen years? Where do the Pittsburgh Crawfords and the 1934 Negro National League fit in our hypothetically colorblind pyramid of baseball talent? First, let's take a look at the league itself, with STARS scores for each of the eight best black clubs in the country:

29.4

1934 Negro National League	STARS Score
Pittsburgh Crawfords	362
Chicago American Giants	346
Philadelphia Stars*	246
Homestead Grays**	240
Nashville Elite Giants	231

1934 Negro National League (*continued*)	STARS Score
Atlantic City Bacharach Giants	184
Cleveland Red Sox	159
Baltimore Black Sox	141

*The Philadelphia Stars beat the Chicago American Giants 4–3 in a post-season championship series. But the Pittsburgh Crawfords actually had the best overall record. During the regular season, the Craws went 15–9–1 against the Stars and 9–8 versus Chicago.

**The Homestead Grays were not officially part of the league but played just as many "league" opponents as anybody else. Judging by their record (they finished about .500), and their STARS scores, they were clearly better than at least three of the NNL franchises.

As a whole, the entire league (including unofficial member Homestead) pencils out at 239, which is a slight improvement over 1920. The area with the biggest difference is among the top teams. The Crawfords, American Giants, Stars, and Grays are significantly more talented than the top four in 1920 (Rube Foster's American Giants, Detroit Stars, Kansas City Monarchs, and Indianapolis ABCs), especially the Craws and Giants, who have ascended into the major league realm.

Let's look at four major league clubs from 1934, the two World Series teams, and the two basement dwellers from each league:

29.5

1934 Major League Teams	STARS Score
Detroit Tigers (1st, AL)	388
St. Louis Cardinals (World Series winner)	341
Chicago White Sox (last place, AL)	330
Cincinnati Reds (last place, NL)	325

It bears repeating: the STARS system measures talent in inches, not millimeters. It's much more effective comparing entire leagues than it is for team-to-team evaluations. But it warrants a reminder that there *is* a strong correlation between a team's STARS score and their place in the standings. The great 1927 New York Yankees, for instance, had the highest STARS score in the American League (391) that year, but it was only slightly higher than that of the Athletics and Senators, who finished in second and third place. And it's only a tick higher than the 1934 Detroit Tigers, who were loaded with great players but lost to the St. Louis Cardinals in the World Series.

Keeping all this in mind, here are the 1934 Negro National League teams interspersed among four of the sixteen major league teams:

29.6

1934 Professional Baseball Teams	STARS Score
Detroit Tigers	388
Pittsburgh Crawfords	362
Chicago American Giants	346
St. Louis Cardinals	341
Chicago White Sox	330
Cincinnati Reds	325
Philadelphia Stars	246
Homestead Grays	240
Nashville Elite Giants	231
Atlantic City Bacharach Giants	184
Cleveland Red Sox	159
Baltimore Black Sox	141

Although not shown here, the Negro National League once again hovers *below* the two white major leagues. Due to the weakness of its second-division clubs, it's mired in the no-man's-land between Triple-A and the big leagues, occupying the same space the old Federal League held for two seasons (1914–15) and serving as a third wobbly wheel at the top of the baseball pyramid.

And oh, after all the due diligence and the implementation of a rather conservative evaluation system, it looks like the Pittsburgh Crawfords (and the Chicago American Giants, for that matter) really *could* have been in the running for a pennant in either major league. Philadelphia, Homestead, and Nashville would have struggled, but not embarrassed themselves, versus big-league competition. Atlantic City, Cleveland, and Baltimore were Triple-A or less.

◆ 30 ◆

FASTBALLS

THREE OF THE MOST INTRIGUING FASTBALL PITCHERS in outsider baseball donned the House of David flannels during the summer of 1934. Two men (one white, one black) and one woman (an Olympic heroine) mesmerized audiences across the country with their speedball exploits. One is still counted among the hardest throwers of all time, while the other two are considered mere historical footnotes.

I want to kill two birds with one fastball in this chapter. We'll tell the story about how the two "footnotes" were given big-league opportunities in 1934, while the most talented of the bunch had to wait thirteen years before getting his chance. And at the same time, we'll try to see if there is any way to estimate how fast these pitchers threw, even though they retired several decades before the invention of radar guns.

◆ ◆ ◆

Minor league pitcher Ben Benson retired from organized baseball at the end of the 1929 season and the next year joined the House of David ballclub. He was only twenty-four years old, but after struggling in the professional ranks—he had a 24–25 lifetime record, with an earned-run average hovering in the 4s—Benson decided to try his hand at barnstorming baseball with the bearded outsiders. A couple years later, when he signed his contract for the 1934 season, there was no way he could have anticipated the bizarre path his career would take.

In the spring of 1934, Mildred "Babe" Didrikson, the most famous female athlete in the world, was invited to Florida to pitch a couple exhibition games versus big-league and minor league clubs. Didrikson first rose to prominence after winning two gold medals and one silver at the 1932 Olympic Games. An immensely talented all-around athlete, Babe excelled at basketball and softball and was one of the great champions during the early years of women's professional golf, winning forty-eight tournaments during her lifetime, including forty-one LPGA events. During the summer of '34, she'd try her hand at baseball full time, pitching for the House of David ballclub from Benton Harbor, Michigan.

Midsummer 1934, Satchel Paige and catcher Bill Perkins left the Negro National League powerhouse Pittsburgh Crawfords to play for the all-white House of David team in the prestigious *Denver Post* Tournament. This was a first, with blacks being allowed to compete in one of the nation's top semi-pro tournaments. In addition to the Pittsburgh duo, the entire Kansas City Monarchs team showed up in Colorado, ready to do battle. At stake was a $6,400 first-place prize, a tremendous amount of money back then, perhaps the equivalent of $100,000 today.

There were five House of David teams operating during the summer of 1934, run by two organizations. Although Ben Benson, Babe Didrikson, and Satchel Paige all played with the House of David during the same season, they were never part of the same particular troupe. Paige, it should be pointed out, moonlighted with the most competitive version, a club fortified with ex-minor leaguers and college stars.

◆ ◆ ◆

When it was announced that Didrikson would pitch in spring training against actual big-league clubs, there was a tremendous amount of curiosity about how she would perform. At an AAU (Amateur Athletic Union) event in 1931, she set the women's world record by throwing a baseball 296 feet. It's a record that still stands since the event was discontinued in 1957.

The top long-distance throws ever recorded, by anybody, traveled in excess of 440 feet. In fact, at forty-five years old, Satchel Paige threw a baseball an estimated distance of 426 feet when he was a member of the St. Louis Browns.

We can actually use some back-of-the-envelope physics to estimate how hard Didrikson threw. Based on the speeds recorded by modern-day radar guns, we know the upper limits of fastball velocity fall from 100 to 105 mph. By my reckoning, this corresponds directly to 440 to 450 feet of distance.

To create a couple other data points, a few years ago I took my son to a local football field where we could accurately measure the distance of our own throws. My son was young at the time, maybe twelve years old, and I was just plain old and worn out, and although I'll spare you the details, I could *not* throw as far as Babe Didrikson had back in 1931. Neither one of us could.

A couple days later, after our arms had fully recovered, we went to a minor league ballpark that had one of those pitching booths where, for a dollar, fans could gauge the velocities of their fastballs, using a radar gun. In three throws, I averaged somewhere about 65 mph; my son was probably in the low 50s. Later on we plotted this data on a chart, with the upper limit of 440 feet equaling 100 mph and our speed/distance schemes at the bottom.

Over the years, I've collected dozens of newspaper accounts regarding long-distance throwing contests from the major and minor leagues. Among other things, we can say that Glen Gorbous and Don Grate (the two top long-distance throwers in history) probably threw harder than 100 mph. Both men could throw a baseball 445 feet. Rocky Colavito, who once threw a ball 435 feet, probably threw 99 mph, by my calculations. Honus Wagner could throw 92. Tony Mullane, a star pitcher in the 1800s, threw 94. Joe Jackson would have hit 90 mph, based on his recorded distances in these contests. Whitey Herzog could throw 86, Harry Hooper 81, and Tris Speaker 79.

So how fast was Satchel Paige? Unfortunately, we only have two recorded throws, both of which occurred well after his prime. At age forty-five, he was said to have thrown a baseball 426 feet, which translates to roughly 95 mph. This is Satch giving it his all in the moment; during actual games he mixed things up, changed speeds, and likely operated at an average speed much less than that. Five years later, when Paige was fifty, Whitey Herzog witnessed the man throw a ball approximately 395 feet. Herzog was known for his arm strength and had just won a throwing contest the night before (380 feet), but he admitted that even at an advanced age, he couldn't touch

How fast could Satchel Paige throw? His long-distance throws and Roger Clemens's odd comeback in 2012 help shed some light on the question. *Courtesy of Scott Simkus*

Paige for distance. Satchel's throw at that juncture translates to about 90 mph.

Can a man really throw 90 mph at age fifty? Well, in 2012, Roger Clemens helped answer this question. Although he was noticeably out of shape, hadn't pitched professionally in five years, and was embroiled in an ongoing PED scandal that ultimately prevented him from induction into baseball's Hall of Fame during his first appearance on the ballot, Roger made a brief comeback with the Sugar Land Skeeters of the independent Atlantic League.

Relying mostly on his command, Clemens made two starts, pitched a total of 8 innings, and allowed only 3 base hits. He didn't walk anybody, didn't allow any runs, and struck out 3 batters in this low-level minor league. And on the radar gun, he consistently hit 87 to 88 mph.

When Roger Clemens was in his peak back in the 1980s and '90s, he operated in the 97- to 98-mph zone. And at the end of his major league career, when he was forty-five years old in 2007, his heater topped out at 94. Using a calculus based on distance, I have Satchel Paige throwing 90 mph at age fifty, Clemens throwing 88. At age forty-five, Satchel was around 95, while Clemens was at 94. If Paige was one or two ticks higher than Clemens later in life, is it possible he was also one or two ticks faster at his peak? Of course.

During his glory days with the Boston Red Sox, Roger Clemens's fastball was regularly clocked at 97 to 98 mph. This means, working backward, the great Satchel Paige *may* have been throwing from 98 to 99 during his prime, give or take a couple miles per hour.

So getting back to the 1930s and Babe Didrikson, how hard did *she* throw? What does 296 feet of distance translate to on a modern-day radar gun? My best guess would be about 70, 71 mph. A typical high school heater. Even today, she probably had enough stuff to pitch for a boy's team at the high school level. Although she took the mound for the St. Louis Cardinals and Philadelphia Athletics in spring training, she obviously didn't make either ballclub and instead signed on with the House of David in April, continuing her career on the outsider circuit.

In nine starts against major leaguers, Negro leaguers, minor leaguers, and semipros, Miss Didrikson coughed up 15 hits in 9 innings pitched and finished with an earned-run average of 12.00. All this, despite the fact that a number of her male opponents were holding back when batting against her.

Newt Allen, a stellar infielder with the Kansas City Monarchs in the 1920s and '30s, explained in an interview with historian John Holway, "We played against her (but) . . . you couldn't treat her like a regular pitcher. Nobody would bunt on her because she couldn't field bunts. And if somebody hit a line drive through the box, it would kill her. You just tried to place your ball away from hitting it directly at her. She was more a novelty act than anything, a drawing card."

◆ ◆ ◆

Satchel Paige, at his peak, throwing somewhere in the vicinity of 98 or 99 miles per hour, left the Crawfords for a couple weeks to pitch for the House of David in the big *Denver Post* Tournament. With Craws teammate Bill Perkins in tow, the integrated House of David steamrolled their way through the bracket, winning their first three games 16–0, 6–1, and 4–0. In his first 19 innings of work, Paige fanned 32 men while allowing only 1 run.

Because it was a double-elimination tournament, the House of David needed to defeat Newt Allen and the Kansas City Monarchs twice to win the prize money. Paige shut down the Monarchs in their first encounter, striking out 12 in a hard-fought 2–1 victory. In the rematch, Paige's white teammate, Miles "Spike" Hunter, shut down the Kansas City boys on 8 hits, as HOD took home the first-place prize, 2–0. Overall, the House of David finished 7–0, and Paige set a record that was never topped: 44 strikeouts in 28 innings pitched.

With their billfolds stuffed with cash, Satchel Paige and his buddy Bill Perkins returned to the Pittsburgh Crawfords and resumed their regular campaign.

◆ ◆ ◆

While Paige was dominating, making national headlines on semipro baseball's biggest stage, and Babe Didrikson was in the backwoods, getting her ears pinned back by line drives with a different version of the House of David, a plot was being hatched in Washington DC.

Clark Griffith, owner of the Senators, announced he was hiring a House of David pitcher and stated this person would make his or her major league debut on Sunday, August 19. The *Denver Post* Tournament had just finished. Could this be Satchel Paige, making his way back from Colorado? Or was Griffith going to alter history forever by inserting a female named Babe Didrikson into the Senators lineup? Nope, on both accounts. Instead, he was going with a right-hander named Ben Benson, the aging, washed-up former minor leaguer. Griffith was opting for the carnival attraction.

We can't say for sure whether or not Clark Griffith was capitalizing on the publicity generated by the House of David's victory in Denver, but it sure seems like it. Frankly, the team had nothing to lose. When Benson took the mound, with his beard intact, the Senators were 52–60, 21 games behind the first-place Detroit Tigers.

Facing the visiting Chicago White Sox, Benson actually did okay in his debut. He had a 7–4 lead going into the eighth inning before things really fell apart. The White Sox strung together a couple of base hits, Benson was lifted for a reliever, and by the time the damage was over the game was tied. The White Sox went on to win the game, but Benson didn't figure in the decision.

The Senators started the bearded righty one week later, in the second game of a doubleheader with the St. Louis Browns, but this time things didn't go too well. Benson was sent to the showers after just 2 innings' work, as 10 of the 14 men he faced collected base hits, good for 7 runs. He was released shortly thereafter, never to return to the major leagues.

I have no idea how hard Benson threw, but I'm guessing it was faster than Didrikson and slower than Paige. His nickname was "Bullet Ben," suggesting he had a decent arm. He struck out 4 batters in 9.2 innings during his brief stint in the majors, giving him a K/9 ratio of 3.7, which was equal to that of Senators team leader Earl Whitehill. I get the impression Satchel Paige would have blown that figure to smithereens, if only he'd been the one given an opportunity.

Just for fun, here are the stats (versus *all* levels of competition) for Babe Didrikson, Satchel Paige, and Bullet Ben Benson in 1934. They're incomplete, of course, but worth the look:

30.1

Pitcher	Age	W	L	ERA	G	GS	CG	IP	H	BB	K	WHIP	K/9
Babe Didrikson	23	0	0	12.00	9	9	0	9.0	15	5	3	2.22	3.0
Ben Benson	26	1	2	5.74	4	4	2	26.2	33	6	16	1.46	5.4
Satchel Paige	28	24	3	1.51	37	28	24	257.0	158	38	289	0.76	10.1

◆ ◆ ◆

Although this doesn't necessarily have *anything* to do with outsider baseball, I'll print the entire speed chart mentioned earlier anyway, mostly because it's fascinating. Aside from Paige and Didrikson, there are a couple other prominent outsiders on the list, in addition to a wonderful cross section of familiar names from baseball's past.

30.2

Year	Name	Distance	Est. MPH	Notes
1957	Glen Gorbous	445'10"	101	Had 10 OF assists in 70-game MLB career.
1956	Don Grate	445'1"	101	Struggled with control in brief MLB stint.
1953	Don Grate	443'3"	100	6'2", 180 lbs (same as Gorbous and Nolan Ryan).
1955	Rocky Colavito	435'10"	99	Everybody knew Rocky had a rocket.
1952	Don Grate	434'1"	98	Liked showing off his hose, if you'll pardon the expression.
1910	Sheldon LeJeune	426'9"	96	Never pitched, never did much in the MLB.
1952	Satchel Paige	426'0"	95	45 years old; 6'3", 180 lbs, dripping wet.
1879	Tony Mullane	416'7"	94	Was a great nineteenth-century pitcher.
1884	Ed Crane	406'0"	92	Nicknamed "Cannonball" because lasers hadn't been invented.
1965	Willie Mays	406'0"	92	In-game throw at Forbes Field, estimated by game reporter.
1898	Honus Wagner	403'8"	92	Threw only 340' in 1907 (see below).
1884	Ed Crane	402'5"	91	Ed's second contest of 1884. He enjoyed the competition.
1890	Farmer Vaughn	402'2"	91	Huge (6'3") catcher with great arm. Good farmer, too.
1910	Sheldon LeJeune	401'4"	91	Second of three appearances on this list.
1872	John Hatfield	400'7"	91	Original long-distance throwing champion.
1888	Ned Williamson	399'11"	91	Hit 27 HR in 1884 when his team played inside a shoebox.
1907	Sheldon LeJeune	399'10"	91	Sheldon also went by the name "Larry."
1884	Ned Williamson	397'0"	90	This one was from his big home-run year.

Year	Name	Distance	Est. MPH	Notes
1882	Fred Pfeffer	396'5"	90	Pfeffer was a rookie when he uncorked this puppy.
1917	Joe Jackson	396'8"	90	Not sure if this was with or without the shoes.
1868	John Hatfield	396'0"	90	Hey, there wasn't even pro baseball yet!
1908	Jose Mendez	396'0"	90	Cuban HOFer made throw at Logan Square Field
1957	Satchel Paige	395'0"	90	Outgunned 25-year-old Whitey Herzog, settling a friendly bet.
1912	Tillie Walker	393'7"	89	Walker clubbed 37 home runs for Connie Mack in 1922.
1911	Fred Toney	392'10"	89	Proof that dead-ball pitchers threw hard?
1931	Ben Chapman	392'10"	89	Chapman was known for his strong arm.
1931	Myril Hoag	390'0"	88	Dominant minor league pitcher after World War II.
1908	Solly Hoffman	388'0"	88	Nicknamed "Circus Solly." Great at making balloon animals?
1907	Art Hoelskoetter	385'8"	87	A utility man, he pitched a little bit, averaging 3.8 K/9.
1943	Phil Cavaretta	385'0"	87	Was a legendary high school pitcher in Chicago.
1889	Ed Crane	384'10"	87	Threw from 87 to 92 mph during his career.
1917	Duffy Lewis	384'6"	87	Pitched one inning in the majors, struck out one batter.
1917	Tillie Walker	384'6"	87	Walker's second appearance on list. Threw from 87 to 89 mph.
1957	Whitey Herzog	380'0"	86	Before becoming a HOF manager, was a great outfielder.
1943	Vince DiMaggio	380'0"	86	Brother Dom was said to have a better arm than Vince.

Year	Name	Distance	Est. MPH	Notes
1932	Josh Gibson	?	?	Both Gibson and Sam Bankhead won throwing contests.
1933	Sam Bankhead	?	?	Nobody ever won an MLB contest with less than 375'.
1934	Hal Trosky	376'2"	85	Made minor league debut as pitcher, switched to first base.
1932	Johnny Dickshot	375'0"	85	Insert your own inappropriate punch line here.
1911	Joe Tinker	374'0"	85	Next to Wagner, best shortstop arm of dead-ball era.
1907	Joe Stanley	372'11"	84	Reserve OF, pitched 4 games in major leagues.
1907	Mike Mitchell	372'11"	84	Considered one of the strongest arms of dead-ball era.
1888	Mike Griffin	372'8"	84	Little guy (5'7", 160 lbs) with big arm.
1889	John Peltz	371'0"	84	Obscure nineteenth-century outfielder from New Orleans.
2004	Vlad Guerrero	370'0"	84	During warm-ups, before 2004 ALDS game.
1914	Happy Felsch	370'0"	84	Made his biggest throw in October of 1919.
1888	Harry Stovey	369'2"	84	Struck out 7 in 9.1 big-league innings pitched.
1910	Dode Paskert	368'0"	84	Never pitched at the professional level.
1904	Doc Marshall	367'0"	83	A rookie catcher.
1888	Farmer Vaughn	366'9"	83	Vaughn's second appearance. Threw from 83 to 91 mph.
1888	Oyster Burns	364'6"	83	Utility man. Pitched a little bit in the bigs (8–5, 4.09 ERA).
1910	Luis Padrón	364'0"	83	Cuban star. Pitched well in minors (33–17 record).

Year	Name	Distance	Est. MPH	Notes
1889	John Grim	362'0"	82	Catcher. Pitched 3 innings in bigs, fanning 3 batters.
1888	Darby O'Brien	361'5"	82	An Illinois boy, died of typhoid fever at age 29.
1872	Andy Leonard	358'7"	82	One of the original Cincinnati Red Stockings of the late 1860s.
1910	Harry Hooper	356'4"	81	Threw farther (faster?) than the legendary Tris Speaker.
1888	Hub Collins	354'6"	81	Second baseman known more for his running speed.
1910	Biff Schaller	354'0"	81	Spent most of his career in the Pacific Coast League.
1888	George Tebeau	353'0"	81	Position player, pitched 13 innings at big-league level.
1872	George Wright	352'1"	81	Hall of Famer proves Civil War–era gents could throw 80+.
1907	Patsy Dougherty	351'0"	80	Big outfielder (6'2") played well during dead-ball era.
1932	Bob Feller	350'+	80	Bob Feller was just 13 years old when he uncorked this throw!
1872	Bill Boyd	345'7"	79	250 lbs., OF/3B, could throw nearly 80 mph.
1910	Tris Speaker	345'7"	79	Is reputation based more on positioning and accuracy?
1888	Bob Gilks	343'11"	79	Outfielder went 9–9, 3.98 ERA in 21 games pitched
1907	Bernie McCay	343'11"	79	Player/manager of Class D Mobile Sea Gulls. Went 1–3 in 1907.
1888	Long John Reilly	341'6"	79	Slugging first baseman threw well for position.
1907	Honus Wagner	341'4"	79	Big discrepancy with 1898 throw. What's going on here?

Year	Name	Distance	Est. MPH	Notes
1889	Cannonball Titcomb	341'0"	78	Lefty, career 30–29, 3.47 ERA. Proof of soft tossers back then?
1908	Ray Demmitt	340'0"	78	Died in 1956, not far from where I live. I have an alibi.
1888	Jack Brennan	339'6"	78	Played catcher, outfield, and third base. None of them well.
1888	Cub Stricker	337'8"	77	5'3", 138-lb. second baseman. His mustache weighed 12 lbs.
1872	Wes Fisler	336'6"	76	Played 1B and 2B. Also from the big 'stache era.
1888	Dave Foultz	335'4"	76	Won 41 games in 1886. Arm was fried at time of contest.
1888	Jumbo Davis	333'6"	75	Since you asked: Jumbo was 5'11", 195 lbs.
1872	Cap Anson	330'6"	75	Hall of Fame hitter, high school arm.
1888	Jack O'Connor	330'0"	75	Rowdy Jack spent most of his time playing catcher.
1907	Eddie Hahn	330'0"	75	Played in Chicago City League with Nixey Callahan.
1931	Babe Didrikson	296'0"	70	Still the world's record for women.

◆ 31 ◆

SPEED TRAP

H OW FAST WAS COOL PAPA BELL?
     Fast enough to inspire a couple dozen tall tales and a handful of genuine mysteries.

Supposedly, he could flip a light switch and crawl beneath the bed covers before the room went dark. One time, he hit a grounder up the middle and the ball hit him in the back as he slid into second base. He stole 175 bases in 1933 (but they "only recorded 91 in the scorebook," said Bell). He could tag up from second and cross home plate on sac flies. He regularly scored from first base on singles and went from first to third on sac bunts, and one time (in an exhibition game versus major leaguers), he scored all the way from first on a bunted dribbler in the infield.

And then there was something else.

Once, during a Field Day competition, he circled the bases in 12 seconds flat, allegedly becoming the only man to ever lap the sacks in less than 13 ticks. In fact, he was said to have turned the trick 1.2 seconds faster than any other human being. Ever.

Where did this stuff come from? Well, Satchel Paige, mostly. Especially the apocryphal stuff. Cool Papa said as much, during a 1970 interview with historian Charles Korr. Referring to the story about the hotel room light and the ball plugging him in the backside as he slid into second, Bell explained it's "just something that Satchel says."

Satchel was a master storyteller, the self-appointed griot of blackball.

Without calling out Paige specifically, Bell confessed he'd prefer his former teammates and opponents simply "tell the truth" instead of "adding stuff on" when interviewed about the Negro leagues. The exaggerations partly undermined the efforts to present a serious history of segregated baseball.

Interestingly, in the same interview, Bell expressed his personal frustration that the old black leagues didn't record the numbers and preserve the type of baseball statistics fans crave. Specifically, Bell said, "The public doesn't know about these black ballplayers and, you know, it's just a shame."

This was back in 1970, and yes, it was a shame.

Since then, of course, there have been various armies of people rebuilding the numbers. Every month new box scores are uncovered, having been buried in dusty newspapers, digital archives, and crumbling microfilm. The boxes aren't necessarily easy to find, or without their imperfections, but enough of them are out there to compile meaningful batting averages, slugging numbers, and fielding percentages. When you consider the explosion of Negro league–inspired websites, books, and magazine articles that have emerged in the last couple decades, I believe the late Cool Papa Bell would probably be shocked at how well we're getting to know some of his former teammates and opponents.

But what about the other stuff? The stuff not included in the box scores? What about the areas where the chalk line between tall tales and reality has been smudged?

I mean, could Cool Papa Bell really circle the bases in 12 seconds flat?

◆ ◆ ◆

Before sprinting into the Bell legacy, let's take a brief look at the history of base-running competitions among ballplayers.

I don't know the exact origins of what came to be known as the "circling the bases event" in baseball skills competitions, but anecdotal evidence suggests they date back to the late part of the nineteenth century. After an event at the Polo Grounds in 1904, John McGraw claimed he and Willie Keeler ran a 14-second race years earlier but had been "defeated by Billy Sunday." At the very least, we know baseball Field Day events, where players participated in various throwing and fungo hitting competitions, date back to the earliest days of organized baseball.

But using a stopwatch to time men as they ran around in circles? It seems to have come into vogue (at least in the baseball community) at the beginning of the 1900s, and especially *after* 1904. Commercially available stopwatches date back to the mid-1850s, so what was so special about '04?

My hunch is it had something to do with Olympic fever. The modern Olympic Games debuted in 1896 in Athens, Greece. The 1900 games were held in Paris, France. Then in 1904, the third edition of the modern games was hosted right here in the United States, in St. Louis. For months, newspaper readers across the nation followed the amazing feats of athletes from around the globe. In black-and-white ink, they became obsessed with how fast, how high, and how far people could run, jump, and throw, and suddenly everybody was caught up in the mania. Churches were running competitions. Police forces competed against firemen. Married men squared off against the single chaps. And professional baseball followed suit.

Almost immediately, the Field Day competitions became more elaborate. No longer just fungo hitting or long-distance throws, they added other events as well. There was the "Bunt and Run to First Base" contest, timed with a stopwatch. There was a contest that tested one's throwing arm accuracy from home plate to second. There was an event that tested one's bunting ability, where the batsman tried to deflect the pitched ball into various buckets around the plate. There were straight sprint races, such as 75- and 100-yard dashes. And there was the "circling the bases" event, which joined fungo hitting as one of the marquee attractions. Well, actually, throwing for distance was still a huge deal as well, but by 1904, most pitchers were pulling out of these competitions because several guys, including Old Hoss Radbourne and Rube Waddell, had hurt their arms during these events.

In the earliest contests, the fastest circlers of the bases were usually timed in the 14-second range. In one of the earliest events thus far uncovered, during the fall of 1904, George Browne of the New York Giants won a race versus his teammates with a 14.20 time, just edging out Sam Mertes and Billy Gilbert, who both crossed the plate in 14.40. For comparison's sake, in 2009 Brett Gardner of the New York Yankees (one of the fastest men in the modern major leagues) circled the bases during an inside-the-park home run in 14.68 seconds, according to *Baseball Prospectus*'s Larry Granillo, who tracks such things. It's not a perfect example, comparing a running race to an inside-the-parker, but it helps us calibrate the radar.

So, the 14-second barrier was the sweet spot for quicks, but right away there were a couple speed merchants who exceeded it. In 1907, Bullet Jack Thoney of the Eastern League's Toronto Maple Leafs ran the bags in 13.60. The next year, the great Ty Cobb won a Field Day race with a time of 13.75. Then, in 1921, minor league outfielder Maurice "Flash" Archdeacon circled the bases in a record-setting 13.40 seconds. Archdeacon's mark would be tied in 1929 by two-sport star Evar Swanson, who played in both the major leagues and the fledgling National Football League.

After returning to the minor leagues in 1931, Swanson would break the shared record with an unprecedented 13.20 during a Field Day meet hosted in

Columbus's Neil Park. Maury Wills came close to eclipsing the record in 1953 but fell short with a time of 13.40. To this day, Swanson's record has stood the test of time. The fact these running races died out as a side attraction by the mid-1950s has probably helped a bit. OK, helped *a lot*. But still, it's Swanson's crown.

◆ ◆ ◆

Now, let's get back to Cool Papa Bell. Just about everybody who saw him play, black or white, said he was the fastest ballplayer they'd ever witnessed. But could he circle the bases in 12 seconds flat? Could he really run one *full second faster* than everybody else who'd put on a baseball uniform before 1950?

To uncover the answer, we should probably begin with Bell's own words. For this segment of the investigation, we'll use the interview published in John Holway's *Voices From the Great Black Baseball Leagues*. In Holway's book, Bell speaks extensively about his running ability. Besides comparing himself to Olympic legend Jesse Owens and Jimmie Lyons (another blackball speed merchant), Bell said, "They once timed me circling the bases in twelve seconds flat." Not much detail here, but he's obviously referring to one specific race. Incidentally, in the 1970 Charles Korr interview, Bell mentions this same race, and the fact he was timed in twelve seconds flat, but again—no details.

Almost immediately, we get a red flag. This is supposed to be one of the crowning achievements of Bell's career, along with a 3-home-run game in Cuba and the time he batted .437 in Mexico. But we get nothing here. No year. No opponents. No venue. Nothing. I've spent years looking through most of the major black newspapers from before World War II and have never located a story about this specific incident, and without any details from Bell, it's impossible to track this down using other sources.

But before we start losing hope, it turns out Cool Papa does remember at least one other competition when he was timed with a stopwatch, and he actually provides some details. Again, in his words, "I was supposed to run against Tuck Stainback, who played center field for the Yankees. The major league record was 13.3 by a guy named Swanson with Cincinnati. We were going to try to break it. Well, it rained and it was muddy and Stainback wouldn't run. He said he had a cold. But the fans kept hollering, so I ran alone in 13.1 on a wet ground."

As far as investigations go, this is more like it. There's Tuck Stainback. They were trying to break Swanson's record. It had rained. Unlike the random "twelve seconds flat" assertion, we actually have some details to work with for this race!

◆ ◆ ◆

Let's play a little baseball detective and work through these things, point by point.

First off, who the heck was Tuck Stainback? George Tucker Stainback was born on August 4, 1911, in Los Angeles, California. A prep star, he excelled in track and field, running the 100-yard dash in 10.1 seconds, and he could broad jump more than 22 feet. A speedy outfielder, he tried out for the Los Angeles Angels of the PCL in 1931 but was farmed out to Bisbee in the Arizona-Texas League. The next season, 1932, Stainback was back in L.A., playing for his hometown Angels, where he hit .356 and was second on the club in triples. By 1934, at the age of twenty-two, he'd be the starting center fielder for the Chicago Cubs, batting .306 but stealing only 7 bases in 377 plate appearances.

Did he ever play for the Yankees? Well yeah, during World War II, when DiMaggio and all the good players were defending the country. Amazingly, although he only appeared in more than 100 games one time (his rookie season), Stainback fashioned a thirteen-year career at the major league level, retiring with an uninspiring slash line of .259/.284/.333. Despite his exploits as a prep speed demon, Tuck managed only 27 stolen bases in 817 career games, and his range factor in the outfield was always below league average. Stainback is one of those natural athletes whose raw speed never translated into much on the diamond.

As we already know, Evar Swanson set the official running record in 1929 but bettered the mark in 1931. And we know Tuck Stainback didn't join professional baseball until '31, so it's a good assumption this race must have occurred during the 1930s or '40s.

Did Cool Papa Bell ever barnstorm against the Yankees in the 1940s? Well, not to my knowledge. He played against some Yankees players, but not the team itself. In fact, by the middle-1930s, postseason exhibition series between major black and white teams on the East Coast had almost faded away. Most of the black/white action was on the West Coast, in California. And most of those games occurred in Los Angeles, Tuck Stainback's hometown. They called it the California Winter League, and Cool Papa Bell spent many off-seasons competing out there. The league typically consisted of at least one black all-star team and two or three white teams outfitted with Pacific Coast League players with a handful of major leaguers who'd returned to California for the off-season.

Did Tuck Stainback ever play in the California Winter League? Well, yes, he did. According to William F. McNeil's *The California Winter League: America's First Integrated Professional Baseball League*, Stainback played one full season there, 1933–34, with a team called the Pirrone All-Stars. Cool Papa

Bell was out there as well, playing with an incredibly talented club featuring Satchel Paige, Willie Wells, Turkey Stearnes, and Mule Suttles.

McNeil has a pretty good account of the season. Bell's team steamrolled the triple-A level competition, going 35–8–2. Bell hit .362 to lead the loop and stole 23 bases in 45 games. Stainback's team managed only a 3–22 mark, and Tuck scratched out a meager .194 batting average in the ten box scores thus far uncovered. But did they run against one another? There's no mention of it in McNeil's book, which means we need to hit the newspapers.

That winter, the league was covered very well by the *Los Angeles Times*, and it doesn't take long to stumble across a doubleheader played on Sunday, December 17, 1933. Satchel Paige grabbed most of the headlines, striking out 12 as he and the Royal Giants defeated Buck Newsom and the Pirrone All-Stars. But what caught my eye was this: "Between tilts a field meet was held with Bell featuring by winning the race around the bases in 13-3/5, just one fifth of a second slower than Archdeacon's world record."

So there it is, the only field meet of the season, and it featured Stainback and Cool Papa Bell's ballclubs. This has got to be it, but can we corroborate this any further? There's no mention of Stainback, and in fact, Tuck didn't appear in the Pirrone lineup that day. If he was actually nursing a cold, as Bell recalls, or fighting some other illness, this probably makes sense. I wouldn't expect him to play.

But what about the 13.10 time Bell recalled? The *Los Angeles Times* says 13.6. Matter of fact, the *California Eagle*, an African American paper, posted the same time in its coverage of the event. In fairness, Bell was talking about these events nearly thirty-seven years after they occurred. And in fairness, I don't know any ex-jocks, whether they're former high school teammates or retired major leaguers, who can resist the temptation to revise their own athletic history a little bit.

Which brings us to the wet field. Cool Papa said it "had rained and it was muddy." The weather that week was cool and cloudy; lows dipped into the mid-30s, highs didn't go above the low to mid-60s. There was no report of rain the day of the game (Sunday). In fact, there was no report of rain the preceding two days, before the doubleheader and field meet. But if you go back to Wednesday's *Times*, you find the curious headline STORM BESTOWS NEARLY THREE INCHES OF RAIN. One man was killed in a landslide, roads were cut in half by running water, trees were uprooted, and one estate, near La Crescenta, was covered in four feet of debris that swept down from the mountains.

The storm finally moved out of L.A. on Thursday morning, three days before the doubleheader. In all, the city took on 2.97 inches of rain in less than forty-eight hours. Prior to the storm, they had less than .40 inches of rain the entire season. The farmers in the area had been suffering, there had been multiple brush fires, and the big storm was seen as a relief. Two days later a representative of the agricultural community said, "Many of the farmers, particularly the grain growers, were waiting for the rain to moisten the ground for plowing and seeding. There was sufficient rain to wet the ground to a considerable depth."

So there you have it: wet diamond. You had a field (White Sox Park II) that was likely uncovered, a huge storm, cool temps, and overcast skies, which certainly would have slowed the evaporation process. Three days after the historic storm, the field was playable but soft.

By gum, I think we got it!

◆ ◆ ◆

Do I believe Cool Papa Bell ever ran the bases in 12 seconds flat? Nope. But I'm not going to be the one to put the final nail in this James Bell myth. Somebody out there may find another story, another running race, or some more details we can follow up on. Maybe, just maybe, in hot weather and on a dry diamond, Cool Papa Bell *did* break the 13-second barrier. We just don't know. We may never know.

Following is a list of all the Top Finishers in the circling-the-bases competitions thus far uncovered during my research. I want to thank Larry Granillo, whose wonderful "Tater Trot Tracker" has captured the speeds for many inside-the-park home

COOL PAPA BELL	centerfield-1 leftfield-1 rightfield-1	stealing-AA running 1-17

SOM Hall of Famer

1	2	3
2-groundball (1b)B	2-lineout (2b)	2-lineout (2b)
3-groundball (p)B	3-groundball (2b)A++	into as many outs as
4-lineout (ss)	4-flyball (lf)B	possible
5-flyball (cf)B	5-SINGLE	3-groundball (2b)A
6-groundball (3b)B	6-DOUBLE**	4-groundball (ss)A
7-WALK	1-4 SINGLE**	5-SINGLE*
8-WALK	5-20	6-SINGLE*
9-groundball (2b)A++	7-groundball (ss)A	1-17
10-lineout (1b)	8-HOMERUN	lineout (1b)
11-popout (2b)	1-7	18-20
12-foulout (c)	TRIPLE	7-popout (3b)
	8-20	8-SINGLE**
	9-TRIPLE	9-flyball (rf)B
	1-7	10-groundball (1b)B
	DOUBLE	11-groundball (3b)B
	8-20	12-groundball (p)A
	10-DOUBLE	
	11-SINGLE	
	12-strikeout plus injury	

BATTING RECORD

AVG	AB	2B	3B	HR	RBI
.332	609	32	18	10	43

BB	SO	SB	CS	SLG%	ON BASE %
59	41	27	9	.495	.393

Cool Papa Bell's Strat-O-Matic card, based on the author's research. Bell was the anchor in the Pittsburgh Crawfords' outfield during the mid-1930s and the fastest Hall of Famer before 1950. *Courtesy of Scott Simkus*

runs from the last couple seasons. Cool Papa Bell may not have broken the record, but he *is* the fastest Hall of Famer before 1950! You know, he's sandwiched in between Maury Wills and Ty Cobb, and I think that says something, don't you?

31.1

Year	Name	Time	Notes
1931	Evar Swanson	13.20	Besides baseball, played pro football for several seasons.
1929	Evar Swanson	13.30	12 triples, 33 steals with Cincinnati Reds in 1929.
1921	Maurice Archdeacon	13.40	Nicknamed Flash or Comet. Stole 13 bases in 127 big-league games.
1953	Maury Wills	13.40	Only 20 years old. Later stole 104 bases in 1962.
1926	Roland Locke	13.40	NCAA sprinting champion while at Nebraska. Didn't play baseball.
1930s	Tetelo Vargas	13.40	Legend from Dominican Republic, played in Negro leagues.
1940s	Cliff McClain	13.50	Minor leaguer, 21 triples in 1949 (Albuquerque).
1940s	George Case	13.50	Lost 100-yard dash to an aging Jesse Owens.
1933	Cool Papa Bell*	13.60	Only reliable time for Bell thus far, fastest Hall of Famer ever.
1907	Jack Thoney	13.60	Nicknamed Bullet Jack because of his blazing speed.
1908	Ty Cobb*	13.75	Can't find any information about this guy.
2012	Billy Hamilton	13.80	Set modern-day minor league record of 155 stolen bases in 2012.
1931	Ethan Allen	13.80	Sprinter in college. Stole 21 bases in 1929, good for 4th in National League.
1910	Hans Lobert	13.80	82 triples and more than 300 stolen bases in his career.
1943	Al Rubeling	13.88	Over 100 triples in the minors, Towson University track star.
1955	Carlos Bernier	13.90	PCL legend, stole 65 bases for Hollywood in 1952.
1910	Hans Lobert	14.00	Second race in 1910, 0.2 second separated his times.
1943	John Barrett	14.00	Wartime star, led NL in triples (19) and steals (28) in 1944.

Year	Name	Time	Notes
1943	Lennie Merullo	14.00	Lennie's son and grandson played professional baseball.
1917	Ray Chapman	14.00	Stole 52 bases for the Indians in 1919, hit by 19 pitches in his career.
1910	Vin Campbell	14.00	Averaged 25 stolen bases per season in the Federal League.
2011	Peter Bourjos	14.02	Led American League with 11 triples in 2011.
1921	Guy Chamberlain**	14.03	No pro baseball. Did make NFL Hall of Fame, though.
1921	George Halas**	14.04	Helped found National Football League. Played briefly with Yankees.
1931	Denny Sothern	14.10	Was considered one of the fastest outfielders in baseball in the 1930s.
1907	Dode Paskert	14.15	While with the Reds, he stole 51 bases in 1910.
1904	George Browne	14.20	Averaged 25 stolen bases per season during his prime.
1910	Eddie Collins*	14.20	741 stolen bases, 187 triples.
1911	Jimmy Austin	14.20	Dead-ball era speed merchant, averaged 25–30 SB during prime.
1928	Tom Nash	14.20	Obscure minor leaguer, 15 triples in 1930 (Asheville).
1907	Wally Clement	14.20	30 stolen bases with Jersey City (Eastern League) in 1903.
1931	Dusty Cooke	14.20	30 triples with Ashevile in 1928, 10 triples with Boston Red Sox in '33.
1927	Bill Cissell	14.40	25 steals for White Sox in 1929 (2nd in the American League)
1934	Evar Swanson	14.40	Record holder has added a full second to his time after three short years.
1907	Hans Lobert	14.40	In three races, Hans had times of 13.8, 14.0, and 14.4.
1904	Billy Gilbert	14.40	Averaged 36 stolen bases from 1902 to 1904, always top 10 in league.
1904	Sam Mertes	14.40	Almost 400 steals in career, always near leaderboard.
1907	Jack Thoney	14.40	Second race in 1907, timed at 13.60 in first meet.

Year	Name	Time	Notes
1912	Joe Riggert	14.40	Had minor league highs of 27, 23, and 20 triples from 1910 to 1921.
1938	Pepper Martin	14.40	34-year-old, past prime. Led NL in steals three times during career.
2010	Angel Pagan	14.48	Nicknamed "Crazy Horse," led NL with 15 triples in 2012.
1931	Ernie Orsatti	14.50	Stole 14 bags in 1933 (5th in National League).
1907	Larry Piper	14.50	10-year career in minors, topped 10 triples twice.
1934	Pepper Rea	14.50	Career minor leaguer.
1931	Earle Combs*	14.60	Hit more than 20 triples three times in the major leagues.
1907	Billy Maloney	14.60	Led the NL in steals with 59 in 1905 (Chicago Cubs).
1913	Billy Zimmerman	14.60	Cup of coffee in majors, hit 13 triples for Newark in 1913.
1907	George Browne	14.60	Second time on list. Other time was 14.20.
1910	Jimmy Austin	14.60	Like George Browne, also timed at 14.20 in his other race.
1910	Tris Speaker*	14.60	Number six all-time in triples with 222, also stole 436 bases.
1931	Lefty O'Doul***	14.70	One of the fastest going home to first; surprising, forgotten foot speed.
2010	Cameron Maybin	14.75	Stole 40 bases for the San Diego Padres in 2011.
1907	Cliff Blankenship	14.75	Stole 15 bases in 73 games with Toledo in American Association (1903).
1907	Bert Noblett	14.80	Second baseman, spent entire career in minor leagues.
1911	Jimmy Austin	14.80	Timed at 14.20 and 14.80 in his two Field Day appearances.
1905	John Kane	14.80	5'6", 138 pounds. Stole 30 bases for the 1908 Cincinnati Reds.
1907	Danny Hoffman	15.00	Led AL with 46 steals in 1905 (Philadelphia Athletics).
1913	Hans Lobert	15.00	31 years old and the slowest time in his four different Field Day events.

Year	Name	Time	Notes
1924	Julio Rojo	15.00	Cuban-born Negro league catcher. Only full-time backstop on the list.
1919	Pie Traynor*	15.00	20-year-old amateur at this point. Stole as many as 28 bases with Pirates.
1921	Walt Meinert	15.00	14 triples in 109 Three-I League games (1922, 1925).
1905	Art Kruger	15.00	Stole 38 bases in 365 major league games.
1905	Jim McHale	15.00	Speedy minor league CFer. Stole 4 bases in 21 major league games.
2010	Tony Gwynn Jr.	15.02	Son of Hall of Famer. Timed during inside-the-park home run.
1932	Joe Chamberlain	15.20	Shortstop, spent most of his career in the minor leagues.
1937	Kiki Cuyler*	15.20	36 years old, but still beat rookies in a spring training race.
1932	Steamboat Struss	15.30	A pitcher! Had 3 triples for Peoria in 68 at-bats.

*Member of Baseball Hall of Fame in Cooperstown

**Member of Pro Football Hall of Fame

***Member of Japanese Baseball Hall of Fame

◆ 32 ◆

THE MILLION-DOLLAR ARM

As Matsutaro Shoriki exited his limousine in front of the *Yomiuri* building, a stranger emerged from the crowd and withdrew a short samurai sword from beneath his winter coat, striking the newspaper executive full force in the back of the neck.

Shoriki, owner of *Yomiuri Shimbun*, Tokyo's most powerful daily newspaper, collapsed onto the building's steps, clutching the back of his neck as the swordsman disappeared into the chaos. Bleeding profusely from a six-inch gash, the business mogul was quickly hustled into his building's infirmary, where he lost consciousness.

◆ ◆ ◆

A member of the ultranationalist War God's Society, swordsman Katsusuki Nagasaki was part of a larger conspiracy. When he attempted to assassinate Shoriki on February 22, 1935, he was the frontman representing a group of right-wing thugs, sponsored by a conservative newspaper called *Tokyo Nichi Nichi*.

With Japan's economy crippled by the Great Depression, the ongoing struggle between the country's progressives, who advocated a transition to Western business ideologies, and the conservatives, who favored the authority of the emperor and a return to Japan's traditional values, was reaching a fever pitch. The ongoing squabble between the United States and Japan over naval supremacy in the Pacific only helped exacerbate the situation.

When brought to court on charges of attempted murder (Matsutaro Shoriki spent nearly two months in a hospital but made a full recovery),

Nagasaki explained he had tried "to maim, not kill Shoriki" because, among other things, the newspaper man had defiled the memory of Emperor Meiji by allowing Babe Ruth and his baseball team to play in the stadium named in the ruler's honor.

Ruth and a group of American League All-Stars had just concluded a triumphant (and incredibly popular) tour of Japan just two months earlier, in December 1934. What Nagasaki didn't explain to the judge was that the tour, sponsored by Shoriki and his *Yomiuri Shimbun* newspaper, was crushing the circulation of the *Tokyo Nichi Nichi*, which had paid Nagasaki a couple hundred bucks to cut the man's head off. Turns out the assassination attempt was just as much business motivated as it was anti-Yankee sentiment (as in Americans, not the New York baseball team).

◆ ◆ ◆

Much has been written about the actual baseball tour. By far, the best book published on the subject is Robert K. Fitts's *Banzai Babe Ruth: Baseball, Espionage, & Assassination During the 1934 Tour of Japan*, which provides a richly detailed narrative centering around the tour and the development of baseball (and fascism) in the Far East.

Ruth's team, which featured future Hall of Famers Lou Gehrig, Jimmie Foxx, Charlie Gehringer, and Lefty Gomez, completely annihilated their hosts, beating the All Nippons (a Japanese all-star team) by scores of 17–1, 21–4, 22–1, and 23–5. All told, 22 games were played in Japan, China, and the Philippines, and the Americans never lost. Versus Japanese pitching, Ruth batted .408 with 13 home runs (running his overall season total to 46). It was truly the Babe's last hurrah, as he'd be cut loose by the Yankees, and out of baseball completely, in less than six months.

Not to be outdone, in 1927 a group of Negro league stars, playing under the "Royal Giants" moniker, toured Japan, winning 23 of 24 games. Their one loss was tainted because the Japanese umpires mistakenly disallowed the Giants' tying run, which the Americans chose to take in good stride.

It was pretty clear where the Japanese stood in relationship to the white *and* black American professional clubs. Um, they weren't even close.

◆ ◆ ◆

After returning to the States, Philadelphia Athletics skipper Connie Mack (who had accompanied Babe Ruth's bunch as a goodwill ambassador, *not* as manager of the team) lauded the Japanese for their fine fielding and base-running ability but said they lagged far behind with the stick. The general consensus at that point (the mid-1930s) was that the Japanese were no better than lower-level, Class D minor leaguers.

Seventeen years earlier, Vernon Ayau, a Hawaiian shortstop who would become one of the first Pacific Islanders to play minor league baseball here in the States, had made a similar assessment after playing against a touring club of Japanese college stars. "If the Japanese could only hit they would also cut a figure in league ball," Ayau said, in the April 8, 1917, edition of the *New York Tribune*. "They are certainly fast and good fielders, but do not seem to catch the knack of slamming the ball."

The same stuff was said of the early Cuban teams. After their successful 1911 junket in Havana, John McGraw of the New York Giants said of the locals, "These Cubans are only fair players, they are as fast as lightening [*sic*] on the bases and can throw to beat the band. They have picked up all the knacks of fielding, but they cannot bat."

◆ ◆ ◆

In 1974, eccentric Oakland A's owner Charlie Finley hired Herb Washington, an All-American track star at Michigan State University, to join his club as a designated base runner. Washington neither batted nor played defense for the A's but appeared in 105 games during his career, during which he stole 31 bases as a pinch runner.

After the death of his father, NBA legend Michael Jordan took a hiatus from the hardwood to pursue his childhood baseball dreams. He hadn't played the game since Pony League, when he was just fourteen years old, but he joined the Double-A Birmingham Barons of the Southern League, where he hit .202 with just 3 home runs and 51 RBI. In 127 games, the speedy Jordan stole 30 bases. As an outfielder, his fielding percentage was .952, which is bad but he wasn't the worst of the Southern League regulars during the season of 1994.

In different ways, the development of the Japanese and Cuban teams, as well as the experiences of individual athletes such as Herb Washington and Michael Jordan, teach us much about our own game.

Apparently, Ted Williams was right: hitting a baseball *is* the most difficult thing to do in sports. When looking at the development of baseball in various places around the globe, offense is *always* the last skill set to develop. The other stuff—catching, throwing, and running—ain't really all that elusive.

And time and time again, when people do break through from different demographics, it's often as pitchers. The pitchers come first.

◆ ◆ ◆

In 2008, American sports agent J. B. Bernstein helped create a reality television show in India called *The Million Dollar Arm*. The objective was to scour this country of 1.2 billion people in order to find the person who could throw a baseball the fastest and most accurately. Thirty-seven thousand people entered the competition, vying for a $100,000 prize and a chance to play professional baseball in the United States.

They don't play baseball in India, so most of the men who entered the fray came from the cricket pitch. As the forebear of baseball, scouring the best cricket bowlers for an unknown baseball prodigy would be like interviewing Amish farmers about the latest technological advances from their cornfields. They use an entirely different kind of throwing motion in that game. Rinku Singh, a twenty-year-old former *javelin thrower*, won the contest by chucking his fastball 88 mph. Later on, he and the contest's runner-up, Dinesh Patel, traveled to America where they worked briefly with a pitching coach, before showcasing their wares for nearly two dozen major league scouts.

Singh's fastball was now up to 92 mph, with Patel not too far behind. Both were signed by the Pittsburgh Pirates and placed on the team's rookie league roster. Neither man had ever *seen* a baseball game, let alone played in one.

Patel washed out after two seasons, but as of this writing, Singh was still learning the game and plying his trade in the Pirates' lower minor league system. In his first four seasons of professional baseball (his first four seasons of *any* baseball, actually), Singh had appeared as a reliever in 96 games, going 11–7 with a 3.29 ERA, while striking out an impressive 7.7 men per 9 innings pitched. Relatively speaking, his control has been outstanding, as the lefty had allowed only 57 walks in 167 innings pitched.

Rinku Singh may never make it to the major leagues, but he proves one thing: regardless of your experience, if you can throw 90+ miles per hour, and get the little round white ball somewhere in the general vicinity of the flat rubber plate, somebody will pay you money to perform this trick.

◆ ◆ ◆

For the Japanese, the one bright spot during the All-American tour of 1934 was the legendary pitching performance of seventeen-year-old wunderkind Eiji Sawamura. Unlike Rinku Singh, Sawamura had plenty of baseball experience and was perhaps Japan's most revered high school ballplayer. At the time, Japanese high school baseball stars were showered with the same kinds of media attention and admiration our country bestows on our *college* athletes today. Although only a teenager, Eiji was already famous.

Sawamura had to be persuaded to join the All Nippons because doing so would likely ruin his college eligibility, prematurely ending his baseball career. Ultimately, the prospect of pitching to Ruth and Gehrig (and the promise of a career in the forthcoming professional baseball league in Japan) provided the tipping point.

By the time Eiji took the mound in Kusanagi Stadium, nine games had already been played, with the Americans scoring more than 10 runs in six of them. In Tokyo, the teenager had faced Ruth's team twice as a reliever and taken his lumps. This time he'd get a start, and the conditions couldn't have been more ideal.

This was the first game played in Kusanagi, a place where the midday sun glared in from above the right-field bleachers, directly into the batter's eyes. Nobody from either team could see the damn ball. Earl Whitehill, who had gone 14–11 for the Washington Senators, was virtually unhittable, as was the Japanese kid.

During one stretch, Eiji Sawamura fanned Charlie Gehringer, Babe Ruth, Lou Gehrig, and Jimmie Foxx in succession before Earl Averill (another Hall of Famer) grounded out to second, ending the string. It wasn't until the fourth inning, when Ruth lined a clean single into center field, that the All-American All-Stars were able to scratch a hit off the kid.

The score was knotted 0–0 in the seventh inning when the Japanese righty hung a curveball to Lou Gehrig, who crushed it over the right-field fence for a homer. All Nippon was able to get runners on base in both the eighth and ninth innings but couldn't drive them home. Although they had lost the game, 1–0, a legend was born.

Eiji Sawamura allowed 7 hits, walked only 1, and struck out 9 men. Although known for this one legendary contest, his overall performance versus the All-Americans wasn't quite as stellar:

32.1

Eiji Sawamura vs. All-Americans									
W	L	ERA	G	GS	CG	IP	H	BB	K
0	4	7.85	6	2	1	28.2	33	25	25

After his outstanding start, Mack met with Sotaro Suzuki, one of the envoys of the trip, inquiring about the possibility of signing Sawamura. Suzuki later met with the kid, who said he "was interested, but afraid to go." Mack decided not to press the issue any further.

◆ ◆ ◆

Far less well known than the 1934 series in Japan is the fact the All Nippons (now calling themselves the Dai Nippon "Tokyo" Giants) traveled to the United States in 1935 and 1936. Many of the same men who tested their mettle against Ruth and company (including star pitcher Eiji Sawamura) came here and performed in two coast-to-coast tours, playing a mix of minor league, college, semipro, and Negro league teams.

It's here in the States, with Sawamura and crew squaring off against teams *not* loaded with several future Hall of Famers, that we get a much clearer sense of where their development as baseball players stood. In 1935, they did very well against amateur and college players, going 72–14 in those contests. But against the American minor league teams, things proved much more difficult.

Over the course of their two tours, the Tokyo Giants won only 8 of 28 games versus

Japanese star pitcher Eiji Sawamura was courted by Philadelphia Athletics manager Connie Mack but declined the overtures, preferring to stay in his home country. *Courtesy of Scott Simkus*

Pacific Coast League teams, which represented the highest minor league classification in the United States. The Tokyo Giants weren't getting blown out, as they had against the major league All-Stars, but they struggled mightily from one game to the next. They seemed to find their level when traveling to Texas, though, where they went 4–5 against teams from the Class A Texas League and Class C East Texas League. These teams were two and three steps down the ladder from the PCL outfits and, realistically, in an area where an all-Japanese team would have found its competitive comfort zone. In their one recorded game versus a Negro league team, they lost 9–5 to the independent Cincinnati Tigers. Overall, against white minor league teams and the Negro league Tigers, the Tokyo Giants finished 12–26 (.316).

They were one World War and three decades away from becoming a genuine reservoir of major league–caliber talent.

That being said, Eiji Sawamura was, in fact, an interesting prospect in the same way African American Frank Grant had been in the 1880s. In the eight box scores that have thus far been unearthed, Eiji Sawamura was 4–3 against minor league teams, including a shutout of the Pacific Coast League's Oakland Oaks and a 14-strikeout performance versus the Hollywood Stars second-string club. Considering he was still only eighteen years old, Eiji's numbers versus higher-level minor league competition were not too shabby. In fact, his 5.5 strikeouts per 9 innings pitched (in an era when the typical major league leader hovered around 6.0) is an indication of a lively arm. If they'd had radar guns back then, I'm guessing Sawamura would have been in the same neighborhood as Rinku Singh, topping out at somewhere from 88 to 92 mph.

32.2

Eiji Sawamura vs. American Minor League Teams (1935–1936)									
W	L	ERA	G	GS	CG	IP	H	BB	K
4	3	5.20	8	7	6	64.0	76	13	39

If we add in his work versus the All-Americans and a relief appearance against the Negro league's Cincinnati Tigers, teenager Sawamura's (nearly complete) career record against American professional baseball teams looks like this:

32.3

W	L	ERA	G	GS	CG	IP	H	BB	K
4	7	5.89	15	9	7	94.2	110	38	69

◆ ◆ ◆

Just before the 1936 American tour, Eiji Sawamura published a piece in a popular Japanese magazine, sharing his thoughts on professional baseball. Reading the essay today, it's difficult not to see Sawamura as a petulant, immature kid.

Although he said he'd "love to pitch against the major leaguers," he didn't see it as a realistic possibility because he "hated America" and didn't care for the food there. The lack of rice in the American diet wouldn't allow him to pitch at full strength, he claimed. Plus, he wasn't wild about the prospects of living in a place "with formal customs" where "men weren't allowed to tie their shoes while in the presence of women."

"American women," wrote the eighteen-year-old expert in Western culture, "were arrogant."

Back in the 1880s, Frank Grant wasn't allowed to play Major League Baseball because the American majority's culture had no interest in giving an African American a chance. In the 1930s, Eiji Sawamura didn't pursue a major league career because the Japanese culture *had no interest in taking a chance on America*.

These things take time.

Japanese pitcher Masanori Marakami pitched (and pitched *well*) for the San Francisco Giants in 1964–65, but it wasn't until the arrival of Hideo Nomo thirty years later that a real infusion of top Japanese talent began trickling into the major leagues.

I don't believe the modern Japanese baseball legends, such as Sadaharu Oh and Isao Harimoto, shared the same pre–Pearl Harbor venom of Eiji Sawamura and his generation, but Japanese baseball stars of the 1960s and '70s didn't appear to have a strong desire to play here, even though they beat visiting major league clubs on a fairly regular basis. A change of mind-set needed to occur before stars like Ichiro Suzuki and Yu Darvish would come to the United States to play professionally.

◆ ◆ ◆

During the winter of 1935–36, Matsutaro Shoriki and his newspaper minions formed the Nippon Professional Baseball League. Sawamura was one of the earliest stars. Shoriki (the man who nearly lost his head for daring to import America's national game) sponsored the Tokyo Yomiuri Giants, who quickly became the most famous, most dominant franchise in Japanese baseball history.

◆ 33 ◆

1943: THE WORLD WAS BURNING

THE BUS RIDE TOOK ABOUT AN HOUR AND A HALF, as the Chicago American Giants motored from the south side of the city due north through some of the metropolitan area's most wealthy suburbs, all immaculately manicured lawns and families with generational wealth. They were headed to the Great Lakes Naval Training Station, a one thousand six hundred-acre compound nestled along the western shores of Lake Michigan. This would be perhaps their biggest game of the year, with more than ten thousand people on hand for the Saturday afternoon contest, and a national radio broadcast featuring Bob Elson, a future recipient of the Hall of Fame's Ford Frick Award, behind the microphone.

Manager Ted "Double Duty" Radcliffe's club was in first place in the Negro American League, having recently defeated their archrivals, the Cleveland Buckeyes, in a 14-inning contest. Their opponents would be the Great Lakes Bluejackets, helmed by the legendary Mickey Cochrane who, despite a head injury that had ended his Hall of Fame baseball career early, had enlisted in the navy to help the cause.

The Bluejackets were one of the premier military teams during World War II, their roster loaded with former and future white major leaguers. No fewer than sixteen of the twenty-five men who played with them in 1943 had major league experience; the others had all logged time in the high minors. Their starting lineup included outfielder Joe Grace, who batted .309 with a .410 OBP for the St. Louis Browns in 1941; Barney McCoskey, who led the American League with a .340 batting average and 19 triples for the Detroit Tigers back in 1940; and first baseman Johnny Mize, who just the year before had batted .305 with 26 home runs and a league-high 110 RBI for the New York Giants.

Great Lakes Bluejackets skipper Lt. Cmdr. Mickey Cochrane and his star player Johnny Mize in 1943.
National Baseball Hall of Fame Library, Cooperstown, New York

Not surprisingly, this big league–caliber team had run roughshod over its competition, winning 41 of 49 games against other military teams and factory clubs, most of whom were also augmented by the presence of former professional players. In fact, before meeting the Chicago American Giants, Cochrane's Bluejackets had made national headlines by defeating six *major league* squads and four American Association teams. Of their eight losses, six were to big-league teams. They would ultimately finish with a .538 record versus major league outfits during the 1943 season, going 7–6.

After their 8–7 victory over the Brooklyn Dodgers in late July, manager Mickey Cochrane beamed, "I'd like to have this Great Lakes team and a franchise in *either* major league, and we'd be the team to beat for the championship." Considering how depleted the major league ranks were due to the war, Cochrane probably wasn't too far off.

The Chicago American Giants were the first African American team invited to challenge the all-white Bluejackets at Constitution Field. In light of what had occurred in Detroit just six weeks earlier, this was not insignificant. On the bus were several Negro league veterans. Double Duty Radcliffe's brother, thirty-seven-year-old Alex Radcliffe, would man third base. Thirty-one-year-old Lloyd "Ducky" Davenport patrolled center field, while John Bissant (twenty-nine) and Henry Smith (twenty-eight) manned the corner outfield spots. And Double Duty, who had just turned forty-one on July 7, would be behind the plate. By far, the youngest man on the field that Saturday afternoon (on either team) was a twenty-year-old middle infielder named Art "Superman" Pennington.

◆ ◆ ◆

On June 20, a massive fight erupted between the white and black citizens of Detroit. Due to a shortage of labor in the war factories, more than three hundred and fifty thousand people had immigrated to the Motor City, most of them coming up from the Deep South, seeking a fresh start and attractive wages. About fifty thousand of these southerners were African American.

There was an extreme shortage of housing, and blacks found themselves living in lousy neighborhoods, sometimes paying double the amount whites paid for rent, for places that had no indoor plumbing. In the factories, where the war demands required seven-day, twenty-four-hour shifts, companies tinkered with progressive scheduling.

Just weeks before the riot, the Packard Motor Car Company promoted a handful of blacks to work on their assembly lines next to whites. The next day, 25,000 whites walked off the job, crippling the company's production schedule. They had no problem with blacks working, mind you, they just didn't want to work *next to them*.

Crazy, unfounded rumors about violence and rape perpetrated by both races ignited the powder keg on a Sunday afternoon. Soon thereafter, mobs of white and black men crisscrossed into one another's neighborhoods, vandalizing homes, burning streetcars, toppling vehicles, and assaulting random people in the streets. The Detroit Tigers baseball game was postponed as the city burned.

City officials finally asked President Roosevelt to send in the National Guard in order to restore peace. In three days of rioting, thirty-four people died, hundreds were injured, and $2 million in property damage was caused. Most of the folks who died were black, the majority of whom were shot by police.

◆ ◆ ◆

Clark Griffith wrestled with his conscience. The seventy-three-year-old owner of the Washington Senators had been involved with professional baseball since 1888. He was there in 1901 with John McGraw at the Eastman Hotel in Hot Springs, Arkansas, pitching batting practice to African American Charlie "Chief Tokohama" Grant, as Mac concocted an ill-fated scheme to integrate the upstart American League. Griffith had been perhaps the game's most aggressive owner, in terms of signing Cuban ballplayers, and in 1943 he had Alex Carrasquel (the big league's first Venezuelan) on his pitching staff.

Surely these things must have been clicking through his mind when he called Josh Gibson and Buck Leonard up to his office for a secret, in-season meeting. Both men had been designated as 4-F, ineligible for military service, and were still with the Homestead Grays, tearing up the watered-down Negro National League in 1943.

◆ ◆ ◆

Eiji Sawamura returned to Tokyo in January 1943 and shortly thereafter rejoined the Yomiuri Giants. The world was going to hell in a handbasket, but baseball was struggling onward in all corners of the globe. The lad who had come close to beating Babe Ruth and the All-Americans in 1934 was neither the same man, nor the same pitcher. Three years in the Imperial Army had taken its toll. He was supposedly shot in the left hand and had suffered through a bout of malaria while stationed in the Philippines. His pitching shoulder was said to have been injured as well during his multiple tours of duty.

In just four appearances with the Tokyo Giants in 1943, he was 0–3 with a 10.64 ERA. He was persuaded against coming back in 1944 by Sotaro Suzuki (one of the men who had organized the '34 tour) and instead retired from the game at the age of twenty-six. With the war tilting in favor of the Allies, Sawamura was recalled by the Imperial Army. On December 2, 1944, Sawamura was killed when his transport was sunk by an American submarine, off the coast of Taiwan.

◆ ◆ ◆

In the spring of 1943, Lieutenant Jackie Roosevelt Robinson walked over to the baseball diamond at Fort Riley, Kansas, asking for a tryout with the all-white baseball team. He was told he needed to play on the black team (they didn't have one) and sent on his way.

Robinson had been an All-American athlete and letterman in four sports at UCLA. When the Fort Riley athletic director approached him about playing on the integrated *football* team, he refused, even though a colonel had insisted he must. If he couldn't participate on the baseball team, he said, he had no interest in football. After this incident, Robinson was transferred to Fort Hood, Texas.

On July 6, 1944, Lieutenant Robinson refused to adhere to a southern bus driver's orders to move to the back of the bus, "where the coloreds belong." Robinson was aware the military had just ordered the desegregation of military buses, but when the base provost marshal sided with the driver, he found himself in a tremendous amount of trouble. Robinson faced a court-martial for insubordination. At his trial, he was exonerated by the judge. In November 1944 he was honorably discharged. The next year, he signed with the Kansas City Monarchs of the Negro American League, becoming teammates with Satchel Paige and Hilton Smith, among others.

◆ ◆ ◆

On New Year's Day in 1943, slugger Josh Gibson was rushed to Pittsburgh's St. Francis Hospital, suffering from what was likely alcohol poisoning. After ten days in the hospital, he'd return home. Shortly thereafter, he'd travel to Hot Springs, Arkansas, where he would spend five weeks drying out.

Four hundred and seventy-five miles to the southeast, in Toulminville, Alabama, a nine-year-old boy named Henry Louis Aaron played pickup ballgames with other boys from his neighborhood on a makeshift diamond in a pecan grove across the street from his family's new home. The Aaron house, which was built for less than $300, had six rooms, no windows, no electricity, and an outhouse in the backyard.

◆ ◆ ◆

Like Eiji Sawamura, who supported the Japanese war efforts by authoring pro-war propaganda pieces, Babe Ruth was here in the states, helping raise money for the Red Cross.

On July 28, 1943, Babe Ruth made one of his last appearances on a baseball diamond, managing a group of All-Stars versus Ted Williams's military team. Although forty-eight years old and hopelessly out of shape, Ruth pinch hit against Johnny Sain late in the game, drawing a base on balls.

The game raised $30,000 for the Red Cross.

◆ ◆ ◆

Back in Washington, DC with the Homestead Grays, Josh Gibson began dating a lady named Grace, whose husband was serving in the military overseas. He quickly lapsed back into the demons that had apparently been plaguing him for a couple years, pounding whiskey and beer and smoking marijuana. He gained weight and sometimes struggled to crouch behind the plate while catching.

Amazingly, his batting eye and power never abandoned him. In 40 games at Griffith Stadium (he didn't miss *any* of the scheduled home contests), Josh batted .503 with 21 doubles, 6 triples, 10 home runs, and 59 RBI in 1943. The entire American League didn't hit 10 home runs in Griffith Stadium in 1943.

◆ ◆ ◆

Just like everybody else in the game, owner Max Rosner's Brooklyn Bushwicks, the preeminent semipro baseball team in New York City, were decimated by the war. Buck Lai and Eddie Gerner were long gone. Oddly, it was the talent-starved major league teams, and *not* the military, who were cherry-picking Rosner's best players. In March 1943, the Chicago Cubs signed the Bushwicks' two best pitchers—Wally Signer and Bill Sahlin. Later on, shortstop Gar Del Savio got scooped up by the Philadelphia Phillies, and catcher Tony DePhillips was signed by the Cincinnati Reds.

Signer would go 16–7 in the Southern Association and get called up to the big club in September, fashioning a 2–1 record and a 2.88 ERA in four appearances. Sahlin would spend the entire season with Nashville in the minor leagues. Del Savio had a cup of coffee with the Phillies, then found himself with the Syracuse Chiefs in the International League for the remainder of the summer. DePhillips appeared in 35 games for the Reds, mostly as a defensive replacement.

As an indication of how bizarre things were in the baseball world, future Hall of Famer Lefty Gomez, who made one mediocre appearance with Clark Griffith's Washington Senators in 1943, finished the year pitching full time for the Brooklyn Bushwicks, with most of his starts being against military and Negro league clubs.

◆ ◆ ◆

Mickey Cochrane smoked a cigarette and shook hands with Double Duty Radcliffe in the dugout as both their clubs limbered up on the Great Lakes ballfield. They went over the ground rules and exchanged lineup cards. The Bluejackets had more than twenty men on their roster, while the American Giants had traveled with no more than the usual fourteen or fifteen, like a high school team.

During batting practice, future Hall of Famer Johnny Mize drew gasps from the overflowing grandstands with his exhibition of power.

A reporter for the *Chicago Defender*, the black weekly newspaper that had supported the Negro leagues since the days of Rube Foster, made note of the crowd's indifference toward their opponents. The ten thousand white folks in the grandstands—mostly naval recruits—settled in, seemingly expecting an easy victory for their vaunted Bluejackets. No record exists of how Cochrane felt about his competition, but I'd assume he'd have nothing less than the most supreme confidence in his troops. He truly believed they could compete for a major league championship, after all.

Just six days earlier, three of the American Giants, including Double Duty, his brother Alex, and Ducky Davenport, had appeared in the East-West All-Star Game in Comiskey Park, beating Josh Gibson and Buck Leonard's team

2–1, in front of a record 51,723 (mostly black) patrons. The great Satchel Paige started for the West, pitching 3 scoreless innings, while striking out 4.

The crowd wouldn't be nearly as large at Constitution Field, but with Bob Elson and the national radio broadcast, it's likely their game against the military juggernaut would be "experienced" by more people.

◆ ◆ ◆

Back in 1938, Clark Griffith confessed that integration was inevitable: "There are few big league magnates who are not aware of the fact that the time is not far off when colored players will take their places beside those of the other races in the major leagues."

Griffith could see what was coming, perhaps as far back as 1901, but what weren't clear were his motivations for speaking with Buck Leonard and Josh Gibson in 1943. According to Buck Leonard, in an interview conducted by historian John Holway, Griffith asked the two men point-blank if they believed they could succeed in the white major leagues during a private meeting in his office. Both players answered in the affirmative, and Griffith assured them that if integration *did* occur, they would certainly be among the first two selected, as they were the two best players in the league.

But the Senators owner also tried to explain to Josh and Buck that the existence of the Negro leagues would be in jeopardy if the majors began signing the top black stars. Leonard said he hadn't thought of that but was more interested in what was better, overall, for the players.

This, according to Leonard, was the end of the conversation. Integration, and the possibility of playing for the Washington Senators, was a subject never broached again. Historian Brad Snyder (author of *Beyond the Shadow of the Senators: The Untold Story of the Homestead Grays and the Integration of Baseball*) has argued rather convincingly that neither Griffith nor Homestead Grays owner Cumberland Posey may have been all that motivated to expedite the integration process.

African American businessman Cumberland Posey had owned and operated the Grays for more than twenty years. It provided a nice income for his family, as well as that of his brother, Seward, who was a partner in the operation. On the flip side, Clark Griffith's company earned roughly $160,000 in 1943 by renting their ballpark and floodlights to Posey's Homestead Grays when the Senators were out of town. Both owners—one black, one white—seemed satisfied with this arrangement.

It doesn't take a Harvard business degree to understand that the Negro leagues would suffer if their top stars were lifted.

It doesn't take a certificate in sociology to understand (especially considering the violent race riots in Detroit) that the owners in 1943 *feared* truly horrific (though in hindsight, *unlikely*) outcomes.

And it doesn't take an insurance actuary to understand that any potential increase in attendance generated by signing Josh Gibson and Buck Leonard probably wasn't going to offset the $160,000 earned by leasing the park when the Senators were out of town.

Toss in the prospects of potential violence, and from Griffith and Posey's point of view, it simply wasn't good business.

This is just my personal opinion, but I get the impression the Senators owner felt compelled to pull Leonard and Gibson aside to acknowledge that he respected them as ballplayers and believed in his heart they were worthy of the major leagues. He wanted to tell them that. He wanted them to know that. He was hedging his bets on the off-chance the doors did open. But, for reasons he could only partially articulate (business reasons, basically—and fear), he was explaining why they shouldn't get their hopes up.

◆ ◆ ◆

On July 6, just two weeks after the race riots in Detroit made national headlines and postponed one American League baseball game, Clark Griffith elected to back off on his long-standing policy preventing black and white clubs from competing against one another in the Senators' home park.

Ten thousand people showed up, without incident, to see the Homestead Grays whip the visiting Brooklyn Bushwicks in a battle of the best black and white outsider clubs in the nation. Josh Gibson launched a homer into the farthest reaches of the left-field bleachers, hit a triple, and walked twice. In the lineup for Max Rosner's Bushwicks was a twenty-two-year-old named Chuck Connors. Connors would later play briefly in the major leagues with both the Dodgers and Cubs, but he achieved greater fame portraying the Rifleman on the hit television series in the 1950s.

On the outsider baseball diamond, from one game to the next, you really had no idea what (or whom) you might see on the ballfield.

◆ ◆ ◆

Tom Ferrick, who'd been a relief pitcher and spot starter for the Cleveland Indians the previous year, started for the Great Lakes Bluejackets on August 7, 1943. He shut down the Chicago American Giants in the first inning, which didn't come as much of a surprise. In 31 appearances in the American League in 1942, he'd fashioned a fine 1.99 ERA.

In the second, the American Giants broke into the scoring column when left fielder Johnny Bissant singled to center, stole second base, then scampered home on Double Duty Radcliffe's base hit. In the third and fourth innings, Ferrick and the Bluejackets' defense fell apart.

Ducky Davenport started things in the third with a liner in the gap, which Glenn McQuillen (St. Louis Browns outfielder in 1942) muffed, allowing Davenport to race around the bases for an unearned run. Superman Pennington, the twenty-year-old phenom who was batting third in the American Giants lineup, singled, then went to third on cleanup man Pep Young's base knock.

Twenty-year-old Superman Pennington had a big day against Mickey Cochrane's military team, collecting two critical base hits while handling eight chances flawlessly at second base. *Courtesy of Scott Simkus*

Both men scored on a base hit by Henry Smith, putting the Negro American Leaguers ahead, 4–0.

In the meantime, Chicago pitcher Gentry Jessup was setting down the sailors with relative ease, holding them scoreless through the first four frames. Johnny Mize would wind up 4-for-5 with a double, triple, and an RBI, but overall, the servicemen would only manage to score 3 runs off the American Giants right-hander.

In the top of the fourth, Ralph Wyatt doubled, and Superman Pennington knocked him in with another single. Pep Young's base knock put runners on first and third, and on a hit-and-run play, Henry Smith drove in both men with a liner up the middle. The American Giants held on for a 7–3 victory.

Jessup, who had just pitched 14 innings versus Cleveland, didn't have his best stuff but muscled his way through a workmanlike, complete-game victory. He allowed 12 hits, walked 7, and struck out only 1.

It was the defense, particularly the work of the kid at second base, that helped keep the Bluejackets at bay. Superman Pennington handled eight chances flawlessly and helped twist two of the Giants' three rally-killing double plays.

Both the *Chicago Tribune* and *Chicago Defender* lauded the twenty-year-old's performance.

Manager Mickey Cochrane's crew would recover, beating the American Association's Indianapolis Indians a couple weeks later. With most of his players being shipped out for active duty, the Great Lakes team shut down their schedule in early September, finishing with an overall record of 52–10–1.

◆ ◆ ◆

Three days before the Grays played the Bushwicks in Washington, DC, a hulking mass of a man named Luscious "Luke" Easter (6'4", 240 pounds) walked out of the gates of Fort Leonard Wood, Missouri, a civilian once again. He'd been discharged from the military, due to a bum ankle, which he'd injured in a car accident two years earlier while driving to a baseball game.

Luke moved his wife and children to Chicago, where he took a job working in a factory. Easter was originally from St. Louis, where he had been a sandlot baseball legend who had a labor job during the day but earned extra money playing for the black minor league St. Louis Titanium Giants during the evenings and on weekends. Near the end of 1945, Easter approached Chicago American Giants manager Candy Jim Taylor (the same man who'd signed Superman Pennington six years earlier) about getting a chance to play in the Negro leagues. Taylor connected Easter with Abe Saperstein (the Harlem Globetrotters guy, who also happened to be a major booking agent in the world of outsider baseball, and confidant of Hank Greenberg), and in 1946, the first baseman joined the Cincinnati Crescents.

At thirty-one years old, Luke Easter would *finally* play professional baseball full time, albeit for the equivalent of a Triple-A-caliber Negro league club his first season. He'd sign a contract with the Homestead Grays the next year, then move on to the Pacific Coast League and, eventually, the Cleveland Indians. He'd wind up playing pro ball until he was forty-nine years old, slugging no fewer than 498 home runs against Negro league, winter league, major league, and minor league competition. Among these were some of the longest, most majestic shots ever witnessed, in dozens of ballparks from coast to coast.

If Eddie Gerner had been the "(almost) real Roy Hobbs" of the 1920s, then Luke Easter was the black Roy Hobbs of the postwar era. Half his career, what literally should have been his best years as an athlete, simply doesn't exist. There's no telling what kinds of records this man may have set had he enjoyed the luxury of a traditional career path. In fact, men like Luke Easter and Superman Pennington became the poster boys for baseball's Lost Generation. This was the class of ballplayer for whom integration was just five or ten years too late.

Those who preceded the Lost Boys (greats like Satchel Paige and Josh Gibson) had their legends cemented during the golden age of Negro league coverage. Those who followed the Lost Generation (Hank Aaron, Willie Mays, and Ernie Banks) were given the opportunity to prove themselves on the game's biggest stage.

Guys like Easter and Pennington (and dozens of other Negro league vets) get folded into a different category altogether. There were men like Easter who had partial (albeit late) opportunities in the big leagues. There were those, like Pennington, who excelled in the minors after integration but never got a shot because of their advanced age or other factors.

◆ ◆ ◆

In the spring of 1945, the *New York Times* published an article stating that of the 5,800 professional baseball players active at the time of Pearl Harbor (1941), nearly 5,400 (93 percent) had gone into the military, supporting the war effort. Not everybody served at the same time, or for the entire duration of the conflict, of course, but the talent was certainly depleted at the major league level.

Stars Bob Feller, Hank Greenberg, and Ted Williams missed several seasons while in the armed services, as did Negro league standouts Willard Brown, Bus Clarkson, and Leon Day, among others. Both white and black baseball at the top level were affected.

Out of desperation, a one-armed outfielder named Pete Gray appeared in 77 games for the St. Louis Browns, and dozens of teenagers, including Joe Nuxhall (fifteen years old), Carl Scheib (sixteen), and Tommy Brown (sixteen), appeared in big-league games. Whenever you read about baseball during the war, you'll see mention of Gray and Nuxhall. Although the teams were legitimately strapped for talent, the example of one disabled athlete and emphasis on the teenagers distorts the reality quite a bit.

Fact is, the teenagers didn't appear in too many games. During the height of the war (1942–44), the schoolboys accounted for only 581 total at-bats and 430 innings pitched, over the course of three entire seasons. For comparison, in the three years *prior* to the war's escalation (1939–41), teenagers accounted for far more at-bats (1,443) and nearly as many innings pitched (304), but nobody ever writes about this. And when you check this record against just about any three-year stretch in big-league history prior to the war, you'll discover the number of teenagers, and the amount of playing time during WWII, isn't in any real sense out of the ordinary. In terms of on-field contributions, the teeny boppers actually made less of an impact than in many nonwar years.

From 1942 to 1944, about three dozen teenagers made their debuts in the big leagues. During the years spanning 1911–13, back when Ty Cobb and

Walter Johnson were kings of the diamond, the number of teenagers getting their start in the bigs was close to sixty. Those dead-ball years might be considered the golden age of schoolboy opportunities. During that short, three-year span, the kids compiled 1,294 at-bats and pitched more than 500 innings, dwarfing the teenage numbers during the beleaguered war years in the 1940s.

By intuition, big-league clubs were still trying to field clubs with athletes in their middle to late twenties as much as possible. It's just a large percentage of these men were culled from the minor league rosters, 4-F lists, semipro teams such as the Brooklyn Bushwicks, and from the rolls of those recently retired.

In the middle of this global hell, how did the talent on the diamond compare to nonwar years? We can use the STARS method to show how the National, American, and Negro National leagues were affected from 1939 to 1947. And we'll put it in an easy-to-understand table:

33.1

Year	American League	National League	Negro National League
1939	360	343	237
1942	349	338	230
1944	298	300	207
1947	365	341	195

With this system, a higher STARS score represents the better-quality league. In 1939, the AL and NL are virtually neck and neck, with the Negro National League a step behind. Everybody takes a slight dip in 1942. By 1944, at the height of the war overseas, all three leagues hit rock bottom. The hierarchy remains the same, but in terms of percentage, the AL has been hit far worse than the other two loops. In simple terms, this is probably the impact of losing stars like DiMaggio, Feller, Greenberg, and Williams.

By 1947, everybody bounces back to prewar levels, except one: the Negro National League. It's a new world, with Jackie Robinson donning a Brooklyn Dodgers uniform. Blacks are being siphoned from the Negro leagues and given opportunities in the white minors. Integration is just getting started, but already the Negro leagues are in a death spiral. By the early 1950s, the black league would sport a STARS score near the very bottom of the talent rung. And the National League, whose teams were much more aggressive in signing blacks and Latinos, would see its STARS scores soar past those of the rival American League during the 1950s and '60s.

✦ 34 ✦

LUKE: .274

Luke had as much power as Mickey Mantle, if not more. The only man I ever saw with more power was the Babe.
—Bob Feller, *Cleveland Plain Dealer,* March 1979

IT WASN'T AS IF HE DIDN'T SEE IT COMING. Almost midway through the season, his batting average sputtered around .200 and he'd driven in fewer than three dozen runs from the cleanup spot. He was thirty-six years old, and his legs felt like wooden two-by-fours, knees hinged together with rusted steel. He struggled to reach ground balls to his left and right and butchered those slapped directly at him. He couldn't come up with scoops that had once been routine. For the first time in his life, playing first base was a challenge and hitting a ball squarely was a complete mystery.

No, it didn't surprise him one bit when general manager Hank Greenberg called him upstairs on the last day of June 1952 and told him he was being sent down to Indianapolis in the American Association. It soured the taste inside his mouth, but a demotion was perhaps the most merciful thing the organization could do.

✦ ✦ ✦

Rod Thomas brushed snow off the windshield as Victor Pritchett sat inside, nursing a stale gas station coffee, blasting Sister Sledge on the radio. This was going to be the Big One, the job they'd been planning for several months. In the glove box was a loaded .357 Magnum. Under the passenger's seat, sandwiched in between Victor's feet, was a sawed-off shotgun. It had been almost a year since Rod had been fired by the Aircraft Worker's Alliance, and this morning he'd get a little payback.

It was March 1979, and the two men were one hour away from justice. Get in, get out. Nobody gets hurt, no more money problems for a long, long time, brother.

◆ ◆ ◆

Hank Imrey's stomach felt as if it was going to twist inside out, rip through his abdomen. His ears were still ringing from the honky-tonk jukebox, and although he'd dozed off for an hour or two in the gravel parking lot, he couldn't shake the fog out of his eyes. Hank kept one hand on the wheel, used the other to jiggle a couple Kents out of their box, onto the empty passenger's seat.

He was headed home, to his father's house, going 50 mph through a residential neighborhood where 20 would have been considered too fast. The sun was rising, Saturday, springtime in suburban Ohio.

◆ ◆ ◆

After meeting with Greenberg, big Luke Easter gathered his equipment and personal effects from the clubhouse. He needed to be in Indianapolis the next day, but before making the six-hour trek, he'd go through the fan mail rubber-banded at the bottom of his locker one last time. The 6'4" first baseman didn't know when, or if, he'd ever return to Cleveland Municipal Stadium. For a thirty-six-year-old batting .208, there were no guarantees of another major league opportunity.

A couple years in the big leagues and most of these fan letters looked exactly the same, but one envelope caught Easter's eye. Handwritten in pencil by a young boy from the suburbs, the note beseeched Luke to "keep his head up through the tough times" and "keep plugging away." Usually these envelopes were stuffed with requests, people asking for something: an autograph, a photograph, free tickets. This one, though, offered heartfelt encouragement at a time when Luke needed it most. And from a child, of all people.

Easter studied the author's name—Daniel Jack—eight-years-old, from Willoughby Township, Ohio. He sent the kid an autograph and a sincere thank-you. Luke folded the letter and tucked it inside his billfold. This was a rarity: he always appreciated the well wishes, but this was one fan letter Luke Easter actually felt compelled to keep.

◆ ◆ ◆

Victor said he had a bad feeling about this thing, and Rod told him to shut the fuck up, put the blanket over the shotgun. He didn't want the gas station attendant seeing the steel as they filled up before heading to Euclid, just outside the city limits.

They'd been through something of a dry run, two weeks earlier. Rod wanted to make sure the union steward still cashed the checks for the night crew. Wanted to be sure he still did this alone. Wanted to confirm it was the same gentle old-timer running the show. Wanted everything to be easy peasy, bro.

Two weeks earlier, they watched from across the street as the union steward entered the bank, then exited with a large canvas bag. Sure enough, same dude taking care of payroll from back when Rod still worked there. They took note of where he parked, how he hobbled gingerly on the ice, and in which direction he steered his vehicle when leaving the strip mall parking lot.

Victor had been there with Rod, plotting their getaway route fourteen days ago, but still his stomach felt as though it would twist inward on itself and rupture.

◆ ◆ ◆

Hank tried to keep the wheel steady as he groped for one of the loose cigarettes bouncing on the passenger seat. Fished his Zippo from his front breast pocket, popped it lit with a quick flick of the wrist, and began cursing.

The sun was in his eyes, he smelled of whiskey, and he'd done that thing where he put the Kent in his mouth backward and lit the goddamn filter. He tossed the butt out the window and noticed he'd drifted into the wrong lane, headed straight for an oncoming car.

Hank turned his wheel hard to the right as the other guy veered in the other direction. Although it seemed a head-on was unavoidable, their vehicles only sideswiped one another lightly, which was nothing short of a minor miracle. The oncoming car wound up in a ditch and, aside from some scratches along the side, was otherwise in decent condition. The driver was safe but shaken.

Hank was traveling at a much higher rate of speed, and his wheels screeched as he slammed the brakes, ran over four mail boxes, and crashed hard into an electric pole. The Buick's front end was so badly mangled, it was actually difficult to believe it had ever been a motor vehicle at all. Hank was alive but bleeding.

Steam whistled from a cracked radiator, dogs howled in the distance. This was a Saturday morning that would haunt those who lived along this stretch of road the rest of their lives.

◆ ◆ ◆

Luke stayed with the Indianapolis Indians for only two weeks before Hank Greenberg summoned him back to Cleveland, which in its own way was nothing short of a minor miracle. With Daniel Jack's letter in tow, he went on a tear against minor league pitching, batting .340 with 6 home runs and 12 RBI in only 14 games. His confidence was back, and he believed he owed at least part of his good fortune to little Danny's letter.

Easter kept the handwritten note the remainder of the season, and his groove continued, even after returning to the Indians' starting lineup. The old man batted .319 in the second half, with 20 homers and 64 RBI in just 57 games. After being concerned his career might be over, on July 1st, Luke rallied in inspired fashion, finishing thirteenth overall in the race for American League MVP.

The Indians, 37–32 when Luke was sent down, finished the 1952 season 93–61, just 2 games behind the eventual World Series–champion New York Yankees.

Luke Easter was famous for his tape-measure home runs. *Courtesy of Scott Simkus*

◆ ◆ ◆

The two men waited for the union steward to exit the Cleveland Trust Bank branch.

Things, Rod pointed out to his jittery partner, were going "exactly as planned." Victor lit a roach that had been buried in the ashtray, took a couple hits to calm his nerves. Rod kept his eyes fixed on the glass doors.

When the old man finally emerged with the canvas sack, Rod put the car in drive and rolled up on the union steward, cutting him off before he could reach his car. Rod and Victor jumped out of the El Camino, pointing their guns at the big dude with thick glasses, and told him to fork over the loot.

The man was startled, but instead of conceding, he pulled a revolver from his coat pocket. Inside the Cleveland Trust Bank, a loan officer noticed the ambush outside the front window and nervously dialed the police.

A single shot rang out, several pigeons scattered upward. Somebody screamed for help.

◆ ◆ ◆

Luke Easter peeled the rubber band off the Sunday *Cleveland Plain Dealer* and studied the large, front-page photograph of twisted metal that had once been a child's bicycle. On the front page, there were other pictures—those of three smiling little boys, two brothers and their friend—each of whom had been killed in the same tragic accident one day earlier.

The story said Hank Imrey, thirty-eight, from Mayfield Heights, lost control of his vehicle, careening into the three boys as they delivered newspapers out in Willoughby Township. After questioning by police, Imrey admitted he had been on a two-day drinking binge and may have been intoxicated at the time of the collision.

The names of the victims were Peter Allen, twelve years old; his younger brother, Fred, nine; and their best friend, Daniel Jack Jr., nine. The newspaper story noted the three fatalities raised Lake County's traffic death toll to ten for 1953, as if it were a box score. Luke Easter looked at the names three or four more times, then pulled out his billfold and opened the handwritten letter.

"Keep your head up," it began. At the bottom, signed in pencil, it said, "Daniel Jack, Willoughby Township—8 years old."

Luke pushed his unfinished breakfast away and stood up from the table, shaking. He called for his wife, asked her to come downstairs, but his voice had become too small for her to hear it.

◆ ◆ ◆

Near the end of the funeral service, a huge black man entered the back of the church. This was the early 1950s in a part of suburban Cleveland where black folks were rarely seen anywhere, let alone inside a white house of worship. He approached the parents of Daniel Jack, the young boy lying inside the casket, and apologized for being late. He wasn't familiar with the neighborhood, he explained, and had a hard time finding the church.

Luke produced the letter Daniel had written ten months earlier, explaining how much it meant to him when he was struggling with the Cleveland Indians. With tears welling up in his eyes, the hulking man tried to put into words the devastation he'd felt when he heard the news. He tried to explain how sorry he was for the loss of Daniel, as well as that of the other two young boys.

◆ ◆ ◆

"This ain't how things was supposed to go," Victor said, deadpan.

"No shit, blood," snapped Rod, and for the second time in the morning, he told Victor to shut the fuck up. Chill. They were driving 80 mph with two squad cars on their ass, trying to get back to Cleveland where they figured they could shake them in the labyrinth of decaying neighborhoods.

Rod hooked around a corner, nearly hitting a pedestrian, then gunned it south, down East 140th Street, into an industrial part of the city. In the rearview, he noticed the fuzz were keeping pace, and this is where Rod lost control of the El Camino, as the road dipped toward a railroad underpass. They bounced off a cement pillar, spinning into a 720, before the vehicle finally came to a steamy halt. They were surrounded by sirens and people headed to work in the old factories and others leaving after overnight shifts.

Instinctively, Victor opened his door and fired his shotgun toward the nearest squad car, shattering its windshield, but he failed to injure anybody. He then jumped into another car, which had stopped to avoid their spinning wreck, and told the shocked motorist—some dude on his way to work—to slide over, or he'd kill him. The cops riddled this second vehicle with bullets, flattening the tires before Victor finally gave up. Rod unloaded a couple shots from his .357 Magnum, and the cops returned fire; then Rod tried to get away on foot. Coming out of the underpass, the road was steep and icy, and Rod slipped, fumbling his gun, a couple wads of cash, and an 8-track tape he'd inexplicably grabbed when bolting the El Camino. He decided to lie on the pavement, prostrate, and surrender.

The ballgame was over. They were going to lose this one.

◆ ◆ ◆

The body of the union steward lay motionless on the icy pavement outside the Cleveland Trust Bank in suburban Euclid. He'd been killed instantly, by a single shot to the chest, dumdum bullet from a .357 Magnum. Scattered around his body was $35,000, cash, abandoned by Rod and Victor during their frantic getaway. The union steward's revolver, with all its bullets still chambered, lay a couple feet away, in a crimson puddle.

The union steward's name was Luke Easter. He was sixty-three years old now, husband of nearly thirty years, father of three grown children. He'd been employed by the Aircraft Workers Alliance for nearly fifteen years. Played first base for the Negro National League's Homestead Grays in the 1940s, and the Cleveland Indians back in the early 1950s, then later starred in the minor leagues where he made friends from Buffalo, New York, to San Diego, California.

Back in April 1953, Luke Easter walked into a church in suburban Cleveland to pay respects to one of his biggest fans, a little boy whose life had been tragically cut short by a reckless drunk driver. A little boy whose handwritten letter had helped Luke during perhaps the darkest moment of his professional baseball career.

When Luke Easter's own life was taken, just a mere six miles from where young Daniel Jack had passed away two and a half decades earlier, the eulogies poured in. They came from former teammates and opponents, from co-workers and managers at the Aircraft Workers Alliance, from friends across the country.

People wrote about how Luke had inspired them when he was a player, signed an autograph, or shared a kind word. Luke's superiors at AWA talked about Easter's ease with people, how he had a natural gift for making everybody feel important. And there was a letter from a grown man who was a cousin of Peter and Fred Allen, and good friends with Daniel Jack, back when he was younger. He wrote the newspaper to offer his condolences and acknowledge the role Easter had played in his own healing, many years earlier, when his idyllic childhood was turned upside down one early Saturday morning, after his cousins—and their best friend, Daniel Jack—were killed instantly by a drunk driver.

◆ ◆ ◆

One of the odd revelations after Luke Easter passed away was his date of birth. During his career in Cleveland, the big first basemen had always been coy about his age, never giving a straight answer about when and where he'd been born.

Courtesy of the records at the Aircraft Worker's Alliance, the public finally discovered the truth: Luscious Luke Easter had come into this world on August 4, 1915, in Jonestown, Mississippi. This meant that when he finally made his debut with the Cleveland Indians, back in 1949, he was already thirty-four years old, an age when most slugging ballplayers were ending their careers, not starting them.

Exactly where had this man been the first fifteen years of his baseball career? People knew he'd played a couple seasons with the old Homestead Grays of the Negro National League, but the vast majority of his baseball past was a mystery. It was outside the game's written record.

◆ 35 ◆

ROSETTA STONE (PT. 2)

FOLLOWING ARE TWO TABLES BASED on the results of 7,652 games played from 1901 to 1950. Every one of these games featured professional ballplayers, including the very best of all time. Babe Ruth, Ty Cobb, Joe DiMaggio, and Ted Williams all appeared in these games, as did Oscar Charleston and Buck O'Neil and Turkey Stearnes. The Yankees and the Red Sox and the Cardinals are included in these contests, as are the Kansas City Monarchs and St. Louis Stars and all the other great, good, and mediocre Negro league clubs. They're all here, in the tables.

The paid admissions for the games often exceeded ten or fifteen thousand fans, but sometimes, when the weather was cold or rainy or the promotional team had dropped the ball, there'd be fewer than a couple hundred fans on hand, sitting in the bleachers. A conservative estimate is that a minimum of seven million people paid to watch these games. And although we've assembled the records and placed them in a nice, tidy chart, these contests aren't part of any official, unofficial, or superficial baseball record book. They're just *there*, waiting for us to figure out what to do with them. This is the Baseball Rosetta Stone, Part 2.

To refresh our memories, let's take a look at table 35.1, which contains the same data found in Table 2.3:

35.1

MLB vs. Various Levels	W	L	T	PCT.	RF	RA
Negro Leagues	115	128	7	.473	4.10	4.29
Triple-A	731	394	23	.649	6.12	4.33
Military	151	61	5	.712	7.12	4.02

MLB vs. Various Levels *continued*	W	L	T	PCT.	RF	RA
Double-A	517	175	17	.747	6.66	3.74
High Single-A	302	85	7	.780	6.99	3.61
Semipro	690	155	17	.817	6.92	3.03
Low Single-A	140	23	2	.859	8.13	3.28
College	143	11	0	.938	9.88	2.57

Table 35.2 features the Negro league teams versus the same levels of competition, during the same period of time, as the white major leaguers. You'll notice some extremely familiar patterns lining up, but there are some differences in winning percentage and scoring environments that those with keen baseball eyes may find revealing.

35.2

Negro League vs. Various Levels	W	L	T	PCT.	RF	RA
Major League	128	115	7	.527	4.29	4.10
Triple-A	86	58	4	.597	4.34	3.41
Military	6	4	0	.600	4.30	2.70
Double-A	45	24	2	.652	4.89	5.39
High Single-A	26	15	0	.634	5.78	5.34
Semipro	2,279	1,020	70	.691	6.17	3.78
Low Single-A	56	19	2	.747	7.34	8.78
College	33	7	0	.825	8.28	3.90

There's little doubt the top two brands of baseball from 1901 to 1950 were the major leagues and the Negro leagues. One would have to completely redefine deductive reasoning to believe otherwise. So, using these tables (and common opponents) as the gauge, how would these two groups of talent fare, overall, had they played a 154-game balanced schedule, including 21 games against one another?

35.3

1901–1950	Wins	Losses	Pct.
Major League	113	41	.734
Negro League	100	54	.649

This seems plausible. Overall, an average major league team would fare better than an average Negro league team over the course of an equal, balanced schedule. The big dogs, the New York Yankees and Homestead Grays of the world, would have certainly fared better, while the lowly Washington Senators and Negro league basement dwellers would have lagged further behind.

This seems to dovetail with everything else we've covered in the book thus far.

◆ 36 ◆

SATCH

H E WAS LATE.

The fried chicken was already served, an emcee had spilled his guts, and five dozen acne-challenged boys were getting antsy. School superintendent Philip Falk, who had nearly put everybody into a mass coma by sharing a few words of scholarly encouragement earlier in the evening, got up to speak for a *second time* after finishing his plate of mashed potatoes.

Things were getting desperate; somebody—it may have been Alderman Harold Rohr—suggested the boys have a singing contest. You know, each table could belt out their school fight song, and the dignitaries in attendance would vote on who they believed was best. This was *American Idol*, circa winter 1960, an awkward twist in an already uncomfortable evening.

Everybody moaned.

Rohr was a square.

People began taking turns at the podium. Jim Atkins, president of the West Side Business Men's Association (WSBMA), butted his cigarette and killed a couple minutes in front of the group. Secretary of State Bob Zimmerman, representing Wisconsin governor Gaylord Nelson (who apparently had more important things to do than attend the banquet), finished up his highball and took a stab as emcee, as did Ron Nord, assistant basketball coach at the University of Wisconsin, who used his impromptu speech to extol the virtues of hard work and persistence and how these young men should take the lessons learned on the hardwood and apply them to life.

The whole damn evening had devolved into an amateur Toastmasters convention hell.

The high school boys, being teenagers and all, had completely tuned out the speakers by this point and were thinking about getting laid or coming up with excuses for the homework they didn't complete. Some of them were thinking about getting some sleep: they had school the next day.

Nearly two hours after his scheduled arrival, the keynote speaker for the evening, legendary fastball pitcher Satchel Paige, was still nowhere to be found.

The event was an annual affair in the state capital; a high school basketball banquet, hosted at the swanky Madison Club, honoring four local hoops teams, as well as the state champion Wausau group. Coach Marsh Taylor and his trophy winners had motored sixty-five miles due west from the outskirts of Milwaukee to attend the dinner.

Just as Superintendent Falk was threatening to get up for a third speech, a telephone echoed in the lobby. It was Satch, and although he had reached the Madison city limits, he needed directions to the clubhouse. He was at a filling station just a couple miles away, where the slightly inebriated clerk behind the counter, relieved he wasn't going to be robbed, let the tall black stranger make a call.

This was 1960, and Leroy "Satchel" Paige was at a crossroads in his life, toeing the line between being a part-time ballplayer and full-time celebrity. Just a year earlier, the ageless right-hander had gone 10–10 with the Miami Marlins of the International League, featuring a 2.95 ERA. Although well into his fifties, he was still a legitimate pitcher at the minor league level but couldn't hook up with anybody from organized ball in 1959. Instead, he went Hollywood.

For a reported $10,000 (about $70,000 in today's money), he traveled to Durango, Mexico, playing the role of Sergeant Tobe Sutton in *The Wonderful Country*, a romantic western starring Robert Mitchum. He'd later call his acting experience one of the most gratifying (and profitable) projects of his life.

"I loved it. You get to sit down a lot and the money's good."

Upon arriving at the Madison Club, Satch grabbed a frosted mug of Blatz and found a chair in the corner of the wood-paneled room, where he caught his breath for a few minutes. His trip to the basketball banquet had apparently been a harrowing, white-knuckle affair.

Paige had been on the road for more than thirty years at this point, having first left his family's Mobile, Alabama, home back in 1926 to join the Chattanooga Black Lookouts of the Negro Southern League. Thirty-three years later, he'd taken the mound in just about every state across the union, plus Mexico, Cuba, the Dominican Republic, Puerto Rico, and Canada. If he won just 15 games during each of those seasons (and keep in mind, there were years where he won more than 30 on the outsider baseball circuit), he'd approach 500 for his career.

After settling himself, Satch lit a smoke and then grabbed the microphone, apologizing for his tardiness.

"It became so foggy twenty miles out of Beloit, I open th' window so I could see," Paige explained to the room. "The fog drifted in, and I didn't see my partner in the front seat 'til we got to town."

The region had been blanketed in heavy, wet snow just a few days earlier, and on the day of the event, the rubber-ball temperatures of late March had bounced up into the high fifties, saturating the air with moisture, wreaking havoc on visibility.

Satchel put everybody at ease with his charm and humor, telling a few well-worn stories he had probably told a million times before. Then he opened up the room to questions, where coaches and basketball players lobbed batting practice fastballs his way:

> Q: *Who were the best hitters you ever faced?*
> A: *Josh Gibson and Ted Williams.*
>
> Q: *What was your best year as a hitter?*
> A: *There are two things in baseball I never was: a runner or a hitter.*
>
> Q: *How do you keep your arm from getting sore?*
> A: *I don't put anything on it except hot water; I don't give it a chance to get sore. You can get out of shape sitting on the bench.*
>
> Q: *What advice would you give young pitchers?*
> A: *Learn one good pitch and control; that gives you five or six pitches.*

At the end of the session, Satchel told the boys he planned on returning to the major leagues but "didn't know when."

Around this same time, an interview with Chicago White Sox owner Bill Veeck appeared in Wendell Smith's *Pittsburgh Courier* column. "I talked to Leroy," Veeck explained, "and he tells me he's in training.

"He's up in Beloit, Wisconsin, getting ready to throw for anyone who will hire him."

Veeck went on to explain how he had six scouts follow Paige the previous summer, during the barnstorming games, and they all believed the old man was a better reliever than Gerry Staley or Turk Lown, who, he pointed out, "are two of the best relievers in the majors today."

Veeck said they decided against pursuing Paige, as the team was doing well already (they'd wind up in the World Series against the Dodgers) and that adding him might have proven to be a distraction.

"I've seen most of 'em," said Veeck, "Including Bob Feller and all the others, and he knows—and knew—more about pitching than any of them. He's the greatest."

Then why didn't you sign him? Smith wondered.

"Because Staley and Lown were going good. They would have had to sit on the bench if Satch had been with us. That would have made them angry."

By the time Paige reached the podium at the Madison basketball banquet, it had already been a busy couple months. After returning from Mexico, his wife, Lahoma, gave birth to a baby girl (Rita Jean) on February 9. Then it was up to Wisconsin to finalize arrangements for a 150-game barnstorming tour (and attend the first of what would be dozens of paid speaking engagements). Around January, he had inked a deal with writer David Lipman and Doubleday & Company to pen his memoirs. It might not be the "easy" Hollywood money, but he was lining up a nice ten- to twelve-month revenue stream. He now had a wife and seven kids to take care of.

The man who got fogged out of the car with Satchel on the ride up to Madison was a booking agent from Beloit named Dempsey Hovland. Hovland was putting together an outfit called the "Caribbean Kings," who would travel the country and Canada, playing charity ballgames for a flat fee. The Wisconsin entrepreneur had cut his teeth years earlier, playing with the House of David, and had already secured the services of ex-major leaguer Virgil Trucks and several young Cuban ballplayers.

The tour started as planned in April, but Trucks, who had retired two years earlier and was about twelve years younger than Satchel, came up with a bad hamstring and got hit hard in several outings. He was unable to field his position and often gave way to Paige to clean up his mess. He wasn't used to throwing every other day.

Traveling through New Mexico and Arizona, the Kings won some, lost others, and struggled to put fans in the seats. At the end of May, Paige simply disappeared: he hopped in his car and drove home.

Dempsey Hovland, who had put some time and money into the venture, was livid. "I can't run a business like this," he was quoted in several nationally syndicated newspaper stories. "I have to give the fans what they pay to see . . .

playing in the majors might have been the worst thing that could have happened to Paige.

"When a guy gets a taste of a certain kind of living, it's hard for him to leave it. Some fellows just never adjust to the change."

Two weeks later newspaper stories reported Satchel Paige had signed with a semipro team near his home in Kansas City. He was going to pitch for the Salina Bluejays of the Victory League and hoped to participate in the national semipro tournament in Wichita come August.

Salina, a couple hours west of Kansas City, is known as the geographical center of the continental United States. After thirty-one years of beating the bushes, traveling to all corners of the Western Hemisphere, Satchel Paige had returned home, smack dab in the middle of the country.

In his first game with the Bluejays, Satch pitched well: 3 innings of shutout ball, with 1 hit and 2 strikeouts. That night, after the game, Paige claimed he was robbed on his way back to his hotel room.

According to newspaper accounts:

> Paige called the police department about 2 AM to report a Negro man and woman, about 30 to 40 years old, met him on the street and stopped to talk to him.
>
> They chatted about baseball for some time, when Paige asked the couple where he could get something to eat. They told him they knew a place and would be glad to get something for him.
>
> He gave them a $10 bill, and they left. Paige waited for about 1-1/2 hours in his car but they did not return. Then he called police.

Interestingly, C. F. Leiker, the man who ran the Salina ballclub, was a policeman in town. There were no reports that the perpetrators were ever caught (or that they ever actually existed). Paige shrugged off the incident and pitched well for the team. They had a decent ballclub: a half-dozen or so former minor leaguers, college kids, and several high school baseball stars. Their opposing teams were similarly constructed. After Salina was upset in the state tournament, Paige joined the powerful Wichita Weller Indians and won their first game in the National Semipro Tournament, an event he had electrified while pitching for a semipro club from Bismarck, North Dakota, back in 1935.

As for the Caribbean Kings, with Paige gone their tour completely fell apart. Fidel Castro, who was now running Cuba, contacted Hovland, demanding the return of the seven or eight teenagers who were on his active roster. Virgil Trucks, in a *Sporting News* article dated August 25, was still hot about how things unfolded. "I lost $5,000 on the tour, mainly because Satchel Paige could never be counted upon to show up. We had contracted to play throughout the country and Paige was supposed to be with us. The guarantees were no good in those cities where he failed to show."

Before the Kings' baseball junket blew up, Trucks wrote a letter to Pittsburgh Pirates general manager Joe Brown to see if he could get a job throwing batting practice, which he did for the last couple months of the season.

The next year, Satchel Paige finished "writing" his autobiography, hit the road to pitch some barnstorming games again, and wound up in the Pacific Coast League for a few games, where he struck out 19 men in 25 innings, while issuing only 5 free passes.

Satchel Paige didn't lie to those kids at the basketball banquet. In 1965, at the age of 58, he made one last appearance in the major leagues, pitching 3 scoreless innings for the Kansas City Athletics.

◆ 37 ◆

THE SCARLET NUMBERS

Turns out, Clark Griffith was right: as soon as integration occurred, the Negro league's days were numbered. The mighty Homestead Grays, perennial champions of the East, founded in the days preceding the First World War, folded in 1951, just three short years after Jackie Robinson made his debut with the Brooklyn Dodgers. The two Negro leagues consolidated their operations when various franchises folded, then collapsed entirely in the mid-1950s, with individual teams struggling on for several years after that.

The same would be true for the white semipro teams and the outsiders who dominated municipalities or barnstormed around the country every summer. The House of David folded after the 1955 season. The Brooklyn Bushwicks shuttered up their operations after 1951. The Chicago City League was long gone, replaced by slow-pitch softball. With a massive influx of Cuban and other Latino players into organized baseball in the 1950s and 1960s, mostly at the minor league level, winter baseball lost much of its luster. Fidel Castro built political gates around Cuba's baseball paradise.

When pressed for reasons why barnstorming baseball was collapsing, George Anderson, who'd been a star for the House of David baseball team for more than twenty years, simply replied, "Television." Nobody could have recognized the irony when Chuck Connors, the Rifleman, suited up for the Brooklyn Bushwicks during their series with the Homestead Grays in 1943, that his medium, even more so than integration, would forever change the landscape of professional baseball at its fringe.

Baseball was still wonderful and all, but people simply had better things to do after World War II. At their peak, the Brooklyn Bushwicks averaged 350,000 paid customers in eighty home dates, exceeding the attendance figures of several major league franchises. Owner Max Rosner, who became wealthy through outsider baseball, noticed things turning for the worse in the early 1930s, much sooner than the Robinson signing, citing the popularity of radio and the creation of highway systems that allowed folks to venture out of city neighborhoods on weekends. After the end of World War II, there was no reversing this flow, as the tides of change surged furiously toward the little screen, the weekend getaway, and everything else one could possibly do with their spare time.

The Robinson signing, which provided a temporary bump in attendance for the Dodgers, only delayed the inevitable in Flatbush. People were leaving the city already, moving to new, affordable housing in suburban Long Island. Just seven years after the Bushwicks collapsed, and two years after Jackie Robinson retired, the Brooklyn Dodgers moved clear across the country to sunny Los Angeles.

Postseason barnstorming limped through the 1950s and into the early 1960s, a diamond-shaped anachronism. Teams of both black and white (and mixed) major leaguers toured the country, but the profitability of these junkets shriveled with each passing year.

One of the greatest teams ever assembled, the 1956 Willie Mays All-Stars, which is virtually forgotten today, toured the South from mid-October through early November without losing a single game, yet they played in front of only nine hundred fans in Birmingham, Alabama; eight hundred and twenty in Corpus Christi, Texas; and five hundred in Brownsville, Texas. High school football teams in the area were playing in front of larger audiences than a squad featuring Mays, Hank Aaron, Frank Robinson, and Ernie Banks, the Mount Rushmore of superstars in the National League at that time. After returning to New York, Willie Mays echoed the House of David's George Anderson, blaming the poor turnout on television.

"We hit some towns in Texas," said Mays, "where they had television down there for the first time this year . . . I guess they just got a little too much baseball and didn't want to see us play." To be clear, it wasn't televised *baseball* that was killing attendance at barnstorming ballgames, it was all of the other fun stuff on the boob tube: the game shows, westerns, and variety programs.

Mays, who had organized his first all-star team the previous fall, conceded that attendance was down nearly 60 percent from the 1955 figures, owing not just to TV but to high ticket prices and poor promotion as well. Or at least that's what he believed. Although not part of the Mays tours, one of the more popular opponents in the 1950s postseason exhibitions was the Indianapolis Clowns of the Negro American League. In 1953, the Jackie Robinson All-Stars played an ongoing series versus the Clowns, representing something of a milestone: black major league All-Stars playing against Negro league teams in the postseason. They played in front of crowds of 1,500, 1,200, and 2,659. Besides TV and cars and all the other fun stuff folks could do with their time, integration had demystified the black ballplayer. People could follow their exploits throughout the summer, in the major leagues, playing with (and against) the best in the world. They could buy a baseball card with Roberto Clemente's mug on it and rubber-band him in a pile with Warren Spahn and Eddie Mathews.

The Indianapolis Clowns, the Negro league team that gave Hank Aaron his first opportunity in professional baseball, somehow lasted into the 1960s, albeit as a bizarre, county fair–type operation, under new ownership and featuring only white players.

◆ ◆ ◆

If you look up the all-time minor league home-run leaders, you'll notice the man on top of the career list is Hector Espino. During his twenty-five seasons in professional baseball, Hector popped 484 home runs, of which only 3 were hit here in the United States. Espino, who was from Chihuahua, Mexico, played almost his entire career in his home country, in a league technically classified as Triple-A but in terms of actual talent was something much less than that. Espino hit 481 home runs in a league roughly the equivalent of today's Single-A.

Google *Sadaharu Oh* and you'll discover this Japanese first baseman hit 868 home runs during his twenty-two-year professional career, all of which was played with Tokyo's Yomiuri Giants. He added 29 home runs in the Japanese World Series, 13 all-star game bombs, and another 25 during exhibition games with major league teams (including one off of Tom Seaver). He hit no fewer than 935 home runs during his career, playing minor league competition that was certainly equal to—and arguably superior to—the Mexican League, and yet his name isn't included on that list with Hector Espino. The Japanese League is ignored here, but Mexico is included.

Buck Lai played roughly fifteen seasons with the Brooklyn Bushwicks after several years in the minor leagues. The Bushwicks' roster, peppered with former and future major leaguers, was the equivalent of that of a high minor league–caliber club; they played thousands of games against Negro league, semipro, and barnstorming major and minor league outfits. The statistical record of Lai, and his Bushwicks brethren (including Chuck Connors, Dazzy Vance, Jeff Tesreau, Lefty Gomez, Eddie Gerner, and others), is simply uncollected at this point—and unclassified. It's a gap in the record.

◆ ◆ ◆

Back in 1985, I remember watching Pete Rose loop a ball into left-center field, breaking Ty Cobb's all-time record with base knock number 4,192. The Reds' home field, Riverfront Stadium, was jam-packed, and a national television audience looked on as Rose battled the San Diego Padres' Eric Show. After the single, Rose's teammates hoisted him on their shoulders, flashbulbs erupted, and tears flowed. Pete Rose's son met him at first base and hugged his father. It's something I'll never forget.

And I bet Pete won't either.

Later on, some nitpicker went through all the records, discovering Ty Cobb had only amassed *4,190* base hits in his career, meaning Rose had actually passed the Georgia Peach a couple days earlier, with a hit off of Chicago Cubs journeyman right-hander Reggie Patterson. I'm a Cubs fan, so I happened to be watching that game, too. Like fans who paid to see Oscar Charleston and the Pittsburgh Crawfords play their village's local semipro team back in 1933, sometimes you're unaware of history being made, but it's not because you're not paying attention. Sometimes it's because the numbers aren't right.

Hack Wilson was the all-time single-season RBI leader with 190, which he piled up with the Chicago Cubs in 1930. I have a 1979 Topps baseball card with Hack Wilson on there, commemorating the accomplishment. It was a record he held for sixty-nine years, then broke decades after he was already dead. Thanks to accounting, Hack Wilson topped himself with 191 RBI after a newly discovered "run batted in" became part of MLB's official record book in June 1999.

Commissioner Bud Selig commented on the change: "I'm sensitive to the historical significance that accompanies the correction of such a prestigious record, especially after so many years have passed, but it is important to get it right."

Indeed.

MLB has a records committee to address these kinds of issues. There have been other semi-notable changes:

◆ Roger Maris used to be credited with 851 career RBI but now has only 850.

◆ Lefty Grove once had only 140 losses in his big-league career but now has 141.

◆ Lou Gehrig has somehow added *four* runs batted in to his ledger since he died in 1941.

Some of the earned-run averages from the nineteenth century used to be italicized, designating them as *estimates* in the old *Baseball Encyclopedia*. Today, the slanted numbers have been straightened out and presented as fact in the new digital statistical compilations, without qualification.

Fueled largely by the passionate folks in the Society for American Baseball Research (SABR), there is a never-ending audit taking place behind the scenes, as historians and amateur sleuths uncover errors and omissions.

Getting things right is a worthwhile pursuit, and yet there are still Astrodome-sized gaps in the game's statistical record. With every hit or run batted in properly ledgered, hundreds of teams and thousands of players remain exiled in an unclassified wing of baseball history.

Oddly, the categorized and easily accessible information is often grossly misunderstood. This is how we get an MiLB (minor league baseball) sanctioned list of the "greatest minor league teams of all time" featuring the 1920 Fort Worth Panthers at No. 14, when we demonstrated earlier in the book that this club probably wasn't one of the best fourteen minor league teams in 1920, let alone all time.

So how did we get to this point?

◆ ◆ ◆

Major League Baseball is a brand, like BMW, Ford, or Chevrolet. These days, MiLB is basically a subsidiary of MLB. When we talk about the major league record book, or the all-time minor league leaders, we're referring to a certain level of excellence or quality; this much is true. But we're also talking about one brand here, not all three—it's BMW, Ford, *or* Chevrolet. Before 1950, there were several other brands of baseball being played here and around the globe. They were initially brushed under the rug by Major League Baseball, then eviscerated of their talent, and later embraced as a marketing tool by organized baseball.

Jackie Robinson's jersey No. 42 is retired throughout baseball, which is both wonderful and bizarre at the same time. It's difficult to see it painted alongside Bobby Doerr's No. 1 and Ted Williams's No. 9 at Fenway Park and not view it as an uncomfortable, permanent apology for the sins of people who have been dead for decades. The Red Sox were the last team to integrate their roster, signing Pumpsie Green in 1959, three years after Jackie Robinson had already retired. No. 42 has become baseball's scarlet number.

Every year, there are numerous Negro league "tribute" days, where teams don the faux flannels, simulating the uniforms worn by the old Homestead Grays or Kansas City Monarchs. And there have been fundraisers to assist the aging veterans of the blackball leagues, which is a noble thing to do. But should MLB do *more* for the Negro league legacy?

No, they shouldn't.

They've done enough.

It ain't their brand . . .

◆ ◆ ◆

I had an ending in mind when I began writing this book, but it fell apart almost immediately after starting the project. The research process, modest insights, and epiphanies generated by the STARS system, as well as some of the other newly reconstructed statistics, blasted gaping holes in many of my preconceptions. Initially, I'd considered ending this book with an appeal to MLB to include the old Negro league statistics as part of the official major league record book. It's pretty obvious now that many of the teams, and some of the leagues, were as talented as the major leagues, and no worse than the high minors. I figured full statistical citizenship would be more effective and more important than putting No. 42 on the outfield walls of every major league ballpark. It would have been interesting to see Josh Gibson's .361 lifetime batting average sandwiched between Ty Cobb's .366, Rogers Hornsby's .358, Joe Jackson's .356, and Lefty O'Doul's .349.

You would have had a helluva one-through-five in your starting lineup:

◆ A southern racist who became a millionaire through shrewd investments but was considered a pariah by his own immediate family. Near the very end of his life, a man who had once beaten up a crippled black man and kicked a black woman down a flight of stairs, allegedly said Willie Mays was the only player he'd pay to see.

◆ A black guy whose life and career spiraled into drugs and alcohol abuse. More than half of Josh Gibson's career is still unrecovered, hidden in the moldering newspapers and microfilm at various libraries around the country.

◆ A former member of the KKK, who later helped young black ballplayers in the late 1950s and early 1960s, including Ernie Banks, who'd started his career with the Kansas City Monarchs in the Negro leagues.

◆ A man permanently banished from the game for throwing the 1919 World Series, he'd end his career with an outsider team in Georgia.

◆ And finally, the first American inducted into the *Japanese* Baseball Hall of Fame. (Although not discussed in this book, Lefty O'Doul accompanied the Babe Ruth/Japan tour in 1934 and was instrumental in getting professional baseball off the ground in that country, even giving the Yomiuri Giants their name, inspired by the late John McGraw's men in New York City.)

Could you have crafted a more quintessentially American baseball list than that? Talent, ambition, contradiction, and all the nasty demons that make one human. That the gatekeepers of the Hall of Fame assume the moral high ground today in excluding performance-enhancing drug abusers such as Barry Bonds and Mark McGwire from induction, in light of those imperfect souls already bronzed by the Cooperstown institution, is a belly laugher.

No, I no longer wish to lobby for the integration of pre-1950, ebony-hued statistics with the statistics of Ty Cobb, Babe Ruth, and Rogers Hornsby. This would make about as little sense as asking BMW to include the new Ford F-150 in their latest catalog of offerings. They're different brands, man.

I'm a huge fan of the MLB brand and have a renewed appreciation for the sanctity of its record book. To shoehorn the blackball stats into the major league statistical ledger would be unnecessarily revisionist. The major league records tell us the history of their league, and we shouldn't tamper with that.

But if we care about having a full understanding of our game's wonderful history, the entire history, perhaps there *is* something worth pursuing.

◆ ◆ ◆

In fifth grade, students are required to learn the names of each and every one of the fifty state capitals. Leading up to the big test, they spend a few weeks working with online tutorials, flash cards, and reading assignments. They take mini-quizzes and have discussions in class. There's a lot of memorization in play, but teachers try to expose students to the various city names in a variety of ways, so that kids with different learning styles have opportunities to absorb the information.

Ultimately, students may not remember every one, but they will have been presented with all the data, many different times, and in many different ways, before finally sitting at their desk to take the exam. Imagine if a teacher withheld, forgot, or simply didn't know the capital cities of fifteen states and never shared this missing information. Unless students took the initiative and tracked down this information on their own, the best score they could hope for would be thirty-five out of fifty, or 70 percent—a low C. And that's if they ace everything they've been given access to.

I would argue that if we only focus on the history of baseball as presented in the official major league records, the best we can hope for, in terms of truly understanding our game's past, is a 70 percent grade. We'd be low-C, high-D students. By focusing on one brand, MLB, we're missing a sizable chunk of the story. Sure, the more curious baseball fans can find books and articles about the Kansas City Monarchs and Brooklyn Bushwicks today, but when it comes to the game's DNA—its statistical record—nobody has yet presented a workable solution for integrating the major league, Negro league, Japanese League, and the historically significant independent professional teams, such as the Brooklyn Bushwicks, into one platform.

I'd suggest the only way we can do this is to create something entirely new, independent of the official major and minor league record books. By using a combination of the STARS system, which does a nice job of categorizing teams by talent level, and major league equivalencies, we could engineer a rational restructuring of the game's statistical history. That is to say, we could incorporate the missing 30 percent of the game's DNA into a new set of leader boards: the Universal Baseball Database, featuring Babe Ruth, Sadaharu Oh, and Josh Gibson under one tent but not necessarily in the same categories.

◆ ◆ ◆

The **Universal Baseball Database (UBD)** would be modeled after organized baseball's present structure with five divisions, each representing a particular threshold of quality.

DIVISION 1: This is the UBD's equivalency to "major league" baseball. You would find Ty Cobb, Babe Ruth, and Hank Aaron here. The Yankees, Red Sox, and Cubs would be here, as well as (probably) teams such as the Pittsburgh Crawfords. Based on some preliminary STARS work for the 1930s Negro leagues, it's likely Josh Gibson, Satchel Paige, and Cool Papa Bell would find their way into this category as well, and we'd be able to mix, match, and compare their figures with those of their white contemporaries.

The UBD would not only allow us to add new data but also correct old errors. The 1884 Union Association, which is considered top-notch by the official MLB record, would probably not be included here, with its teams and player stats sliding down to the appropriate level. The Federal League may or may not make the grade, depending on the standards established. And then there are those oddball aggregations, such as the 1911 Minneapolis Millers, who may have been major league quality but performed in a lower-level association. What to do with them? Those could become very interesting conversations down the road.

Using new organizational principles, the statistics of legendary Japanese slugger Sadaharu Oh could be included alongside baseball's all-time greats, regardless of skin color or country of origin. *Courtesy of Scott Simkus*

DIVISION 2: Like Triple-A, D-2 includes the Pacific Coast League, International League, and other high minors. It's likely some of the Negro leagues, such as those from the early 1920s, would fall into this category. I'm not positive, but I'm guessing Sadaharu Oh, the Yomiuri Giants, and the Japanese Leagues of the 1960s and 1970s would slot here or in D-3, one step lower. Mickey Cochrane's star-studded military teams of 1943 and 1944 might fall here. Heck, depending on how they shake out during our evaluation, the major leagues might grade as a D-2 in 1944, when their talent was severely depleted by the war effort.

DIVISION 3: Equivalent to the Double-A category in today's organized baseball. Outsider clubs such as the Brooklyn Bushwicks might find recognition in this division. The UBD will have a slew of subcategories, where Bushwicks games versus D-1 and D-2 teams (such as the Negro league clubs) could be accounted for and added to the database.

DIVISION 4: The same as Single-A in the modern game. I believe the Mexican League which, as previously mentioned, is considered Triple-A by organized baseball, might fall into this division. If Hector Espino is going to be on top of any home-run list, it would probably be as the D-4 leader.

In 1949, there were fifty-nine minor leagues in operation, not including the Negro leagues, Japan, or Latin America. Today, there are roughly thirty-six professional leagues around the entire globe, including the majors, minors, independent teams, and leagues in Asia, Latin America, and Europe. This means that even though the United States population has doubled and the world population has nearly tripled, there were actually more men playing professional baseball in 1949 than there are today. The jobs are harder to come by; the money is incredibly enticing at the highest level.

Major League Baseball hasn't just monopolized the global talent, it has all of the real money. In the past, a man could carve out a living playing twenty years of minor league baseball or supplement his livelihood in the semipros. Those days are gone.

When the new UBD sorts through those fifty-nine minor leagues in 1949, it should be interesting to see how the leagues get shuffled under the new five-division grading system.

DIVISION 5: Low Single-A to Rookie ball. There would be a lot of outsider clubs, such as the Paterson Silk Sox of New Jersey and Jimmy Callahan's Logan Squares of Chicago, who would likely grade out no lower than D-5, depending on their STARS scores. Although not covered in this book, there were also dozens of white "outlaw" leagues before 1950, some of which included members of the Black Sox, that could be graded, classified, and given proper recognition by the UBD.

◆ ◆ ◆

To understand the importance of such an undertaking, we need to revisit the story of Hack Wilson's 191st RBI in 1930.

In 1977, Cliff Kachline, a founding member of the Society of American Baseball Research and former editor at the *The Sporting News*, was working as the official historian at the Baseball Hall of Fame and Museum in Cooperstown. In November of that year, he received a letter from a former co-worker at TSN, asking for clarification on Hack Wilson's RBI figures for 1930.

A man named James Braswell had written to the *Sporting News*, suggesting Hack Wilson's name should have appeared alongside Mel Ott's in the latest edition of the *Sporting News' Baseball Record Book*, under the category of "Most RBI in Consecutive Games." Braswell said the box scores from July 24 through August 5, 1930, showed Wilson had knocked in runs in eleven consecutive games, matching the National League record held by Mel Ott.

Kachline checked the official daily logs from the archives and saw that Wilson had only driven in runs in ten of the eleven scheduled contests. But upon reviewing the newspaper accounts, he was surprised to discover there had, in fact, been a mistake. In the second game of a doubleheader played on July 28, 1930, Hack Wilson singled home Kiki Cuyler from second base in a game the Cubs eventually won, 5–3. Although the newspaper accounts from multiple papers clearly showed Wilson should have been credited with an RBI, the official record showed Cuyler with 3, first baseman Charlie Grimm with 2, and Wilson with zippo. Wilson and Grimm should have each been credited with one.

A month later, Kachline prepared a report on the finding and presented it to the Baseball Records Committee, which thanked him and told him to go away. A journalist from TSN joined Kachline in the Wilson project and suggested collaborating on a story for the magazine about the phantom RBI, but they were shot down by the editor, citing the publication's policy against correcting official records unless they had been approved by the Baseball Records Committee.

By this time, the records committee had apparently canned Kachline's report and moved on, saying the evidence he'd presented was "inconclusive." Twenty years would pass before anything else happened. The steroid era, of all things, would reopen the can of worms.

As Bill Chastain wrote in *Hack's 191: Hack Wilson and His Incredible 1930 Season*, "The need to make sure the RBI mark indeed was accurate became dire in 1998 when Juan Gonzalez of the Texas Rangers arrived at the All-Star break with 101 RBIs."

Kachline went public with his findings, citing the importance of correcting the record as there was a legitimate chance of somebody challenging the mark. When he approached Elias Sports Bureau, the official statistician of MLB, they shot him down, saying they didn't believe the record should be altered.

Fortunately, Jerome Holtzman, the game's official historian, stepped in on Kachline's behalf, getting Major League Baseball's attention. After a lengthy review of the material, Bud Selig announced the correction.

The entire process for one lousy RBI took twenty-one years.

◆ ◆ ◆

Today, my favorite brand of baseball is MLB. From the inception of the National League in 1876, it has been at, or near, the very top in terms of on-field talent. The game we see played in the major leagues today is without question the greatest it has ever been, and it includes virtually every great player from around the world.

This hasn't always been the case. The Players League of 1890 was better than the NL, and yet it wasn't officially designated as major league until a committee was formed in 1968 to address the matter. Before 1950, there were hundreds of Negro league players and dozens of blackball teams who were major league (or high minor league) caliber but have *no* place in the game's statistical record. In this book, I've argued that there were many white independent clubs of professional caliber and players, such as Eddie Gerner, whose greatness has been thus far hidden because they played outside the dominion of organized baseball. Sadaharu Oh, who hit 868 homers in a foreign league, doesn't appear on any minor league leaderboards.

I love MLB, but it shouldn't be in charge of anything other than its own legacy. By establishing the Universal Baseball Database, we have an opportunity to reclaim the history of our game—the full story, without strategically convenient omissions or twenty-one year delays for what are obvious corrections.

This won't be just a rational restructuring of professional baseball's statistical history: there's an entire world of outsider baseball waiting to be explored.

◆ ◆ ◆

The bad news is it would take an army of people, and many years, to assemble the new Universal Baseball Database. All sorts of important decisions will need to be made regarding thresholds of quality for each category, the tools to be employed, and even the matter of where, precisely, to begin this process. As for the latter issue, I'd suggest three starting points: first, let's shore up the Negro league statistics, which are the most important of unclassified professional baseball leagues, using the scholarly standards established by historian Gary Ashwill and the crew at seamheads.com. Second, we need a thorough study and classification of the most historically important foreign leagues, including those in Japan, Cuba, Mexico, the Dominican Republic, and Puerto Rico. And third, we need a full survey of the minor and major leagues to make sure the existing classification designations pass the smell test. The independent (outlaw) minor leagues, white semipros, and other rogue endeavors would come later.

The good news is this army of dedicated historians, fans, researchers, and analysts already exists. The Society of American Baseball Research, formed in 1971, when fifteen people (including Cliff Kachline, the Hack Wilson–RBI guy) gathered in Cooperstown, has grown to include more than six thousand members today. I'm one of them.

Perhaps the biggest misperception of SABR is that it is a conclave of numbers-oriented stat nerds, when in fact the analysts represent just a small fraction of the organization. It's really a history club populated by men and women who love the game of baseball and its storied past. These are, perhaps, the most passionate fans in the country. There are dozens of committees dedicated to writing biographies of players and teams, researching demographic data, and studying foreign leagues, minor leagues, and the Negro leagues.

And yes, there are those who focus on the numbers. All of these committees become important in the creation of a Universal Baseball Database, their tireless efforts being of immense value to the cause in a variety of ways.

Having joined the organization just a few years back, I'm new to SABR—an outsider, really, just getting my feet wet—and I am humbled by the work of those who have come before me. Whether or not you feel this book is a clarion call forecasting the new road forward doesn't matter to me nearly as much as one thing: I hope you've enjoyed the journey.

ACKNOWLEDGMENTS

NINE YEARS AGO I LAY IN INTENSIVE CARE, hooked up to various tubes, a nine-inch gash running up my abdomen, all held together with industrial-strength staples, tape, and crimson-stained gauze. Next to the bed was one of those clear plastic vessels, containing all of the vile fluids being pumped out of my lungs. Machines chirped in a corner, monitoring heart rate and body temperature and whatever else medical machines communicate.

I was there because I had no business pretending to be my own personal physician.

I'd foolishly diagnosed myself with a twenty-four-hour bug, the common flu, perhaps. But it turned into a forty-eight-hour bug, and then a seventy-two-hour bug, and when I simply couldn't stand the pain any longer, and when I couldn't shit, and when my piss had become the color of instant coffee, and when I hadn't slept in two days, and when my body temperature soared to that of planet Venus's surface, my older brother came over and insisted on driving me to the E.R. It was something much worse than the flu, obviously, and if I'd toughed it out a few more hours at home, the doctor said I wouldn't have made it.

My lower intestines had ruptured.

After three months, there was a follow-up surgery, and under heavy doses of morphine and various other pain killers, I tried to read books. I *love* books. History, biography, fiction. And if they are *baseball* history, and *baseball* biography, and *baseball* fiction, all the better. One of them, *The Pride of Havana*, by Roberto González Echevarría, was a richly detailed history of baseball in Cuba in the days predating Castro. I don't remember much of anything else during my second stint in recovery, but reading Echevarría's passionate account of a nearly forgotten corner of baseball history penetrated my narcotic fog. His accounts of Josh Gibson, Martín Dihigo, and Babe Ruth playing ball in the tropical paradise nourished my imagination and refueled dreams that had stalled somewhere in the past.

I know, I know . . .

If this all seems a bit melodramatic, I agree. But it's true, and it *is* the turning point that led to many wonderful things, including the eventual publication of this book. Before moving any further, I'd like to thank my brother, Rob Simkus, for taking me to the hospital when I didn't want to go. And Dr. Altimari—and the staff at Central DuPage Hospital—for gutting me like a fish, stitching me up like a monster, and saving my life. Thanks to compassionate people, and medical science, I was given a second chance. And of all the things to do with a second chance, I became interested in baseball history again.

My passion for the game's backstory dates almost all the way back to the time when I first learned to read. By the time I was in my teens, I'd built up a decent library, interviewed aging ballplayers, and had designs on writing books at some point in the not-so-distant future. After college, I covered baseball for small newspapers in the Chicago suburbs, wrote a weekly humor column, and cobbled together human interest stories for insignificant regional magazines—none of which amounted to much, either in the way of money or personal satisfaction. And so I moved on, and the things I dreamed of as a teenager faded away. I sold copiers for a living and snuck off to the library to dig through old microfilm, but it was a fuzzy pursuit with little focus and no economic rewards. As I mentioned in the introduction to this book, I was the worst salesman in the history of the industry and soon found myself driving a limousine and doing all manner of other shitty jobs for a living.

Years went by, and it wasn't until I was thirty-five years old, walking out of the hospital with *The Pride of Havana* tucked beneath my arm, that I decided to get serious. I basically challenged myself to commit, full bore, seven days per week, to see where writing and research would take me. I literally had no money, no job, and no contacts in the industry at this point. We had a roof over our head and one car, but the same exact day I was being rushed into surgery was my wife's last day as a part-time school teacher in a district that had just let her go. She'd been fired due to budgetary cuts. We didn't have health insurance. We didn't have anything. Our kids were in grade school, and we'd hit rock bottom.

After regaining my strength, I found steady work as a dispatcher for a limousine company, and my wife landed a full-time teaching position. I started chipping away at the baseball research again, pitching ideas to magazines and game companies and building a massive archive of newspaper stories and baseball box scores and an exclusive database. For the first couple years, nothing. Six or seven days per week, forty hours on top of the forty-plus hours invested at my full-time job, and I didn't make a penny. I realize now those were the years I was becoming a stronger writer and researcher . . . and building relationships with people. It's impossible to *overstate* the importance of personal relationships.

One person can write a book. Anybody can, really. But for that book to be worthy of publication, and worthy of a reader's attention, it usually requires an army of talented, generous folks behind the scenes. *Outsider Baseball* is no exception. Dozens of people have helped me improve my craft and sharpen my understanding of our national pastime's history. Dozens of others have been there as inspiration, or as motivators, or cheerleaders, or to be there to listen to me when I was hitting the wall, ready to obliterate my keyboard with a sledgehammer. Not sure I'll be able to remember everybody, but I'll try my best.

Hal Richman, founder of the Strat-O-Matic Game Company, first fueled my imagination with his amazing tabletop game when I was a kid, then later became the first person to open a door for me professionally, showing me what was possible in the baseball business. Gary Ashwill has taught me more about writing and researching baseball history than anybody else on the planet. I'll be forever in his debt. Dr. David Lawrence has become the mentoring college professor I never had, showing me how to think critically about not just baseball history but about *everything*—and always with good cheer and humor. Keith Scherer read several chapters early on, helped save an important section of this book from the scrap heap, and has become a terrific friend in the process. Josh Wilker opened the gates and waved me inside. My agent, Kate McKean, stuck with the project (and stuck with it some more!), even after it seemed my anonymity was conspiring against what was otherwise considered promising. To my editor Yuval Taylor: thank you for saying yes! You gave me the keys, let me go pedal to the metal on the accelerator, then saved me several times from driving this book off a cliff. Gary Joseph Cieradkowski, Jeff Polman, Mike Lynch, and Kevin Johnson—the four of you have been extremely supportive and influential.

Other folks, without whom this book might not exist, or exist in its present form: Steve Barkan, Kevin Baxter, Eric Beato, Craig Calcaterra, John Cywinski, Doug Drotman, Tom Dunkel, Paul Dylan, Robert Fitts, Sean Forman, Gary Gillette, Glenn Guzzo, Dan Hirsch, Dave Hoekstra, John Holway, Ted Knorr, Michael Lusk, Stuart Miller, Bill Mullins, Peter Nash, Rod Nelson,

Dayn Perry, Todd Peterson, Adam Richman, Joe Sheehan, Pam Smith, Wayne Stivers, John Thorn, Tim Wiles, and all the other helpful folks at the National Baseball Hall of Fame and Museum in Cooperstown, New York.

Besides spending an afternoon with former Negro leaguer Art Pennington (and communicating with him via telephone), several interviews and/ or e-mail correspondences with the descendents of former ballplayers and baseball promoters proved fruitful. Chris Tremper, Tom Smith, Bob Harris, George Case III, Erin Hovland, and Marita Rivero were generous with their time and input.

How can I ever repay the sacrifices made by those closest to me? My wife and kids have given me the freedom to work odd hours and drift off into the solitary place writers need to go on a regular basis. More importantly, they've always welcomed me back with open arms when the daily work is finished. Life simply wouldn't be worth living without Joyce, Joe, and Libby Simkus. You guys are everything to me.

Other family and close friends who've had an impact on this project include Bob and Barbara Simkus (again), Matt and Diana (Ding) Bell, Karen and John Batke, Sharyl and Shawn DeWane, Laura Simkus Lynch, Robert Simkus Jr., and Leticia Aurelio Dino. Al Kosek and John Paraoan are my home boys, from the way-back, wiffle-ball, and Strat-O-Matic days. The late Jim Billon will never be forgotten.

Special thanks also to the current (and former) members of the West Sub Limo crew: Pickles, Larry, Wez, Shane, Sully, Aldo, Big D, Hilty, Tony C., Gianni, Bruce, Dan, Aamir, Gus, and Pat.

When boiled down, more than anything else, the good folks mentioned here are the ones who've helped me get things *right* in the book. They've helped make this better. On the off-chance any factual errors emerge in *Outsider Baseball*, I take full responsibility.

BIBLIOGRAPHICAL NOTE

THE GLORY DAYS OF INDEPENDENT BASEBALL have long since passed, but a great variety of research material is readily available, literally at our fingertips, often in the comfort of our own homes. Thanks to the digital revolution, we are living in the golden age of baseball research. Not only have thousands of historic newspaper archives been made accessible on the Internet; there are also photographs, videos, personal correspondences, census information, memorabilia, legal documents, essays, scholarly papers, and detailed statistical compilations just a few keyboard clicks away. It would be impractical to list every newspaper and website consulted during the writing of this book, but hopefully a general overview of source material will prove sufficient for those wishing to explore further the world of outsider baseball.

The African American newspaper archives are arguably the most important, as they covered the great black teams, and many independent white clubs as well since the two groups were regular competitors of one another. Among these, the best are the *Chicago Defender, Pittsburgh Courier, Baltimore Afro-American, Philadelphia Tribune*, and New York's *Amsterdam News*. Among the mainstream daily newspapers, the archives of the *Chicago Tribune, New York Times, Brooklyn Daily Eagle, Pittsburgh Post-Gazette, Cleveland Plain Dealer, Philadelphia Inquirer, Detroit Free Press*, and *Indianapolis Star* proved invaluable. There were hundreds of other newspapers, from big cities and small towns alike, that helped fill gaps or open new leads.

The most popular newspaper search engines are genealogybank.com, newspaperarchive.com, chroniclingamerica.loc.gov, fultonhistory.com, and the free Google news archives. The historical papers available via ProQuest are a must for any serious researcher. The Mid-Continent Public Library of Kansas City, Missouri, helped me gain access to these archives.

Not every important newspaper has been digitized. During the writing of this book, I perused more than 200 rolls of microfilm. The most helpful libraries were the Chicago Public Library, Detroit Public Library, Easton (PA) Public Library, Monroe (LA) Public Library, Carol Stream (IL) Public Library, and the Berwyn (IL) Public Library.

This book could not have been written without the information available via ancestry.com. At the popular genealogy site, one can access census records, social security death records, city directories, family histories, and military data.

Researching baseball without being a member of the Society of American Baseball Research (SABR) would be like climbing the monkey bars with one hand tied behind your back. The organization, founded back in 1971, is an excellent reservoir of information. Their digital portal provides access to important magazines, including the *Sporting News*, *Sporting Life*, *Spalding Base Ball Guides*, and *Reach Base Ball Guides*, among others. The crown jewel of SABR's collection is the digital archives of their very own *Baseball Research Journal*, with important popular and scholarly research pieces dating back more than forty years. Perhaps even more important than its digital resources are SABR's vast *human* resources. With more than 6,000 members, there is always somebody ready and willing to answer a question, help locate a difficult resource, or point a fellow time traveler in the right direction. Several of these folks were mentioned specifically in the acknowledgments.

One of the pleasant research surprises of the past few years has been the emerging web presence of auction houses such as Robert Edward (robert-edwardauctions.com) and Hakes (hakes.com), whose online catalogs often feature detailed images of old player contracts, photographs, programs, and other rare items that would otherwise be hidden in private collections.

As for general baseball websites and blogs, the most helpful for the purposes of this book have been baseball-reference.com, seamheads.com, agate-type.typepad.com, retrosheet.org, and the infinitecardset.blogspot.com.

If the Internet is the place for quantity, then books still remain the place for *quality*. It's very difficult to surpass the combined efforts of professional writers and editors from the traditional world of publishing. I read more than 300 books during the research phase of this project. Following are the most important, without which this book could simply not exist:

Thomas Barthel, *Baseball's Peerless Semipros: The Brooklyn Bushwicks of Dexter Park* (Harworth, NJ: St. Johann Press, 2009); Barthel, *Baseball*

Barnstorming and Exhibition Games, 1901–1962: A History of Off-Season Major League Play (Jefferson, NC: McFarland, 2007); Bill Chastain, *Hack's 191: Hack Wilson and His Incredible 1930 Season* (Guilford, CT: Lyons Press, 2012); Pedro Treto Cisneros, *The Mexican League: Comprehensive Player Statistics, 1937–2001* (Jefferson, NC: McFarland, 2002); Dick Clark and Larry Lester, *The Negro Leagues Book* (Cleveland: Society for American Baseball Research, 1994); Robert W. Creamer, *Babe: The Legend Comes to Life* (New York: Fireside, 1992; orig. publ. 1974); Phil S. Dixon, *Phil Dixon's American Baseball Chronicles: Great Teams, The 1931 Homestead Grays, Volume I* (Kansas City, KS: Xlibris, 2009); Dixon, *Phil Dixon's American Baseball Chronicles: Great Teams, The 1905 Philadelphia Giants, Volume III* (Charleston, SC: Xlibris, 2010); Dixon, *John "Buck" O'Neil: The Rookie, the Man, the Legacy, 1938* (Bloomington, IN: AuthorHouse, 2009); Tom Dunkel, *Color Blind: The Forgotten Team That Broke Baseball's Color Line* (New York: Atlantic Monthly Press, 2013); Jorge S. Figueredo, *Cuban Baseball: A Statistical History, 1878–1961* (Jefferson, NC: McFarland, 2003); Robert K. Fitts, *Banzai Babe Ruth: Baseball, Espionage, & Assassination During the 1934 Tour of Japan* (Lincoln, NE: University of Nebraska Press, 2012); Timothy M. Gay, *Satch, Dizzy & Rapid Robert: The Wild Saga of Interracial Baseball Before Jackie Robinson* (New York: Simon & Schuster, 2010); Roberto González Echevarría, *The Pride of Havana: A History of Cuban Baseball* (New York: Oxford University Press, 1999); Joel Hawkins and Terry Bertolino, *Images of America: The House of David Baseball Team* (Chicago: Arcadia Publishing, 2000); Hobe Hays, *Take Two and Hit to Right: Golden Days on the Semi-Pro Diamond* (Lincoln, NE: University of Nebraska Press, 1999); Lawrence D. Hogan, *Shades of Glory: The Negro Leagues and the Story of African-American Baseball* (Washington, DC: National Geographic, 2006); John Holway, *Voices From the Great Black Baseball League, Revised Edition* (New York: De Capo Press, 1992; orig. publ. 1975); Holway, *Josh & Satch: The Life and Times of Josh Gibson and Satchel Paige* (New York: Carroll & Graf, 1992); Holway, *The Complete Book of Baseball's Negro League: The Other Half of Baseball History* (Fern Park, FL: Hastings House, 2001); Holway, *Black Giants* (Springfield, VA: Xlibris, 2009); Holway, *Black Ball Tales: Rollicking, All New, True Adventures of the Negro Leagues by the Men Who Lived and Loved Them* (Springfield, VA: Scorpio Books, 2008); Bill James, *The New Bill James Historical Baseball Abstract, Revised Edition* (New York: Free Press, 2001; orig. publ. 1988); Bill Jenkinson, *The Year Babe Ruth Hit 104 Home Runs* (New York: Carroll & Graf, 2007); Jerry Kuntz, *Baseball Fiends and Flying Machines* (Jefferson, NC: McFarland, 2009); Mark Lamaster, *Spalding's World Tour: The Epic Adventure That Took Baseball Around the Globe—And Made It America's*

Game (New York: Public Affairs, 2006); Neil Lanctot, *Negro League Baseball: The Rise and Ruin of a Black Institution* (Philadelphia: University of Pennsylvania Press, 2004); Larry Lester, *Black Baseball's National Showcase: The East-West All-Star Game, 1933–1953* (Lincoln, NE: University of Nebraska Press, 2001); Jerry Malloy (editor), *Sol White's History of Colored Base Ball, With Other Documents on the Early Black Game, 1886–1936* (Lincoln, NE: University of Nebraska Press, 1995; orig. publ. 1907); Kyle McNary, *Ted "Double Duty" Radcliffe: 36 Years Pitching & Catching in Baseball's Negro Leagues* (St. Louis Park, MN: McNary, 1994); William F. McNeil, *The California Winter League: America's First Integrated Professional Baseball League* (Jefferson, NC: McFarland, 2002); Peter Morris, *A Game of Inches: The Story Behind Innovations That Shaped Baseball* (Chicago: Ivan R. Dee, 2006); Rob Neyer and Eddie Epstein, *Baseball Dynasties: The Greatest Teams of All Time* (New York: W. W. Norton, 2000); Robert Peterson, *Only the Ball Was White: A History of Legendary Black Players and All-Black Professional Teams* (New York: Oxford University Press, 1992; orig. publ. 1970); Todd Peterson, *Early Black Baseball in Minnesota: The St. Paul Gophers, Minneapolis Keystones and Other Barnstorming Teams of the Deadball Era* (Jefferson, NC: McFarland, 2010); Alan J. Pollock, *Barnstorming to Heaven: Syd Pollok and His Great Black Teams* (Tuscaloosa, AL: University of Alabama Press, 2006); Joe Posnanski, *The Soul of Baseball: A Road Trip Through Buck O'Neil's America* (New York: William Morrow, 2007); James A. Riley, *The Biographical Encyclopedia of the Negro Baseball Leagues* (New York: Carroll & Graf, 1994); Donn Rogosin, *Invisible Men: Life in Baseball's Negro Leagues* (New York: Atheneum, 1985); Harold Seymour, *Baseball: The Early Years* (New York: Oxford University Press, 1960); Seymour, *Baseball: The People's Game* (New York: Oxford University Press, 1991); Brad Snyder, *Beyond the Shadows of the Senators: The Untold Story of the Homestead Grays and the Integration of Baseball* (New York: McGraw-Hill, 2003); John Thorn, *Baseball in the Garden of Eden: The Secret History of the Early Game* (New York: Simon & Schuster, 2011); Larry Tye, *Satchel: The Life and Times of an American Legend* (New York: Random House, 2009); Jules Tygiel, *Baseball's Great Experiment: Jackie Robinson and His Legacy* (New York: Oxford University Press, 2008; orig. publ. 1983).

INDEX